once a·day

worship & praise

DEVOTIONAL

365 days to adore God

The Livingstone Corporation

ZONDERVAN®

We want to hear from you. Please send your comments about this book to us in care of zreview@zondervan.com. Thank you.

ZONDERVAN

Once-A-Day Worship and Praise Devotional
Copyright © 2003, 2012 by the Livingstone Corporation

This title is also available as a Zondervan ebook.
Visit www.zondervan.com/ebooks.

Requests for information should be addressed to:
Zondervan, *Grand Rapids, Michigan* 49530

Library of Congress Cataloging-in-Publication Data

Once-a-day worship and praise devotional.
    p. cm.
    Includes bibliographical references and index.
    ISBN 978-0-310-44076-5 (softcover : alk. paper)
    1. Devotional calendars.
  BV4810.O53   2012
  242'.2—dc23   2012018160

Cover design: Faceout Studio and Jamie DeBruyn
Interior design: Sherri Hoffman and Jamie DeBruyn
Project Manager: Dave Veerman
Project staff: Joel Bartlett, Bruce Barton, Mary Horner Collins, Peter Gregory, Rosalie Krusemark, Kirk Luttrell, Kathleen Ristow, Thomas Ristow, Betsy Todt Schmitt, Ashley Taylor, Linda Taylor, David R. Veerman, Linda Washington, Neil Wilson

Printed in the United States of America

---

12 13 14 15 16 17 /DCI/ 20 19 18 17 16 15 14 13 12 11 10 9 8 7 6 5 4 3 2 1

ABOUT THE LIVINGSTONE CORPORATION

Since our inception in September 1988, Livingstone has helped Christian publishers produce 169 specialty Bibles and more than 500 trade books, devotionals, gift and specialty books, studies and curriculum products. Each year we produce about 70 new titles, including Bibles, reference products, trade books, children's books, studies and curriculum. Our products have won 11 Gold Medallion awards and have been Gold Medallion finalists more than 30 times.

OUR VISION

Our vision is to glorify and enjoy God in and through our lives, relationships and services and support the advancement of the Good News of Jesus Christ.

OUR MISSION

Livingstone's mission is to provide superior ideation, content, design and composition services for religious publishers worldwide.

OUR MOTTO

Ideas to Marketplace. This saying expresses our core brand promise to clients and reflects both the breadth and depth of our capabilities to deliver convenient and effective solutions for marketplace success.

WORSHIP HIM ONCE A DAY

Shout for joy to the LORD, all the earth. Worship the LORD with gladness; come before him with joyful songs.   PSALM 100:1–2

What ideas or songs come to mind when you contemplate worshiping God? Some people think of a huge orchestra—the best in the world—playing full out with a chorale singing Handel's *Messiah* or any other great work. Others might think of an acoustic guitar skillfully played and blending with the voice of a well-known singer in a worship chorus. Still others might draw a blank, either out of a fear of inadequacy—this is the God of the universe we're talking about, a God who has thousands of "professional" worshipers (angels) worshiping him all day—or a lack of knowledge about worship. With the *Once-a-Day Worship and Praise Devotional*, you can see that worship is just as natural as breathing. It is a response of thanksgiving to the God who made everything and gave his life to save everyone.

Each day's reading features an excerpt from a prayer in the Bible, a short meditation on that prayer that will help you focus your thoughts, and then a sentence you can use to start your own prayer. Although these daily readings begin with January 1, you can begin exploring the Bible's prayers on today's date.

The readings in *Once-a-Day Worship and Praise Devotional* express a wide range worship themes and emotions. You'll see the real and the raw—glorious notes of worship, coupled with cries of agony. Through these readings, you'll find the inspiration to come before God in worship just as you are.

Our hope and prayer is that the readings and Scriptures collected in this book will cause you to fall before the God who deserves your worship.

FINE CRAFTSMANSHIP

God saw all that he had made, and it was very good. And there was evening, and there was morning—the sixth day. GENESIS 1:31

"It was very good." That phrase seems an apt description when we look up at the night sky and see the stars God hung there and knows by name. We easily see excellence in a sunset so brilliantly hued that it takes our breath away, or in a pine tree stretching heavenward, its feathery branches moving with the breeze.

But what about when we look in the mirror, or when we look across the breakfast table at family members? The descriptor of "very good" applies to people as well as to nature. Of course, we go astray, wandering from his loving care into sin and its consequences. But in our essence—and in the character of every human no matter how far fallen—is excellence from God's hand, excellence that reflects God's image.

Part of what inspires that wonder is God's creative abilities. Who else could have made the magnificent human body? Who but God could have invented the method whereby infants are conceived, grow and make their dramatic entry into the world? Who but God could have fashioned a solar system in which each part functions in precise relationship to the others?

Ask God to give you a new perspective on his creation, then thank him for his awesome works. ❖

PRAYER

Lord, I stand in awe of you . . .

day2

ONLY MY BEST

And Abel also brought an offering—fat portions from some of the firstborn of his flock. The LORD looked with favor on Abel and his offering, but on Cain and his offering he did not look with favor. So Cain was very angry, and his face was downcast.

GENESIS 4:4–5

Jeff planned to make a large donation toward the costs of the addition to the church's Christian Education wing. But when Jeff got a call from the coordinator of children's ministries asking him to be a volunteer in the nursery, he felt it was beneath him.

"I don't really have time," he responded.

Like Cain, Jeff brought God what he wanted to bring, and he thought that was enough. Like Cain, he wanted to worship God in his own way, without considering what God wanted him to bring.

What about you? Have you brought God what you wanted to give without asking him what he wanted from you? Have you brought him a gift grudgingly?

The offering God wants most is the offering of our hearts, dedicated and fully turned toward him in a lifestyle of continual worship. Release your gifts, talents and abilities to him and ask him what kind of a sacrifice he wants from you. The answer might surprise you. ♣

PRAYER

God, I want to give you ...

GIVE ME A SIGN

I have set my rainbow in the clouds, and it will be the sign of the covenant between me and the earth. Whenever I bring clouds over the earth and the rainbow appears in the clouds, I will remember my covenant between me and you and all living creatures of every kind. Never again will the waters become a flood to destroy all life. Genesis 9:13 – 15

Children delight in rainbows. They want to follow a rainbow to its end or run and jump through it if it appears in a spray of water. We tell children the story of Noah, and how God's rainbow became a sign of God's lasting promise that he will never again send a flood to destory life on earth. God doesn't always seal his promises with a visual sign; sometimes we see God's promises reflected in other ways.

Consider Becky, a single mom with two toddler girls. She received no child support or other assistance from her ex-husband, and while Becky had a hard time making ends meet, somehow they managed. When the week's groceries ran out a day early, a friend brought over a pizza. When she needed to pay a doctor's bill, her tax refund came a month early. When it looked as though her week's vacation would be spent at home with her two girls, a couple from church offered to let them stay in their cottage.

What rainbows do you see? Where do you witness God's faithfulness to you? Look for it in the small needs he meets at just the right time. Credit his goodness when good fortune comes your way. ✤

PRAYER

God, thank you ...

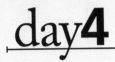

A MONUMENTAL MISTAKE

Then they said, "Come, let us build ourselves a city, with a tower that reaches to the heavens, so that we may make a name for ourselves; otherwise we will be scattered over the face of the whole earth." GENESIS 11:4

Part of what it means to be created in the image of God (see Genesis 1:27) is that we humans have the God-given capacity to make a difference. Yet our desire to "leave a legacy" can become twisted. We may forget that everything—including ourselves—has been created by God *for* God. We exist to do his bidding—not the other way around.

The tower of Babel incident is a continuation of the ugly events begun in Eden. Can you hear the hissing of the serpent behind the scenes? "Fill the earth? Obey God? Don't be ridiculous! You're much better off serving your own desires! Can't you see how he's keeping good things from you? Your only hope for life is to throw off his oppressive rule and do your own thing."

It's easy to want to act like the people of Babel, to desire to build a personal monument to ourselves. Sometimes we do that through elevating our families, our possessions or our accomplishments above our devotion to God.

Fight against that desire today. Humble yourself before God, knowing that he will exalt you at the proper time. ✤

PRAYER

Lord, teach me how to ...

HERE, THERE AND EVERYWHERE

And he blessed Abram, saying, "Blessed be Abram by God Most High, Creator of heaven and earth. And praise be to God Most High, who delivered your enemies into your hand." Then Abram gave him a tenth of everything.　　　　　　　GENESIS 14:19–20

Author A. W. Tozer once observed that what we think about God is the most important thing about us. And surely what we think of him is reflected in the various ways we describe him and in the assorted names or titles by which we address him.

In blessing Abram, Melchizedek, the king and priest of ancient Salem, spoke of "God Most High." In other words, God is lofty and exalted. He sits enthroned above the heavens. But he is not aloof. Notice that he is, in Melchizedek's words, also the God who delivers his people. He is a God who intervenes, who injects himself into the mundane lives of those who follow him.

Amazing, isn't it? Our great Creator rules and reigns. But more than that, he sees and hears. Even better, he shows up, helping, delivering, always desiring to pour out blessings on his beloved servants.

Just as God did for Abram, he will also do for you. What is it that you need most? Protection, guidance, safekeeping? Take your needs to God Most High. He promises to bless you. ✤

PRAYER

God, I lift these requests before you . . .

day6

EYES WIDE OPEN

She gave this name to the LORD who spoke to her: "You are the God who sees me," for she said, "I have now seen the One who sees me." That is why the well was called Beer Lahai Roi; it is still there, between Kadesh and Bered.　　　　　GENESIS 16:13–14

Peekaboo! This game is fun for young children because they know mom and dad won't disappear when they close their eyes. After eight months of age, most children reach a stage in their development where they understand object permanence. They understand that objects continue to exist even when they cannot be seen, heard or touched. Before this phase, babies think that if they can't see someone, the other person can't see them. The world literally vanishes behind their closed eyes.

As adults, we sometimes interact with God as if we are infants before the object permanence phase. We become convinced that if we hide from him, he won't see our true identities. We even play this game with ourselves—"If I don't look at this bad habit, or think about this problem, or talk to others about my sin, then it's not really there." Looking at something—or someone—can be scary.

God saw Hagar. And Hagar responded wisely. She was honest with God about what she was doing. God blessed her for revealing herself to him. And when Hagar stopped getting in the way, her honesty allowed her to see God.

God blesses our open and transparent lives. When we're honest with him, we'll start to see God for who he really is. Only when we see the true God can we worship him in truth. ✤

PRAYER

Lord, it's difficult to let you inside the hidden places within me because ...

RUGGED WORSHIP

The men turned away and went toward Sodom, but Abraham remained standing before the LORD. Then Abraham approached him and said: "Will you sweep away the righteous with the wicked?"
GENESIS 18:22–23

Call to mind a charismatic worshiper. He or she is smiling, right? Almost jaunty. Perhaps even clapping with a joyful look of bliss.

Now behold Abraham, the so-called friend of God. God has just confided in his faithful follower: Catastrophic judgment is coming soon to Sodom. Abraham is upset. He wrings his hands. What is he to do? He has family in the doomed city.

Notice what Abraham doesn't do. He doesn't pout, or stew, or complain to friends. Instead, he takes his heavy heart straight to God. His questions aren't rhetorical. His words aren't self-talk. This is a desperate plea with the Divine. A crisis conversation with the Creator.

If worship is giving God our undivided attention, then the careworn, distraught Abraham is worshiping even at this sobering moment.

Perhaps you are overwhelmed with worry and anxiety. Don't let these feelings alienate you from God. Instead, worship him with your questions and doubts today. Then believe and pray as much as you are able. ✤

PRAYER

Lord, to me, worship means . . .

NO RIVALS

Then God said, "Take your son, your only son, whom you love—Isaac—and go to the region of Moriah. Sacrifice him there as a burnt offering on a mountain I will show you."

GENESIS 22:2

It is one thing to sit in church and sing the old hymn "Take My Life, and Let It Be"—to pledge your silver and gold, to offer God your hands and will. It is another thing altogether to hear God tell you to offer your child to him.

This was Abraham's situation. After waiting many, many decades for God to give him a son, imagine how he felt when called to sacrifice that son. This scene shocks us with its blunt and sobering truth: God will have no rivals. If the great treasure of our hearts is not God, then he will demonstrate that he is all we need by making sure that he is all we have.

Ironically, it is in these dark moments that we discover that he is all we need and that nothing else can ever truly satisfy.

What will it mean for you to make your heart God's throne? Take time to assess any activities or even relationships that are threatening to replace God as the top priority in your life. Offer these to God as an act of obedient sacrifice. ❖

PRAYER

Make me willing, O God, to . . .

PRACTICING THE PRESENCE

Then I put the ring in her nose and the bracelets on her arms, and I bowed down and worshiped the LORD. I praised the LORD, the God of my master Abraham, who had led me on the right road to get the granddaughter of my master's brother for his son. Now if you will show kindness and faithfulness to my master, tell me; and if not, tell me, so I may know which way to turn.   GENESIS 24:47–49

Most people approach each day armed with verbs and phrases like: "Go!" "Get busy!" "Hurry up!" "Produce!" and "Make it happen!" We rush through life, checking off items on our "to do" lists.

When we are tuned in to God, we live each day using a different vocabulary. "Lift up your eyes." "Listen." "Call to me." "Ask." "Seek." "Knock." "Wait." "Trust."

A great illustration of this second, less common approach to life is embedded in the story of Abraham's servant. Sent on a mission to find a wife for Isaac, Eliezer is wholly dependent on help from above. He is faithful, trustworthy and deliberate. He prays nonstop, and his cries for direction and help are amazingly specific. When at last he senses clear leading from God, he erupts in praise. And at the end of the day, his mission is a great success. The Lord has watched over him.

This God-drenched mindset is what Brother Lawrence called "practicing the presence of God." It is simply recognizing that God is ever with us.

As you go through your daily routines, remember Eliezer's example. Slow down and take time to acknowledge God. Trust him to lead you along the right path today. ✤

PRAYER

Lord, today I'm trusting you to . . .

A BETTER PERSPECTIVE

"Look, I am about to die," Esau said. "What good is the birthright to me?"

But Jacob said, "Swear to me first." So he swore an oath to him, selling his birthright to Jacob. GENESIS 25:32–33

Most people view the world through eyes that see only what is happening right *now*. And the result of this self-absorbed, impatient mindset? Not very pretty to look at. We end up with an embarrassing episode like the one cited above: Esau forfeiting enormous privilege and honor, essentially throwing away his prominent place in the eternal purposes of God. And for what? A bowl of stew. How tragic!

However, throughout the Bible, we read of many of God's faithful servants who had a different perspective than Esau's. Rather than becoming obsessed with the small stories of their individual lives, they focused on God's big story. As they did, these worshiping saints remembered the past faithfulness of God, even as they placed their hope in his future promises.

The result is that these people lived steadier lives. They were not susceptible to baser impulses. Because they kept the big picture in view, they finished well.

What are you living for today? When you focus on the present and on your feelings, you can quickly lose sight of God's future and his truth. To put your hope and trust in God is to stand in awe of him and his power with the confidence that God will faithfully perform his Word. ✦

PRAYER

Gracious Father, keep me from the foolish trap of . . .

FAITH, NOT FEELINGS

She conceived again, and when she gave birth to a son she said, "This time I will praise the LORD." So she named him Judah. Then she stopped having children. GENESIS 29:35

If there were such a thing as a time machine and we could use this device to go back in history to the events described in Genesis 28–30, what would Leah tell us? Surely she would describe feeling overlooked, unhappy and dissatisfied. Perhaps she would tell of poignant moments of rejection, of tearful times of prayer, of wrestling with deep-seated jealousy, of heart-wrenching, unanswered questions.

All this is, of course, speculation. What we know for sure is the little bit that God's Word tells us. Leah gave Jacob four sons. And in naming each one, Leah expressed her stubborn faith and desperate hope that maybe Jacob would finally develop deep affection for her.

It didn't happen. Leah's younger sister Rachel remained the delight of Jacob's eyes. A bitter pill to swallow. When you're reading this passage for the first time, you expect resentment to begin to fill Leah's heart. It doesn't. Instead, at the birth of her fourth son, Leah names him Judah, which means "let him (God) be praised."

Living by faith isn't easy. But it's the only way to show that we believe that God wants only the best for us. Today when events or your feelings pull you toward fear and cynicism, remember Leah and choose faith. ✤

PRAYER

O Father in heaven, I choose to focus on you, rather than ...

day12

WRESTLING

Then the man said, "Let me go, for it is daybreak."
But Jacob replied, "I will not let you go unless you bless me." GENESIS 32:26

Scripture paints an unusual portrait for us in the story of Jacob's sweaty struggle with God on the banks of the Jabbok, a struggle culminating in Jacob's receiving the name his people carry to this day.

Jacob always had been determined to do things his own way—whether it was wresting control of his brother's birthright or amassing wealth from Laban's flocks. After years of learning the hard way that his way wasn't God's way, he finally did something right. He seized an opportunity to grab onto God and hold on with all his might.

Worship is composed of familiar elements such as praise, adoration, confession and intercession. Sometimes we forget, however, that worshiping God also involves persistence—pursuing hard after the One who is impossible to see, but who is never at a distance from us.

Worship doesn't always feel good; at times it resembles Jacob's struggle more than Sunday morning singing. Scripture reminds us that problems and trials are good for us because they help us learn to endure, and endurance produces the strength of character God longs to see in us (see Romans 5:3–4).

Are you struggling with God right now and feeling frustrated? Take a lesson from Jacob and hold fast to the One who has promised to never let you go. ♣

PRAYER

Lord, I'm really struggling with ...

IT'S THE PITS

Joseph's master took him and put him in prison, the place where the king's prisoners were confined.

But while Joseph was there in the prison, the LORD was with him; he showed him kindness and granted him favor in the eyes of the prison warden.   Genesis 39:20–21

Whenever we're tempted to think "Woe is me," Joseph's story can remind us that others have it worse. Unjustly accused of the attempted rape of Potiphar's wife, Joseph was thrown into prison.

Believers in Christ are not exempt from unjust accusations. How, then, do we worship in the midst of such awful circumstances?

The key is found in a small phrase in today's verses: The Lord was with Joseph. When God is with us, even a prison cell can become a place of worship. Regardless of our circumstances, we can take comfort in the fact that God has promised to stay close by our side. Remember his promise to Moses? "I will be with you." To Gideon? "I will be with you." And to Paul? "I will be with you."

Worship does not only take place in a sanctuary or even with the companionship of other believers. Learn to welcome those times when life's unfairness draws you closest to the One who has promised never to leave you. He already is there, waiting. ✤

PRAYER

Dear Father, I feel . . .

day14

RESTORED RELATIONSHIPS

Then he threw his arms around his brother Benjamin and wept, and Benjamin embraced him, weeping. And he kissed all his brothers and wept over them. Afterward his brothers talked with him.   GENESIS 45:14–15

Families function in very different ways, but by any comparison, Joseph's family was far from typical. He was the preferred son out of twelve brothers, and his favored status stirred up in his brothers a jealousy so intense that his siblings sold him into slavery. Later, after God had brought Joseph into prominence as a ruler in Egypt, he had his brothers at his mercy. He could either pay them back for the years of pain they had caused him, or he could forgive them and restore their shattered family relationship. Joseph chose to forgive.

Only a soul refined in the fires of adversity can react in such a way. Throughout the years of slavery, and later imprisonment, Joseph found solace and strength in his relationship with his heavenly Father. When opportunity came to bless or curse those who had wronged him, Joseph chose blessing.

Look at your personal family relationships in the light of Scripture. Have you allowed old grievances to separate you from the very people you are to care for? Spend time with God, like Joseph, and allow God's love to change your heart. ✛

PRAYER

Lord, you know my family. Help me to forgive . . .

day15

SITUATION UNDER CONTROL

But Joseph said to them, "Don't be afraid. Am I in the place of God? You intended to harm me, but God intended it for good to accomplish what is now being done, the saving of many lives." GENESIS 50:19–20

Life is full of unexpected situations. A pink slip. A spouse announcing his or her intention to leave. A child in trouble. A job transfer. A heart-stopping lab result. A church split. Events like these suddenly sweep us up and carry us along. Only God knows where we'll end up.

This is the lesson of Joseph's life. And it is the message of Joseph's lips. Sold into slavery as a teenager by his jealous brothers. Falsely accused of attempted rape. Thrown into an Egyptian dungeon. Forgotten. Where is God in all this chaos and injustice?

Answer: Watching. Weaving all these jumbled, seemingly random events together into a purposeful, beautiful whole. And just when we think evil really has won, God orchestrates the ultimate plot twist. Joseph is inexplicably rescued from the depths and set in a position where he is able to save his speechless brothers and devastated father.

Our great challenge each day is to look beyond our circumstances to the One who controls all things. As you listen to, read or watch the news today, use it as a springboard for worship. Thank God that in the reports of chaos and evil, he is working out his good purposes in the world and in your life. ✤

PRAYER

Lord, help me trust your way and your time when it comes to ...

day16 january 16

ATTENTION GRABBER

When the LORD saw that he had gone over to look, God called to him from within the bush, "Moses! Moses!"

And Moses said, "Here I am."

"Do not come any closer," God said. "Take off your sandals, for the place where you are standing is holy ground." EXODUS 3:4–5

Moses wasn't looking for God in the wilderness. God found him there, however. And God's presence gave Moses a gateway to step into a place of true worship.

We often think that if God is present, people should notice him. Moses should have sensed he was on holy ground, right? But the act of "coming into God's presence" doesn't necessarily mean we understand that presence. We take the first step towards worship each time we become aware that God constantly surrounds us.

Moses' awareness of God's presence preceded his training in worship. Out of our desire to worship, we often rush to manufacture forms and feelings of what we believe worship should be. We're missing out on the real thing. Our "It's Sunday, let's worship" attitude skips an important step. Like Moses, our worship only begins after we recognize God and attune our hearts to listen to him.

Looking for holy ground? God will direct you to that place of worship in the most unexpected times. Be ready to turn your attention to him. ✤

PRAYER

Lord God, please help me recognize your presence in my day . . .

GOD'S QUALIFICATIONS

I will take you as my own people, and I will be your God. Then you will know that I am the LORD your God, who brought you out from under the yoke of the Egyptians. And I will bring you to the land I swore with uplifted hand to give to Abraham, to Isaac and to Jacob. I will give it to you as a possession. I am the LORD. EXODUS 6:7–8

We praise people for what they do. Rarely does someone become famous because of who they are. They have to publish, score, invent, sell, win, lead or record.

This standard of praising others is often what we use when we praise God. Our first question is, "What has God done to benefit me?" The quality of his blessing equals the quality of our praise. Using this standard, Pharaoh might not have had much to say to God. God unleashed terror upon terror on Pharaoh's country for holding the Israelites. Did that exempt him from worshiping God? No, God still expected Pharaoh to acknowledge and worship him as the true God.

God tells us a lot about himself in the Scriptures. He also proclaims that he does many things. But when our worship becomes contingent on God doing things for us, we walk on dangerous ground. God will not be managed or manipulated. We have an obligation to worship God for who God is.

In his reintroduction to the Israelites, God begins and ends his address with the declaration, "I am the Lord!" He repeats this phrase over 130 times in the Old Testament when addressing Israel. God wanted his people to know him. He expected that worship would be the by-product of his relationship with them. Take time right now to worship the God that you know. ✣

PRAYER

Lord, I know this about you . . .

REMEMBERING YOUR PASSOVER

The blood will be a sign for you on the houses where you are, and when I see the blood, I will pass over you. No destructive plague will touch you when I strike Egypt.

This is a day you are to commemorate; for the generations to come you shall celebrate it as a festival to the LORD—a lasting ordinance.   EXODUS 12:13–14

For nearly 3,500 years, since the time of their exodus from Egypt, the Jews have been remembering the Lord's "pass over." God instituted the Passover celebration as an integral part of Israel's law. It's a good thing, too. Not long after their deliverance from slavery, the Israelites' praise seemed to be drowned out by mounting complaints.

Sound familiar? So often we forget God's blessings soon after they are bestowed upon us, not reflecting upon his interaction with past generations. Do you know in what specific ways he blessed your great grandparents? Have you told your children about God's blessings in your life? There's value in both looking back and passing on a record of God's work. Worshiping God becomes more and more natural when we take time to remember why we worship.

When you begin to complain, sit down and literally count your blessings. You will never come to the end of God's good deeds. ✤

PRAYER

Here are the blessings, Lord, that I am thankful for today ...

THE BEST DEFENSE

Moses answered the people, "Do not be afraid. Stand firm and you will see the deliverance the LORD will bring you today. The Egyptians you see today you will never see again. The LORD will fight for you; you need only to be still." EXODUS 14:13–14

We take our defense seriously, both personally and as nations. Having a good defense means winning a case or triumphing over an opponent. We naturally connect defending ourselves with action. With this mindset, Moses' instruction for the people to "be still" sounds too passive, or at best, risky.

For the Israelites facing the rushing Egyptian army, standing still tested and demonstrated their trust in God. Standing still helped them to start standing firm in their faith.

The same God who defended the Israelites defends us. While our instincts may scream for us to be proactive, we must remember that these impulses are repeatedly driven by fear and pride. We will all face circumstances that threaten our security. Having an attitude of expectant stillness during these intimidating experiences opens the door for us to trust and worship God.

Although you feel trapped, wait a little longer. Remember the words of the psalmist, "But you, LORD, are a shield around me, my glory, the One who lifts my head high" (Psalm 3:3). Stand firm and worship the One who is already fighting for you. ♣

PRAYER

Lord, I need your defense concerning ...

day**20**

LIFT UP MY BANNER

Moses built an altar and called it The LORD is my Banner. EXODUS 17:15

Winning battles typically involves superior weapons, larger forces or a better strategy. But when God is Commander in Chief, all natural rules of war are thrown out. Consider how Moses, Joshua and the Israelites won this particular battle (see Exodus 17:8–16): Joshua fought, Moses prayed, Aaron and Hur assisted, and the Lord God, *Yahweh Nissi*, was the rallying point—the banner lifted high that carried them to victory.

As long as Moses kept his eyes focused on God and his arms lifted to him, the Israelites prevailed. But as he grew tired and his arms sagged with fatigue, the enemy advanced.

How true that is in our own lives as well. When we are focused on God as our only hope, we are able to overcome the obstacles and conflicts in life. But when we allow fatigue and weariness of spirit to distract us from spending time with God in worship and prayer, the enemy advances and overtakes us.

Let the examples of Moses and Joshua remind you where to turn daily to regain your strength. ❖

PRAYER

Thank you, Lord, for your . . .

MODERN IDOLS

And God spoke all these words: "I am the LORD your God, who brought you out of Egypt, out of the land of slavery.

"You shall have no other gods before me.

"You shall not make for yourself an image in the form of anything in heaven above or on the earth beneath or in the waters below. You shall not bow down to them or worship them; for I, the LORD your God, am a jealous God, punishing the children for the sin of the parents to the third and fourth generation of those who hate me." EXODUS 20:1–5

Idol worship is more subtle for us today than for those in the days of the Old Testament. Instead of a wooden or silver statue, we may choose to worship money and success. Our "healthy" quest to look our best may actually be an idolization of outward beauty.

We naturally find it easier to dedicate our time, money, love and strength to the things we think we control. And there's the trap. Idols always end up controlling us. Even the words we use to talk about our idols reveal their suffocating effect — we get wrapped up in work or addicted to shopping.

In contrast, worshiping God always has a liberating effect. He asks for our total dedication to free us from bondage. God knows our great temptation to worship idols. That's why he highlighted the importance of proper worship from the very beginning of his relationship with Israel.

God spoke about faithfulness in his first commandment to the Israelites. Today, God still asks for our wholehearted devotion. Are there "idols" in your life right now that are preventing you from wholehearted devotion? Ask God to reveal them, and then take steps to remove them. ✤

PRAYER

O Holy God, the idols I see in my life are . . .

HE'S AWESOME!

When Moses went up on the mountain, the cloud covered it, and the glory of the LORD set-
tled on Mount Sinai. For six days the cloud covered the mountain, and on the seventh day
the LORD called to Moses from within the cloud. To the Israelites the glory of the LORD
looked like a consuming fire on top of the mountain. Then Moses entered the cloud as he
went on up the mountain. And he stayed on the mountain forty days and forty nights.

EXODUS 24:15–18

"That's awesome!" we say about many things these days. Yet in the Bible, to be awesome is to command both fear and adoration. God chose certain situations to highlight different parts of his character, including the awesome wonder of his glory, which was "like a consuming fire." With Moses and the other leaders perched on Mount Sinai, God chose to demonstrate this characteristic to the people standing below.

At the time, the Israelites fully understood God's greatness as he seemingly torched the mountain. Sadly, a month later the people were bowing down to a golden calf. Apparently, asking for signs and proof of God's awesomeness did not guarantee they would continue to worship him.

Experiencing God's awesomeness moves us one step closer to knowing him. So how do you get to the place where you personally recognize and respond to God's greatness? Instead of attempting to force a respectful response in worship, begin by looking inward. Seeing God's awesomeness also means acknowledging the truth about yourself—your own frailty and dependence on him for everything. God is greater than you can imagine. ✤

> **PRAYER**

Lord God, help me to experience your greatness . . .

GOD'S MOBILE HOME

Have them make a sanctuary for me, and I will dwell among them. Make this tabernacle and all its furnishings exactly like the pattern I will show you.   EXODUS 25:8–9

Give a child some old sheets and pillows, and watch him or her construct a giant fort. Let a kid loose in enough snow, and a castle will materialize. In the eyes of children, these structures are magnificent and magical. Children like to build and play in forts that replicate their real houses — places that offer shelter, protection and stability.

When God commissioned the Israelites to build a home for him, he obviously wasn't asking them for protection from the rain. He's God. Unlike a child's fort, the tabernacle served a much greater purpose than a shelter or a place of protection. The tabernacle was important for its ability to teach the Israelites about their Lord. The Holy Place and Most Holy Place declared God's perfect holiness and purity. The tabernacle's detailed instructions proclaimed God's creative genius. And the tabernacle's portable nature told a migrant people that their God would always be with them no matter where they went.

Throughout the Bible, from the tabernacle to the temple to the birth of Jesus Christ, God has shown himself as our "God with us." Wherever you go, God is with you. ✤

PRAYER

Almighty God, you are my shelter . . .

CLEANING UP

Then the LORD said to Moses, "Make a bronze basin, with its bronze stand, for washing. Place it between the tent of meeting and the altar, and put water in it. Aaron and his sons are to wash their hands and feet with water from it." EXODUS 30:17–19

In Old Testament times, serving God was serious business. The priests and Levites, God's appointed ministers to the Israelites, were given specific instructions as to how to approach God. The Hebrew word for minister, *meshereth*, means one who serves a superior. Aaron and his descendants understood that what was required of them was humble service to God.

God's directions to the priests and Levites were in two areas: how to minister to the Lord and how to be holy as God is holy. To be a servant required holiness.

In this passage, God gives Moses instructions regarding how the washbasin was to be used in the tabernacle. The washbasin represented the importance of holiness in God's presence. Positioned in front of the Holy Place, it was a reminder of the cleansing process necessary for worshiping God. When the priests and Levites cleaned their hands and feet, their actions represented spiritual cleansing before ministering.

God's Word reveals to us that he delights in both spiritual and physical worlds, and he's willing to use physical symbols like the washbasin to remind us of spiritual realities. God calls us to holiness. Are you living out that spiritual reality? ✣

PRAYER

Cleanse my heart, O God, . . .

day25

SHOCK AND AWE

And he passed in front of Moses, proclaiming, "The LORD, the LORD, the compassionate and gracious God, slow to anger, abounding in love and faithfulness."   EXODUS 34:6

The repetition of God's name here is striking. God is emphasizing his covenant name, and the repetition serves to focus Moses' attention on God himself. God uses repetition later in the Pentateuch as well: "the LORD our God, the LORD is one" (Deuteronomy 6:4). After God says, "The LORD," twice, he provides insight directly into his character. God is compassionate, gracious, forbearing, loving and faithful.

We can never put God in a neat little package. Sometimes people try to describe him as a benign and loving old man, or vilify him as a power-hungry warlord. Neither portrayal fits the God who is beyond comprehension. We grow to know God the same way Moses did—by listening to what God tells us about his character.

The more we know about God, the more we'll be moved to praise him, and the more we will be in shock and awe of him. Thankfully, he keeps telling us about himself. Moses was shown God and instantly responded in worship. Our response can be the same. ❖

PRAYER

Help me, Lord, to respond to you ...

OFFER YOUR GIFTS

They joined five of the curtains into one set and the other six into another set. Then they made fifty loops along the edge of the end curtain in one set and also along the edge of the end curtain in the other set. EXODUS 36:16–17

How many people does it take to make a worship service happen? The pastor, probably an instrumentalist or two, a vocal leader, maybe a choir or ensemble. Just add a congregation, and ... wait a minute.

Does your church distribute a bulletin? Someone typed, printed and copied it. Did someone hand you that bulletin? How about the people who took the offering or greeted you as you entered? What about the nursery attendants? Or the people who cleaned the building?

The point is, a lot more people are a part of the worship experience than the small handful of folks you see up front during the service.

What gifts or talents do you have that could be utilized in worship or serving the Lord?

Consider the Hebrew artisans working on the tabernacle. Their behind-the-scenes labor—making curtains, clasps, coverings, frames, bases—was deemed important enough to be recorded in the Word of God. Worship in the tabernacle would have been greatly diminished—and also much less than what God wanted it to be—without their contributions.

Today, look for ways you can use your gifts and abilities as an act of worship to God. ❧

PRAYER

Lord, I offer you my gifts ...

THE SACRIFICE FOR SIN

If any member of the community sins unintentionally and does what is forbidden in any of the LORD's commands, when they realize their guilt and the sin they have committed becomes known, they must bring as their offering for the sin they committed a female goat without defect. LEVITICUS 4:27–28

We often forget that the Israelite worship center was a slaughterhouse. It was a place where birds were torn apart with bare hands, where the plunge of knives turned livestock into dead-stock, where blood flowed in trenches and the odor of charred flesh filled the nostrils of worshipers. Death was ever present in the house of God — a reminder of the consequences of sin.

We are spared the necessity of this blood sacrifice because of Jesus Christ. His death on the cross paid the penalty due for our sin. Nothing we do adds to the sacrifice Jesus paid for our sin. We are accepted by God because of Jesus' death. It is the only sacrifice that pays for our sin.

God chose to let his own Son pay the penalty for our sin so that we could have a restored relationship with him that is not contingent on a continual sacrifice. We are freed not only by the blood, but from the blood. We have a free relationship with God that allows us anytime access to God. Take time today to thank God for this indescribable gift! ✤

PRAYER

Lord, thank you for the gift of your sacrifice for my sin ...

day28

MAKING IT RIGHT—RIGHT AWAY

When anyone becomes aware that they are guilty in any of these matters, they must confess in what way they have sinned. As a penalty for the sin they have committed, they must bring to the LORD a female lamb or goat from the flock as a sin offering; and the priest shall make atonement for them for their sin. LEVITICUS 5:5–6

Why is it at times we feel so dry, like our inner spirit has shriveled up?

If you're going through a period of spiritual dryness, when worship becomes something you must force or fake, it could be you are experiencing what certain mystics called "the dark night of the soul"—a period in which God removes the sense of his presence in the process of raising someone to a higher level of devotion. Or it could be much simpler than that. You could have unconfessed sin in your life.

The practical religion of the Hebrews made provision for confession, restitution and atonement in its sacrificial system. We're not governed by the same laws. But we, too, have to do something about our sin in order to restore our connection with God.

Is there some unconfessed sin that is preventing you from enjoying God's presence? Take time right now to bring that before God. ✤

PRAYER

Lord, to make things right between us, I confess that ...

FIRE FROM GOD

Fire came out from the presence of the LORD and consumed the burnt offering and the fat portions on the altar. And when all the people saw it, they shouted for joy and fell face-down.
      LEVITICUS 9:24

Who is this God we worship? How nearly do our ideas about him approximate reality?

From time to time, people in Scripture got a glimpse of God. And as at the inauguration of the tabernacle, they responded with powerful emotions such as joy and fear. No tame God here. No illusions that they could master him.

Does your worship generate a thrill in touching something of the real God—at least from time to time? Do you sometimes experience a conflict of emotions such as fear and delight? Do you find yourself moved? If spending time in the presence of God is always comfortable, never anything that would make you fall on your face in reverence, you have further to go.

As you go through the day, take with you a sense of God's majesty, his power, his awesome presence. Fire blazes forth from the presence of the Lord. Feel the heat. ✤

PRAYER

Great God, show me the real you . . .

HOLY BEFORE THE HOLY ONE

I am the LORD your God; consecrate yourselves and be holy, because I am holy. Do not make yourselves unclean by any creature that moves along the ground.   LEVITICUS 11:44

A wedding invitee was digging postholes on his ranch when he suddenly remembered the wedding, which was to begin in less than half an hour. He hopped into his pickup and raced off to the church. At first congratulating himself on managing to slip into a pew before the bride began her procession, he soon noticed other guests casting glances his way. This was a formal church wedding—and he was in dirty work clothes! He was mortified.

The lyric to an angel praise chorus begins this way: "Holy, holy, holy is the Lord God Almighty" (Revelation 4:8). The triple use of "holy" indicates complete holiness. God is not just rather holy or considerably holy but *wholly* holy.

Singing such a song is all well and good for angels who have never sinned. But what about us? How can we, who swim in the sin-polluted pool known as humanity, presume to come near God and declare his holiness?

God chooses to see us as righteous if we ask to be clothed in Christ's righteousness and washed in his blood. Do a mental assessment of your spiritual attire. What is preventing you from worshiping him "in the splendor of his holiness" (Psalm 29:2)? ✤

> **PRAYER**

O Lord, show me my sin ...

day31

THE DRIPPING CROSS

For the life of a creature is in the blood, and I have given it to you to make atonement for yourselves on the altar; it is the blood that makes atonement for one's life.

LEVITICUS 17:11

Those of us who attend churches where the old hymns are still sung can find ourselves singing some pretty gruesome lines:

- "There is a fountain filled with blood drawn from Emmanuel's veins."
- "What can wash away my sin? Nothing but the blood of Jesus."
- "In the old rugged cross, stained with blood so divine, a wondrous beauty I see."

Gruesome, yes, but maybe the old hymns have got something right. Worship is not solely about focusing on the pleasant aspects of the Christian faith. After all, the book of Psalms—Israel's hymnbook—includes songs of lament and sorrow over sin as well as uplifting praises of thanksgiving and gratitude.

The blood splatter of Old Testament sacrifices was like graffiti spelling out, "Death is the only currency that can pay for sin!" And then Christ's death, in the ultimate way, fulfilled God's teaching that atonement comes by blood.

O, bless the Lord for the atoning blood of Christ! May our worship never forget the blood. Rejoice today in the blood of the Lamb. ✤

PRAYER

Lord, when I think of the atoning death of Jesus, I . . .

day32

SEPARATED FOR WORSHIP

Consecrate yourselves and be holy, because I am the LORD your God. Keep my decrees and follow them. I am the LORD, who makes you holy. LEVITICUS 20:7–8

What does it take to create an elite group—whether it's soldiers, athletes or scholars? Elite troops, athletes or scholars need to commit to being isolated, often physically, in order to properly train for their tasks. Separation enhances focus and change.

God gave the ancient Israelites marks to set them apart—marks ranging from peculiar food choices to a unique ceremonial and legal system. We, also, are to be different from unbelievers. Adopting worship as a lifestyle means accepting an identity as something of a holy oddball, for unlike others, our first motivation in life is to know God.

As we write the scripts of our lives day by day, let us make choices that will help conform us to the nature of Christ rather than to any other pattern set before us. Through this choice, we say, "Father, your will be done today," and we commend our spirits to God.

A worshipful life separates us in regard to the world. A worshipful life will allow Christ to mold us into our right shape. ✤

PRAYER

Father, help me as I seek to follow your ways . . .

A VACATION WITH GOD

Consecrate the fiftieth year and proclaim liberty throughout the land to all its inhabitants. It shall be a jubilee for you; each of you is to return to your family property and to your own clan. LEVITICUS 25:10

A common complaint today is that people are too busy. Too busy to sleep, too busy to relate to others, too busy to enjoy life. And all this "too busyness" produces tired, stressed-out people who are hobbled in their ability to enjoy the presence of God.

The year of jubilee was a time to get off the hamster wheel of moneymaking and trust in God's provision. It was a time to relax and let life flow back into the mold God had made for it. Longer than a Sabbath, longer even than a religious festival, jubilee was an extended period in which God's people were given the opportunity to gaze on the face of God until that face became clear, in all its loveliness, through the haze of everyday concerns.

Oh, what freedom! Who among us could not benefit from an extended period in which to put down our tools and spend our time gazing on God?

Our own jubilee experiences can be times when worship goes from being an interlude to being the permanent cast of our nature. It is in these times that we can learn what it means to keep in step with the Spirit and pray without ceasing.

You don't need to wait for an extended period of time to experience jubilee. Make a point to schedule a time of "mini-jubilee" today. ✤

PRAYER

Lord, please meet me ...

A CALL TO WORSHIP

The LORD said to Moses, "Bring the tribe of Levi and present them to Aaron the priest to assist him. They are to perform duties for him and for the whole community at the tent of meeting by doing the work of the tabernacle." NUMBERS 3:5−7

Larry was a recovering alcoholic who became a believer. He asked his pastor one Sunday morning if he could gather in the church office with the staff and members of the worship team for prayer. Pastor Greg was willing.

Standing in a circle, each person took a turn seeking the Lord's blessing on the worship service. When it was Larry's turn, he talked to Jesus with confidence and sincerity. Though his language wasn't eloquent, it was clear he knew who he was talking to. As those who would lead worship prepared to leave for the sanctuary, Larry wrapped his huge arms around them and said, "Go give 'em heaven!"

The next week Pastor Greg asked Larry if he'd be willing to attend the pre-service prayer gathering again. Larry had found a place of ministry.

Just as the Levites were set apart to use their gifts and abilities in corporate worship in Moses' day, so you have been gifted too. Be encouraged by Larry's example. He was affirmed as an intercessor and encourager. And that's not all. As he grew in his faith, he discovered he had the gift of evangelism. Five years after beginning his weekly prayer ministry with the staff, he and his wife, Linda, joined Wycliffe Bible Translators as missionaries in South America.

You have been gifted by God to contribute uniquely to building his kingdom. Discover and celebrate your gifts. Then worship the Giver today by using them for his glory. ✤

PRAYER

Lord, thank you for the ability you've given me to . . .

GOD IS SMILING AT YOU

The LORD bless you and keep you; the LORD make his face shine on you and be gracious to you; the LORD turn his face toward you and give you peace.   NUMBERS 6:24–26

Being validated by a father or a mother is critical. Sons and daughters who have not received their parents' blessing in some shape or form often struggle with self-doubt and feelings of inferiority. They can lose their spiritual moorings and even drift away from worshiping their heavenly Father.

God's heart beats with concern for those in need of validation. It's significant in this passage that the Lord is the one who takes the initiative. He tells Moses to tell Aaron and his sons to speak words of encouragement and blessing on his behalf. God wanted his people to have the assurance that he was smiling on them. He desired to shower them with protection, grace, favor and peace.

The good news is that he still desires to do that for his people today. His heart is one of compassion and care ... and joy! He wants to bestow upon you this day his blessing, his protection, and yes, even his smile. Think about it. Right where you are—whether it's in your office, at the kitchen table, sitting outside on a park bench—God the Creator is smiling at you. Reflect on that image and thank God for his love ... and smile back!

From the beginning of time God has used all sorts of ways to make sure his people know that they are loved, accepted and forgiven. Out of that assurance, draw near to him now, and worship him in spirit and in truth. ✢

PRAYER

Father, I long to know that I have been accepted by you ...

day36

LET'S HEAR IT FOR THE BAND!

Also at your times of rejoicing—your appointed festivals and New Moon feasts—you are to sound the trumpets over your burnt offerings and fellowship offerings, and they will be a memorial for you before your God. I am the LORD your God. NUMBERS 10:10

By definition, worship is coming before God in a set-apart time and place to esteem his greatness: "Great is the LORD, and most worthy of praise" (Psalm 48:1). It's a time when the worth of God should draw out the best we have to offer—coming into his presence with praise on our lips, mindful of him rather than being self-conscious.

One way you can give your best to God is through giving whatever musical ability you have. Whether you are belting out an a cappella solo of "Awesome God" in the shower or singing with hundreds in a performance of the "Messiah," music gives wings to your words. It amplifies your ability to esteem God's worth. There is just something about music that rolls out a red carpet on which your gratitude parades into God's presence.

According to this text, trumpets were appropriate for calling attention to "times of rejoicing." We all can relate to that. The brassy sound of a blaring trumpet can wake the recharged soldier with "Reveille" or invite the weary warrior to rest with "Taps." It can also signal the saints to "give it up" for Jesus. That's why the trumpet is still the horn of choice when we sing "Christ the Lord Is Risen Today" in church on Easter Sunday.

Today, fill the air with praise as a means of celebrating your "times of rejoicing." ✤

PRAYER

I want to thank you, Lord, for ...

day37

NO POWER SHORTAGE HERE!

The LORD answered Moses, "Is the LORD's arm too short? Now you will see whether or not what I say will come true for you."   NUMBERS 11:23

Lloyd John Ogilvie, who once served as chaplain of the United State Senate, also served as the senior minister at First Presbyterian Church of Hollywood (CA). Wearing a royal blue liturgical robe with red piping, he stood before the congregation of that historic church each Sunday at the start of the service. Smiling yet reverent, he called the people to worship by referencing the power of God available to them. He reminded them that every Sunday was Easter Sunday. The power that emptied the tomb of its weekend tenant could be expected to accomplish great and mighty things every day of the week.

This story is reminiscent of the Lord's announcement to Moses that there was no power shortage in the wilderness: "Is the LORD's arm too short?"

The Lord knew the people were beginning to doubt his ability to care for them en route to the promised land. Time and time again he demonstrated the degree to which he was in control. It saddened him to see the children of Israel act like spoiled brats, throwing tantrums instead of allowing their experience of God's power to motivate their desire for more of him.

Yet don't we do the same when we resort to complaining instead of praising, worrying instead of depending, shrinking in fear instead of going boldly forward in God's power? Like the Israelites, we need to pause and remember how God has demonstrated—time and time again—his power in our lives.

Look around you and then inside you. Where do you see God at work, using his awesome power to change lives? ✤

> **PRAYER**

Awesome God, as I contemplate the powerful way you provide for my needs, I can't help but . . .

CROSS PURPOSES

You will have these tassels to look at and so you will remember all the commands of the
LORD, that you may obey them and not prostitute yourselves by chasing after the lusts of
your own hearts and eyes.   NUMBERS 15:39

Just as the tassels in ancient Jewish worship served as visual aids, so the cross is a powerful reminder of the work of Christ for Christians today.

However, what was an obvious symbol of Christianity a century or two ago is no longer so obvious. The cross has become little more than a popular shape for a pendant worn by Christians and non-Christians alike. It is gilded with gold or studded with diamonds to make it beautiful. But actually, there isn't anything beautiful about the cross; it was used as an instrument of torture, suffering and death.

But it is wondrous. To the Christian who knows what Jesus accomplished on it, the cross is a symbol that conveys wonder—wonder that God should love us. Wonder that Jesus would die for us. Wonder that the cross spanned a gulf that separated us from our Creator.

Like the tassels the Lord commanded the people of Israel to attach to their clothing, the cross serves as a reminder each time we see one. When we see a cross, we recall that Jesus tells us to take up our cross daily in order to keep our eyes focused on him. What does that mean for us today? Only as we make the Lord the object of our personal worship can we fully celebrate the benefits he made available to us on that "cross of wonder."

We see many crosses around us—in window panes, in the lower case *t*, through building profiles, perched atop church steeples. Let these remind us of the cross of Christ, the focus of God's love and forgiveness so wondrously displayed through his Son. ♣

PRAYER

Remind me, Father, of . . .

day39

HIS PROVISION IS FOR THE BIRDS — AND US

The LORD said to Moses, "Gather the people together and I will give them water."
Then Israel sang this song: "Spring up, O well! Sing about it, about the well that the princes dug, that the nobles of the people sank — the nobles with scepters and staffs."

NUMBERS 21:16–18

As she looked out her kitchen window, Wendy saw a bright yellow finch in flight. It flew to the birdbath in the backyard and perched on the edge. Sensing this was a moment of wonder, Wendy, a harried young mother of three, stopped scrubbing the grime from the crock pot. She took note of what was going on in the life of this little feathered member of God's creation. The finch lifted its head toward the sky and started to sing. Because she was inside the house and the window was locked, Wendy wasn't able to hear the song. But as she watched one of God's precious creatures, she had no trouble hearing the Creator's voice within her.

"Don't be anxious, dear daughter," she heard. "I know your life is stressful. I know you have concerns for your family. But allow this visual sermon to fill your heart with faith. Just as I provide for the birds of the air and the fish of the sea, I will provide for you."

At that, Wendy began to sing, "I sing because I'm happy ... His eye is on the sparrow and I know he watches me." Like the Israelites of old who sang because of the water God provided, this woman worshiped the One who delights in providing for those he loves.

Stop for a moment and find your own evidence of God's grace and provision — a flower, a friend, a gift, the gentle rain — and use it to turn your heart to the Creator. ✤

PRAYER

Lord, help me today to trust you to ...

day40

COMPASS POINTS

God is not human, that he should lie, not a human being, that he should change his mind. Does he speak and then not act? Does he promise and not fulfill? NUMBERS 23:19

Seeking shelter after an unexpected summer rain, you leave the trail and find a spot where the overhanging branches of giant redwood trees provide a protective canopy. When the dark clouds have emptied their liquid content, you set out to return to the path. The thicket through which you pushed to recline at the trunk of the tree is higher than you remember.

You're becoming worried. You can't find the path. After ten minutes of frantic false starts, you reach into a pocket and pull out a compass. You knew the path on which you were hiking was leading you in a northerly direction. Once you determine where the arrow is pointing, all you need do is follow the needle. Within two minutes you are back on the trail, smelling the fragrance of a summer rain and singing "How Great Thou Art."

Just as the needle of a compass always points to true north, so the God we worship is always reliable. He always does what he says. Promise-breaking Providence is an oxymoron. As the verse above indicates, God is not one to change his mind. His word is a promissory note you can bank on.

Go ahead and ponder that reality. Allow the Lord to draw you to it. That certainty is a blessed assurance with which you can give to God the glory he deserves. ✤

> **PRAYER**

O Changeless One, give me the confidence today to believe . . .

PARTY ON!

"In addition to what you vow and your freewill offerings, offer these to the LORD at your appointed festivals: your burnt offerings, grain offerings, drink offerings and fellowship offerings."
NUMBERS 29:39

An "oldie but a goodie" hit that's often heard at karaoke sing-alongs is "Celebration" by Kool and the Gang. No, it's not a Christian song, but what it calls attention to is the inherent desire people have to enjoy a party. We were born to celebrate!

Judging from what we read in Numbers, our inclination to throw confetti has its roots in history. The Lord established a rhythm of celebration for the Israelites that called for special festivals over and above the regular worship observances that punctuated their calendars. You can't look at the worship life of the people of God without seeing the trappings of ceremony and pageantry. It's everywhere.

Worship was not a casual "oh by the way let's pray and be done with it" sort of thing. The worship of God was an event. There were great numbers of people— adults and kids. There were animals. There was fire and food, tents and music . . . and time. The festivals, sacrifices and offerings took time.

The reason for these celebrations was this: It was all about the Lord. The Creator called his people—and still does—to take time in his presence to fix their thoughts on him while they feasted and enjoyed themselves. He wanted them to have a good time doing it, but he also wanted them to take their time and not rush.

Since he loves being the object of our celebration, he reminds us to celebrate often. Come celebrate! ✤

PRAYER

Lord, as I come into your presence each day, help me not to be so time-conscious . . .

CHARTING YOUR PROGRESS

At the LORD's command Moses recorded the stages in their journey.   NUMBERS 33:2

For as long as she could remember, Star had kept a journal. In addition to charting mundane trivia like weather and what she accomplished each day, she maintained a list of details that might prove helpful in the future.

For example, if she entertained houseguests on a given day, she'd record the menu she prepared—so not to repeat the same recipe each time. But Star's journal was more than facts and figures. It also chronicled her faith: significant milestones of God's intervention. Times of unexpected blessing. Documentations of answered prayer. From time to time she would pick up one of her completed journals and reflect on God's faithfulness.

As Star entered her eighth decade of life and began to struggle with short-term memory loss, she wondered if she would fall prey to the same monster that had destroyed her mother's mind. Tests for Alzheimer's disease were negative, but the fear of what might happen motivated Star to maintain her daily routine of making journal entries before going to bed. "Even if I am spared from coming down with that dreaded disease," she said, "at least I will have a thorough record of my life to pass on to my children and grandchildren."

What this grandmother experienced is the very blessing God gave the Israelites when he commanded Moses to keep a written record of the wilderness journey. The discipline of looking back helps you come to terms with the distance you've covered. Can you think of some pivotal mileposts you've experienced along life's way? Allow those to prompt you to look up in worship today. ✤

PRAYER

Lord, as I look back on how you led me throughout my years, I can't help thinking . . .

day43

NEARER MY GOD TO ME

What other nation is so great as to have their gods near them the way the LORD our God is near us whenever we pray to him?   DEUTERONOMY 4:7

From the earliest times of Israel's faith, the God of Abraham, Isaac and Jacob was not a run-of-the-mill deity. Unlike the distant gods other cultures claimed, Israel's God was never far away. He traveled with his people through the wilderness en route to the promised land.

In the days of the Old Testament, the presence of God was symbolized by the ark of the covenant and the tabernacle. The altar of sacrifice was a tangible reminder that God was engaged with his people. To fully appreciate the reality of God's nearness, you needed to be near the fixtures of faith.

Not today. Now your heart is an altar. It really is. God accepts the sacrifice you willingly lay there. Your pride. Your worries. Your sin. You don't need to wait for church on Sunday to connect with him. Obviously, there are advantages to being in a place where through worship and teaching his grace is so tangible you can almost touch it. But there are also advantages to engaging God at the moment you need him right where you are. Taking a sick child to the doctor's office. Stressing out over a business meeting. Racing to get dinner on the table. God is near.

When the cares of the world have pinned you to the mat, he's committed to being there for you. All he desires is that you call out his name and recognize your dependence on him. With a cry or a whisper, with a song or a prayer, God is listening for those who want to access the "privilege of proximity." ✢

PRAYER

Father, when I consider that I can call on you wherever I am no matter what time of day it is, I...

day44

THE HEART OF WORSHIP

Hear, O Israel: The LORD our God, the LORD is one. Love the LORD your God with all your heart and with all your soul and with all your strength. DEUTERONOMY 6:4–5

Matt Redman, a songwriter, performer and worship leader in England, has committed his life to helping Christians worship. Several years ago the pastor at Matt's church sensed that the praise music and instrumentation had lost its focus and authenticity. The congregation was not entering into worship with their entire selves. In a radical departure from the norm, the minister prohibited the praise team from leading the worship. For several months singing was led with only an acoustical guitar, or the songs were sung a cappella.

Interestingly, the essence of dynamic worship returned. The heart of worship had little to do with keyboards, drums, electric guitars or new and improved lyrics. The congregation was reminded that worship is about encountering the living Lord and loving him.

Deeply moved by what he experienced during the "music moratorium," Matt Redman was inspired to write "The Heart of Worship." In this song, he describes what happens when the music fades and the periphery is stripped away. His song brings into focus what the Lord desired Moses to teach the Israelites. When we understand who God is, the only appropriate response is to come into his presence and offer ourselves. The variety of worship styles, lyrics and instruments aren't that important. Neither is whether we stand or sit or raise our arms.

God wants a voluntary surrender of our mind, emotions, will and spirit. The pressure of performance is gone. So too the need to argue over what is right. Isn't that great news? ❖

PRAYER

Lord, this moment, I give to you . . .

day45

A LITTLE PICTURE OF GOD'S GREATNESS

The LORD did not set his affection on you and choose you because you were more numerous than other peoples, for you were the fewest of all peoples. But it was because the LORD loved you and kept the oath he swore to your ancestors. DEUTERONOMY 7:7–8

Have you ever considered the disproportional influence the land of Israel has had in history given its geographic size? If you look at a map of the world, you'll likely need a magnifying glass to locate it. The "promised land" is dwarfed by huge continents like Africa and Europe. Once you locate Israel on the coast of the Mediterranean Sea near Egypt and Saudi Arabia, you'll be amazed to see that it's only about 150 miles long by 75 miles wide. All that considered, Israel continues to be the focus of world attention—not to mention Biblical prophecy.

It's obvious that God has had his hand on this stretch of real estate, as it was (and is) strategically located between great nations like Egypt and Asia Minor (Turkey). Even a small strip of land can have importance if it is located in the right place.

But then again, Scripture is clear that from the beginning the vulnerability of the people who inhabited Israel was a means by which God was making a point. There would be no way in the world the people of God could take credit for their influence. They were too small. But that was okay. God would get the credit. And seeing that it was God who was choreographing their success, his people were brought to their knees in humble worship.

Paul, in a letter to the early Christians in Corinth, picked up on this principle. He said that it is through weakness that God's glory is made apparent. And that should be the principle that propels us into heartfelt worship each day. And just as a small area of land can have a significant impact, so can a small group of people when God uses them. ❖

PRAYER

Lord, like the people of Israel, I am the picture of creaturely weakness. Help me to give you the glory for all that is around me ...

# day46

HIS PLACE

You are to seek the place the LORD your God will choose from among all your tribes to put his Name there for his dwelling. To that place you must go; ... there rejoice before the LORD your God—you, your sons and daughters, your male and female servants, and the Levites from your towns who have no allotment or inheritance of their own.

DEUTERONOMY 12:5,12

You probably have heard someone say that you don't need to attend church to worship God. In one sense, they are right—certainly, we can worship God anywhere. Our very lives should be an act of reverent worship for the goodness and mercy God showers on each of us. Wherever we are, whatever we are doing, we can seek God and offer our praises to him.

However, we also are called to worship God in a specific place and to share in worship with others. God promises to meet us there at that chosen place. "For where two or three gather in my name, there am I with them" (Matthew 18:20). Whether an elaborate cathedral, a simple clapboard building on a country hillside or an unadorned room in a modern office building, our church provides a sanctuary where we can experience a sense of reverence and peace whenever we enter to worship. There we gather with our families and friends to rejoice in all we have because the Lord our God has blessed us.

Where do you really connect with God? Where is the special place you feel his presence and honor his name? Is it in a building? Your garden? A place in your home? In your car commuting to work? How wonderful that you can seek God wherever you are and honor his name in whatever you do! ✤

PRAYER

Thank you, Lord, that you meet me wherever I am ...

CLAIM VICTORY!

He shall say: "Hear, Israel: Today you are going into battle against your enemies. Do not be fainthearted or afraid; do not panic or be terrified by them. For the LORD your God is the one who goes with you to fight for you against your enemies to give you victory."

DEUTERONOMY 20:3–4

Some days feel like a battle. We fight to keep our heads above water financially. We struggle with depression or a sense of failure. We can't seem to win a battle against an addiction. We wonder if we will ever find another job. We wrestle with a troubled relationship. Everyone's battle is different, but each one of us has at least one.

Do not be afraid, God tells us. Do not lose heart or panic. After all, we do not fight our battles alone. "What, then, shall we say in response to these things? If God is for us, who can be against us? No, in all these things we are more than conquerors through him who loved us" (Romans 8:31,37).

What defines a win for our battles? Sometimes we think we know the right answer, the best outcome, the terms of surrender for our "enemy." We pray only for the outcome we want. But God may fight the battle very differently than how we anticipated, and his victory may not look like what we envisioned. But we can be certain that God's victory is the right one, and his timing will be perfect.

What battle are you fighting? Give it to God and claim victory! Then move ahead, without fear, certain that God is by your side. Praise him for fighting for you, and for the victory that will certainly come. Claim victory, his victory, and feel his presence with you throughout this day. ✤

PRAYER

Lord, please help me fight this battle . . .

FIRSTFRUITS

When you have entered the land the LORD your God is giving you as an inheritance and have taken possession of it and settled in it, take some of the firstfruits of all that you produce from the soil of the land the LORD your God is giving you and put them in a basket. Then go to the place the LORD your God will choose as a dwelling for his Name.

DEUTERONOMY 26:1–2

For the firstfruits offering, the Israelites brought baskets overflowing with vegetables, fruits and grains. Their gifts provided food for the priests, who were chosen by God to serve the people rather than spending their time tilling the soil and growing their own food. For us as Christians, our financial gifts to the church support those who teach and serve, and provide for those who need extra help. The next time you write a check for your tithe, picture yourself carrying a basket of food to someone in need—that's really what you are doing!

But giving back to God is not limited to tithes and offerings. You can give the "firstfruits of your produce" every day. Your gift of time can encourage someone who is ill or cheer a homebound elderly person. You can offer a gift of service by nurturing the budding faith of a child or providing a meal for someone hungry. The list of ways we can give is as endless as the joy that follows when we obey God's request for our firstfruits.

How will you honor God's name today? What firstfruit can you give him? Wherever you are, in your home or running errands, in the office or at school, this is the place God has chosen for you to be this day. Think about what you have to accomplish and offer those tasks to God as an act of worship. Fill your basket with your best efforts, kind words, a helping hand, a grateful heart, a song of praise, and offer these gifts to your heavenly Father. ✤

PRAYER

Lord, today, I will honor you by . . .

BLESSED BY GOD

You will be blessed when you come in and blessed when you go out ... The LORD will establish you as his holy people, as he promised you on oath, if you keep the commands of the LORD your God and walk in obedience to him. DEUTERONOMY 28:6,9

Just as the Israelites were God's holy people of the Old Testament, believers are God's holy people of the New Testament. Therefore Christians can claim the same promise given the Israelites: You will be blessed wherever you go, both in coming and in going. What a wonderful promise! In coming and in going, from our birth to our death, from our awakening each morning to when we go to sleep at night, his love and mercy are always available to us.

For the Israelites, who had been living in tents in the wilderness for 40 years, God's blessings included a land of their own, security and prosperity, the joy of raising a family, and having plenty to eat. How wonderful those promised blessings must have seemed to those homeless wanderers! Yet even during the 40 years of wandering, God kept them safe, gave them manna to eat and quenched their thirst with water from a rock. He forgave them again and again when they complained and turned against him.

How is God blessing your life right now? When things are going well for you, it's easy to recognize God's blessing and respond with joy and thanksgiving. But what about when troubles strike, when you are in pain or suffering or depressed?

Recognize the blessing of God in your life today. Be filled with praise for his goodness to you. God has surely acknowledged you as one of his holy people. Praise God, from whom all blessings flow! ❧

PRAYER

Lord God, I acknowledge that you have blessed me by ...

SAFE IN GOD'S ARMS

The eternal God is your refuge, and underneath are the everlasting arms. He will drive out your enemies before you, saying, "Destroy them!" DEUTERONOMY 33:27

A child cries. We reach out and cradle them in our arms for comfort. Someone we love learns they have a life-threatening illness. We put our arms around them and hold them close. Someone we love dies. We welcome the arms that enfold and comfort us. We all need human touch. No matter how old we are, we all long for someone to hold and protect us when we are troubled, afraid or sorrowing. Here we have the promise that the eternal God holds us in his arms. What a wonder-filled, healing image!

Take a moment and imagine yourself wrapped in the arms of God. Sink into his protection and love and give all your cares to him. God is not distant or unapproachable. He wants to comfort you as a father comforts his child. He wants to protect you like a mother hen who gathers her chicks beneath her wings (see Luke 13:34). He will provide sanctuary for you when troubles come. With his everlasting arms, he will place you out of reach on a high rock (see Psalm 27:5). When you lean on God's everlasting arms, you are safe and loved.

Our heavenly Father will provide the strength to accept the life-threatening illness, the courage to go on living when someone you love dies, the energy and compassion to comfort others, the joy of knowing you are loved by the eternal God. Feel his arms around you today. Draw strength from his presence with you. ❧

PRAYER

Heavenly Father, I am in need of refuge because . . .

THE FEAR FACTOR

No one will be able to stand against you all the days of your life. As I was with Moses, so I will be with you; I will never leave you nor forsake you ... Have I not commanded you? Be strong and courageous. Do not be afraid; do not be discouraged, for the LORD your God will be with you wherever you go. JOSHUA 1:5,9

Joshua had good reason to be afraid: He had just been given the assignment to lead God's people across the Jordan into the land promised to them. He must have been terrified at suddenly being responsible for the fate of so many people. But did you notice the factor that changed everything? The Lord God promised to be with Joshua at all times, in all circumstances and in every place.

A recent ad campaign proclaimed "No Fear." Wouldn't it be fantastic to never experience even a moment of anxiety or doubt simply by buying a product, hiring a body guard or installing a security system? But we know better. Fear seems to haunt us—fear of the future, fear of a doctor's report, fear of a failed relationship.

Just as God promised to go with Joshua, he extends that same promise to you. There is no place you can go that God is not, and nothing he will ask you to do for which he will not first prepare you. When you accept that as truth, you can worship him with a thankful heart no matter what your situation.

What fears do you face? Name them. What personal battles do you have to fight, or what strange land are you about to enter? Like Joshua, remember God's promise to be with you "wherever you go." What an incredible statement! Wherever you are right now, in whatever circumstance, the holy God of Israel is with you. Let that truth build your confidence today. Turn your fear into faith. ❖

PRAYER

Lord, I admit that I am afraid of ...

STONES OF REMEMBRANCE

Each of you is to take up a stone on his shoulder, according to the number of the tribes of the Israelites, to serve as a sign among you. In the future, when your children ask you, "What do these stones mean?" tell them that the flow of the Jordan was cut off before the ark of the covenant of the LORD. When it crossed the Jordan, the waters of the Jordan were cut off. These stones are to be a memorial to the people of Israel forever.　　JOSHUA 4:5 – 7

When you hear the word *memorial*, what comes to mind? Perhaps a marble statue erected in memory of a famous citizen or a tall obelisk of granite stretching into the sky. Cities and towns have numerous memorial buildings, parks, cemeteries and statues to help us remember people and events. That's why they are called "memorials."

God gave Joshua directions for building a very specific memorial — a monument of twelve stones that would stand as a permanent reminder of the people's miraculous crossing of the Jordan on dry ground. God wanted his people to remember and to worship.

Today, we too need memorials — stones of remembrance — that continually remind us of what God has done.

A church on Cape Cod recently named its office building Riverstone because of the miracle God worked in its purchase. A Christian family in Connecticut christened their home Gracehaven to commemorate the presence of grace in their lives. You may not have a building to name or a home to christen, but you will discover countless rock-solid reasons to praise God once you begin remembering all he has done for you in the past.

Drive or walk through your neighborhood or another area of personal victory. Look for "memorials," and use each one as a cause for prayer or praise. ✣

PRAYER

Lord, as I consider the memorials of my past, I think of . . .

COMING CLEAN

Then Joshua said to Achan, "My son, give glory to the LORD, the God of Israel, and honor him. Tell me what you have done; do not hide it from me." JOSHUA 7:19

When we consider what it means to give glory to God, we usually think in terms of praise. Nothing feels better than singing or even shouting our thanks aloud to the Lord as we celebrate his goodness and his activity on our behalf.

Sometimes, however, the most critical component of worship is one that doesn't feel pleasant. When we allow sinful attitudes or actions to infiltrate our lives, our ability to worship God becomes severely compromised. We may continue to observe the outward forms of worship—church attendance, public prayer, perhaps even Scripture reading—but inwardly we know that we are far from God. Sin separates us from the one who is absolutely holy, and the chasm between us grows steadily wider the longer our sin remains unconfessed.

Achan's sin not only brought shame and ruin upon his own family but also judgment on the nation. Rather than come willingly, Achan had to be confronted by the leaders of Israel and asked to confess his sin.

As worshipers who are in continual communion with God, we need to make confession a regular part of our daily experience. Only when we humble ourselves before God can we once again experience the unhindered joy of being in a right relationship with him.

Don't wait for God to call you on the carpet, or for a close friend to pull you aside to confront you with your sin. Reflect on what might be hindering your relationship with God. Confess it and come clean. ✤

PRAYER

Lord, I confess that . . .

AN ETERNAL INHERITANCE

But to the tribe of Levi, Moses had given no inheritance; the LORD, the God of Israel, is their inheritance, as he promised them.   JOSHUA 13:33

The phone rings late one afternoon. You listen to the unfamiliar voice on the other end in stunned disbelief. A distant relative you didn't know even existed has died, and his attorney has just called to inform you that you stand to inherit a fortune. How would you respond to this unexpected good news? With calm complacency or jubilation?

Such a scenario is the stuff of novels and Hollywood movies. Few people can expect an inheritance from a relative they never met. Common sense tells us that. The Scriptures, however, tell another story—one of an eternal inheritance that will never spoil, fade or perish given to undeserving humanity who moved far from their father God. Yet God, in his gracious mercy, adopted us as his children and has given us a share in his Son's inheritance! This inheritance is not made up of possessions that eventually will rot, rust or get stolen. This inheritance is eternal life (see Matthew 19:29).

We invest in the stock market, hoping for a little security in our later years, only to discover that all we have put away can be wiped out literally overnight. The eyes of faith, however, see beyond the gains and losses of this life to an eternal inheritance waiting for us.

God is the inheritance of the one who worships him in spirit and in truth. Go on, get excited about spending your inheritance; you'll have eternity in which to do it. As you go through the day, look at the people you encounter, your possessions, and even your "to-do" list from an eternal perspective and focus on what God has in store for you. ✣

> **PRAYER**

Lord, when I think about the inheritance waiting for me in heaven, I can hardly contain my joy. Today I choose to focus not on what is lacking in this life but what is coming to me in the next ...

YOUR CHOICE

But if serving the LORD seems undesirable to you, then choose for yourselves this day whom you will serve, whether the gods your ancestors served beyond the Euphrates, or the gods of the Amorites, in whose land you are living. But as for me and my household, we will serve the LORD.   JOSHUA 24:15

From the moment you roll out of bed in the morning, you're making decisions—some big, some small. You decide how you'll cover your body with clothing or fuel it with food. You select people to speak to and topics of conversation. You choose between an endless variety of ways that you can spend your time.

Choices. Joshua had them too. Some small and mundane, some large. God placed him in charge of a nation of people who had to decide whether to worship idols made by human hands or to worship the One holding the entire world in his hands.

We face the same choices. Daily, we must choose where we will place our faith and whom we will serve. The only choice that brings life is to serve the living God.

Today, you may be tempted to lie on an expense report or make up an excuse as to why you can't attend the weekly prayer meeting. Ask what it means in each situation to worship and serve the living God. Then choose. ✤

PRAYER

God, give me the strength daily to make the right choices. Today, I choose . . .

day56

NO COMPROMISE

The angel of the LORD went up from Gilgal to Bokim and said, "I brought you up out of Egypt and led you into the land I swore to give to your ancestors. I said, 'I will never break my covenant with you, and you shall not make a covenant with the people of this land, but you shall break down their altars.' Yet you have disobeyed me. Why have you done this?"   JUDGES 2:1–2

You open the Scriptures and read the same words over and over again, unable to grasp their meaning. You set aside time to pray, yet your prayers seem to bounce off the ceiling. Does this sound familiar? We've all been there.

Worship originating from the heart of the believer should be simple. What could be easier than lifting up praise and gratitude to the One who has promised never to break his covenant with us? It should come as naturally as breathing. At times, however, our spiritual breathing becomes heavy and labored. We long for the close bond of fellowship we once enjoyed with God when heaven leaned close and we experienced the intimacy of daily encounters with the divine. Yet it's hard to take faith in when we've failed to push sin out.

Consider the Israelites' story as recorded in Judges. The tribes were given the explicit command to drive out the inhabitants of the land. Instead they allowed them to remain, and in turn, adopted customs and idols forbidden by God. Perhaps they intended to comply with God's command at some point. But they soon realized that God views delayed obedience the same as disobedience. He would never forsake them, but through moral compromise, they had forsaken him.

Their story doesn't have to be yours. As you draw close to God, he promises to draw close to you (see James 4:8). Sin separates, but repentance is a divine U-turn that brings you right back to him again. What a glorious place to be! ♣

PRAYER

Lord, I admit that I . . .

VICTORY SONG

Hear this, you kings! Listen, you rulers! I, even I, will sing to the LORD; I will praise the LORD, the God of Israel, in song. JUDGES 5:3

Everyone has battles. The conflicts we face may not be on the scale of a full-fledged military contest, such as the one Deborah and the Israelites faced against the forces led by General Sisera, but we struggle daily.

Few people enjoy conflict. Deborah and Barak were no exception. Deborah was Israel's judge, and God gave her specific instructions to command Barak to mobilize the Israelites for war. When he refused to go alone, she agreed to accompany him, but warned that any honor due the conquering hero would now be denied him.

When victory was handed to Israel, Deborah responded with worship: "I will praise the LORD, the God of Israel, in song." In a beautiful praise song, Deborah focused on the source of their great victory and recounted for all to hear the wondrous work of God. Such worship not only honors God, but it also encourages others who face battle.

When we see God do something amazing as Deborah did, when we see his hand clearly in our lives, the only appropriate response is worship. "Hear this!" Deborah said.

Look for the many ways that God gives you victories daily. Pay attention to how he is guiding you and carrying you through each struggle. Then you will be able to lift up your song to God in thanksgiving and praise.

What victory has God given to you? Shout thanks to him! How has God provided for you? Offer a song of praise to him! ❧

PRAYER

Lord, I celebrate the victory you gave me over . . .

QUESTIONING GOD

"Pardon me, my lord," Gideon replied, "but how can I save Israel? My clan is the weakest in Manasseh, and I am the least in my family."   JUDGES 6:15

Gideon wasn't posing a rhetorical question here. If God sat down with you for a chat, wouldn't you seize the opportunity to ask a few urgent questions? Maybe your questions would be like Gideon's: "Why are you asking this of me? How can I possibly fulfill this assignment? Lord, don't you think you picked the wrong person?"

The wonderful news is that God welcomes our questions. They don't put him off. He doesn't get angry when we question our circumstances or his plan for our life. Look how he responded to Gideon. Far from being annoyed by Gideon's questions, God actually responded to him with patience, reassurance and a commission for service, "I will be with you, and you will strike down all the Midianites, leaving none alive" (Judges 6:16).

The God whom we worship is not distressed by our questions. He knows that, like Gideon, we often feel inadequate or overwhelmed by life. He desires our honesty in worship and wants us to bring to him those issues, questions and doubts that are on our minds.

As you enter into earnest dialog with God through prayer, you can bring everything to him—your praise, your thanks, your doubts and even your questions. The Lord's response to Gideon's questions is true for you today as well: "I will be with you."

Be honest with God. Don't allow your questions to prevent you from coming to him in worship. Bring your questions as a sacrifice to him. God can handle it. ✤

PRAYER

Lord, here are my questions . . .

BRING ME BACK

But the Israelites said to the LORD, "We have sinned. Do with us whatever you think best, but please rescue us now." Then they got rid of the foreign gods among them and served the LORD. And he could bear Israel's misery no longer. JUDGES 10:15–16

"I'll never leave you," the husband whispered tenderly to his new bride on their honeymoon. Five years later, she came home to a note that read, "I'm leaving you for another woman." Forgotten was the promise given that honeymoon night.

Our faith often resembles that of a wayward spouse. "Lord, I worship you. Only you are worthy of praise," we shout when our faith is new. We study his Word. We tell others of the wondrous things he has done. But, little by little, our enthusiasm wanes. We allow sin to creep in and separate us from God.

The tale is a familiar one. "Far be it from us to forsake the LORD to serve other gods!... We too will serve the LORD, because he is our God" (Joshua 24:16,18). So said the people of Israel in the last days of Joshua. But as years went by in the time of judges, the people forgot the mighty acts of the Lord. They began to worship the gods Baal and Ashtoreth and other gods of the nations around them. Eventually, they did not worship the Lord at all.

We may forget all about the Lord, but he does not forget about us. Just as he allowed Israel to suffer at the hands of their enemies, he allows us to suffer in order to bring us back to himself. The worship God desires comes from a broken and repentant heart. In his mercy, he forgives and restores us.

How far have you wandered from God? Use this time to renew your vows with him as an act of worship. ✤

PRAYER

Lord, I have drifted away . . .

BREAK DOWN THE WALL

Then Samson prayed to the LORD, *"Sovereign* LORD, *remember me. Please, God, strengthen me just once more, and let me with one blow get revenge on the Philistines for my two eyes." Then Samson reached toward the two central pillars on which the temple stood. Bracing himself against them, his right hand on the one and his left hand on the other, Samson said, "Let me die with the Philistines!" Then he pushed with all his might, and down came the temple on the rulers and all the people in it. Thus he killed many more when he died than while he lived.* JUDGES 16:28–30

A stone wall of sin was surrounding Samson. Day after day, stones were added as Delilah tantalized and tempted him. Instead of fleeing his lusts, Samson stayed within the walls. As his desire for Delilah grew, his desire for God diminished. In time, Samson succumbed to Delilah's wiles and betrayed his vow. The wall around Samson was complete.

The wall of separation from God is built by sin. Only repentance can tear it down. Grinding grain in a Philistine prison, Samson had time to reflect on his sin and ask forgiveness. The wall that had separated him from God crumbled. Samson asked the Lord to allow him to defeat the Philistines one last time. The strength of the Lord returned to Samson, and he brought down the Philistine temple in a spectacular crash.

Take a look at the wall that separates you from God. Is the shame of unconfessed sin keeping you from wholehearted worship? Do you worry ceaselessly, or do you humbly trust God with your future? Do you fill up your day with activity, or do you reserve time to worship God? When you cherish sin in your heart, you lose the desire to worship. "If we confess our sins, he is faithful and just and will forgive us our sins and purify us from all unrighteousness" (1 John 1:9). Tear down that wall! ♣

> **PRAYER**

Father, in your mercy, forgive me for . . .

RUNNING IN SIN CIRCLES

In those days Israel had no king; everyone did as they saw fit.   JUDGES 21:25

History does not run in circles, but people do. Generation after generation, children repeat their parents' sins. We claim great progress, yet in the most significant ways remain unchanged. What phrase better describes our cycle of sin than "everyone did as they saw fit"?

The last verse of the book of Judges could serve as a description for every generation, including ours. A government, king or some other authority figure can control external behavior. But inwardly we want to decide for ourselves what is right and wrong.

Notice the irony in the opening phrase above, "Israel [God's people] had no king." Of course they didn't have a king. They had no need for one because they had God. But they forgot God and made themselves kings over their own lives.

Like the Israelites, when we forget God or fail to obey him, what seems right in our eyes usually turns out to be wrong. However, as soon as we acknowledge God's direction in our lives, we begin to break the sin cycle.

When we turn humbly to God, we realize we can't trust ourselves. The cycle of sin can only be broken by the power of the Holy Spirit. "So I say, walk by the Spirit, and you will not gratify the desires of the flesh" (Galatians 5:16). Learning to do what God wants rather than what looks good to us will keep us from running in sin circles. ✤

PRAYER

Dear Father, I need you to break this cycle ...

WHAT SHOULD YOU LEAVE BEHIND?

But Ruth replied, "Don't urge me to leave you or to turn back from you. Where you go I will go, and where you stay I will stay. Your people will be my people and your God my God."   RUTH 1:16

"We're moving." Two words sure to set in motion a flurry of activity. So many decisions to be made. What do we pack? What do we leave behind? How do we say good-bye to family and friends and all that is familiar? Moving is as difficult today as it was in the days of Ruth and Naomi.

Panting from exertion, the two women stopped to rest at the crest of the hill. The high plains of Moab stretched out behind; the road to Judah snaked through the hills ahead. Go home, Naomi urged, and Ruth considered. She could return home to her family and friends, to her culture, to her gods. But with love Ruth replied, "Where you go I will go."

Ruth's decision reached far beyond compassion for her mother-in-law, though, for she added, "Your people will be my people and your God my God." With these words, Ruth abandoned the gods of her ancestors and took refuge under the wings of the God of Israel (see Ruth 2:12). Now she would worship the one true God.

What must you abandon to worship the one true God? False beliefs and practices of the past? A relationship or an activity that does not honor God? Possessions that weigh heavy? A sin that blocks him from your sight? Or is God calling you to leave your home—or your comfort zone—to follow him to a new place?

Worshiping God involves sacrifice, but he "richly blesses all who call on him" (Romans 10:12). God honored Ruth's faith by blessing her new life in Judah and giving her a place in the lineage of Jesus (see Matthew 1:5). How has God blessed you since you put your faith in him? ❖

> PRAYER

Creator of heaven and earth, help me to leave behind . . .

COVER ME!

"I am your servant Ruth," she said. "Spread the corner of your garment over me, since you are a guardian-redeemer of our family."   RUTH 3:9

Walking slowly behind the harvesters, Ruth gathered the grain that had been left behind. This was God's provision, that grain be left in the field for the poor and widowed. Hard work it was, and demeaning. Was this to be her destiny? No husband, no children, no security? Was she to be allotted only the leftovers of life?

With no one left to turn to, she went to Boaz. "Spread the corner of your garment over me," she pleaded. Marry me—for this was a marriage proposal—and redeem my life. Cast the cover of redemption over me. Cover me as a bird covers its young with its wing. Take away my loneliness and despair, and give me hope. Protect me, cherish me, love me, for you are my guardian-redeemer.

We also are in desperate need of a family redeemer. "For all have sinned and fall short of the glory of God" (Romans 3:23). The day of judgment is coming. Our sins will be exposed, and we will stand naked and alone, condemned before a holy God. Yet Jesus, in his love and compassion, will spread the cover of his redemption over us. He will cover us completely, so that only his own glorious work will be seen. Then he will bring us into the very presence of God, and we will be found "holy in his sight, without blemish and free from accusation" (Colossians 1:22). This is only the beginning of redemption, for Jesus seeks to redeem every aspect of our lives.

Turn to him in your poverty and despair, and ask for his redemption. He will take your loss, your failure, your loneliness, and he will use it for God's glory. ✤

PRAYER

Cast your cover of redemption over me, Jesus, my Lord and my redeemer . . .

A PROMISE KEPT

There is no one holy like the LORD; there is no one besides you; there is no Rock like our God.   1 SAMUEL 2:2

Desperate. Tormented. Mocked. Ridiculed. Perhaps you have felt like that when you have been as desperate for a miracle as Hannah was.

Imagine Hannah's pain. Her husband's other wife, Peninnah, mocked and ridiculed her because she had no children. It was bad enough to be childless in her day when childbearing gave women value. But then to be tormented by this woman who had borne sons to Hannah's own husband was too much. Her grief was great.

She poured her heart out to God, and he answered her prayer and gave her a son. Her pain was transformed to joy. Hannah had made a promise to God in her hour of anguish, as many people do, and she kept her promise when he granted her heart's desire. She dedicated her son to God and gave him up to be raised and trained for God's service in the temple at Shiloh.

When have you experienced an answer to a desperate prayer? Was your response praise and thanksgiving? Did you freely give back to God what he had so graciously given to you; or did you clutch it to yourself, now that you finally had what you had longed for?

In Hannah's prayer of praise, she acknowledged the true source of her deliverance. She praised God's holiness and protection. And she lifted up her precious son and returned him to God.

God has given us so much. Too often, we forget what God has done for us, or we simply take him for granted. This day look for his answers, and like Hannah, give him praise. ✤

PRAYER

God, I thank you for ...

GET SERIOUS

So Samuel said to all the Israelites, "If you are returning to the LORD with all your hearts, then rid yourselves of the foreign gods and the Ashtoreths and commit yourselves to the LORD and serve him only, and he will deliver you out of the hand of the Philistines."

1 SAMUEL 7:3

For 20 long years the people of Israel had grieved, feeling as though God had abandoned them. But Samuel recognized that it was the other way around—the people had abandoned God. Samuel gave them the solution to their misery, reminding them of God's faithfulness and mercy. He got right to the point, telling the people what they had to do. If they would get rid of their idols and return to God and obey him, he would rescue them.

Samuel didn't waste words. It was time for the people to stop feeling sorry for themselves and take some action. If you're really sorry, he told them, if you really mean it, then show how serious you are. Do something about it. Get rid of whatever it is that is keeping you from worshiping God, and he will be there again for you.

In response to Samuel's message, the people of Israel destroyed their idols and worshiped God. And God rescued them.

Samuel very well could have been speaking to you. Imagine he is standing in front of you. He begins by saying, "If you are returning to the LORD with all your heart …" How would you finish that sentence? What would it mean for you to get serious about your relationship with God? It might mean removing an "idol" or doing what you know God wants you to do. It might mean changing an attitude.

Today, think about what it might mean for you to get serious about a relationship with God. Then worship him with a clear conscience and with your whole heart. ✤

PRAYER

Lord, show me what I need to do to get serious about my relationship with you …

NEVER, NEVER, NEVER GIVE UP!

"As for me, far be it from me that I should sin against the LORD by failing to pray for you. And I will teach you the way that is good and right. But be sure to fear the LORD and serve him faithfully with all your heart; consider what great things he has done for you."

1 SAMUEL 12:23–24

Samuel was not happy with the people. They insisted upon having a king when they had the Creator of the universe as their leader. Apparently, they had forgotten all that God had given to them and done for them. It would be understandable if Samuel were to just wash his hands of the whole affair and walk away from these ungrateful people. Perfectly understandable.

But note Samuel's response. Instead of giving up on these people, he declared that he would not stop praying for them. And rather than leave the people to their own devices, Samuel said he would continue to teach them. God had given Samuel a call, a duty, a mission, and he was determined to remain faithful to that—regardless of the outcome.

When have you felt like quitting? When the person you've been praying for still shows no interest in God? When have you felt like walking away? When your small group seems more preoccupied with trivial matters than interested in issues of faith? When have you felt that it just doesn't matter? When getting ready for Sunday mornings seems more drudgery than a joy?

Remember Samuel. Remember whom you are serving. God has called you, and God will take care of the results. He wants you to be faithful. Tell him how you feel, and renew your commitment to worship him through your service and obedience. ✤

PRAYER

Lord, I'm glad I can come to you because I feel like giving up on . . .

HIT THE PAUSE BUTTON

But Samuel replied: "Does the LORD delight in burnt offerings and sacrifices as much as in obeying the LORD? To obey is better than sacrifice, and to heed is better than the fat of rams."   1 SAMUEL 15:22

Sacrifices. We make them daily—getting up early to drive the children to school for an activity, assisting a colleague with a difficult assignment, taking time to listen to a hurting friend. Yet it's evident from Samuel's words to King Saul that making sacrifices is not enough.

Saul brought the proper sacrifices to the Lord, but something was missing—his obedience. God had given him an assignment to do that he only did halfway. In addition to his failure to follow God's directive, instead of waiting for Samuel to offer the sacrifices, Saul decided to do it himself. As Samuel reminded Saul and the people of Israel, complete obedience is better than any sacrifice we can offer.

No matter what we're sacrificing, God wants our heart. He wants our obedience. What's your schedule like? Do you sacrifice your time, your energy, maybe even your family, in order to do ministry, leaving precious little time for other important matters?

Hit the pause button on your schedule. Take time to truly listen to God. Instead of frantically changing lanes on the way to the office or doing errands, get in the slow lane and spend that extra time praying to God. Intentionally get in the longer lines at the grocery store so you can offer him thanks for his provisions.

You can wear yourself out serving God and miss out on what he desires most: your obedience, love and worship. ❖

PRAYER

Heavenly Father, I am willing to sacrifice . . .

day68

LEAST BUT NOT LAST

The LORD said to Samuel, "Do not consider his appearance or his height, for I have rejected him. The LORD does not look at the things people look at. People look at the outward appearance, but the LORD looks at the heart."   I SAMUEL 16:7

When have you been overlooked or left out because you just didn't measure up in some way? Maybe you were passed over for a promotion because your colleague landed a bigger deal than you did. Or maybe you didn't get to sing that solo because you just couldn't reach the high notes like the other soprano.

Jessica didn't measure up. She had limped all her life. Complications at birth had left her abnormally short, her leg twisted. She was always picked last for sports teams in school because the other kids knew she was a slow runner. She had never been invited to a school dance.

Despite her obvious physical limitations, Jessica remained cheerful and optimistic. If she minded being left out of activities, she never showed it. She just concentrated on her studies and on being a good friend. So at the end of her senior year in high school, imagine Jessica's surprise when she was voted the "Girl With the Biggest Heart." Although Jessica had often been left out, her classmates recognized her as a valuable member of their class.

It's great to know that God doesn't care if we have a physical deformity or can't sing well. He's not impressed with our bank account, nice house or important job. Instead, he's concerned about what's inside our hearts. That's what he told Samuel when he was looking for a future king, "People look at the outward appearance, but the LORD looks at the heart." The exterior doesn't matter; it's what's inside that counts. ♣

PRAYER

Lord, I'm so glad that you care more about my heart than about how I look . . .

day69

THE GIFT OF FRIENDSHIP

After David had finished talking with Saul, Jonathan became one in spirit with David, and he loved him as himself.   1 SAMUEL 18:1

What does it take to form a friendship? Sometimes it's a bond that develops over years of shared experiences. Sometimes, as in the case of David and Jonathan, the bond forms almost immediately. Whatever the circumstances, friends are those special people with whom we can laugh and cry. They encourage us and stay close to us during the difficult times.

Just the word *friend* can bring a smile. Whether it's the person you call when you get good news or the person who accompanies you through your dark valleys, that friend is a rich gift from God. But the greatest friendship gift that God gives us is a friendship with himself. The Creator of the universe promises to be with us always, to encourage us when we are down and to comfort us when we are grieving.

Just as Jonathan and David were loyal to each other through great difficulties, God is faithful to us when we are facing difficulties in our lives. His promise is true—he will never leave or forsake us (see Hebrews 13:5). He encourages us to lay our deepest burdens and concerns on him. He offers to guide us through the storms. That is a friendship worth keeping and maintaining.

Celebrate the gift of God's friendship—and friendship itself—by worshiping him with a close friend. Share your concerns with that person. Ask that person to lift you up in prayer as you pray for them. ✤

PRAYER

God, thank you for these friendships . . .

REVENGE OR RELEASE

May the LORD be our judge and decide between us. May he consider my cause and uphold it; may he vindicate me by delivering me from your hand.   1 SAMUEL 24:15

David held up a piece of King Saul's robe as he shouted the words from verse 15. Moments before, Saul had been unguarded and vulnerable in a cave where David and his men had been hiding. Saul was at David's mercy, and David had mercy. Instead of killing the king, David sliced off a corner of the royal robe. He spared the king's life out of deliberate trust in God. He refused to take the throne by force. He didn't want to be king unless God placed him in that position.

Perhaps the hardest work we can do during worship is the work of forgiveness. Anytime we are faced with the opportunity for revenge, we have also been given the opportunity to release. And there's nothing like the quietness and reflection of worship to bring to mind offenses, hurts, anger and unsettled issues in our lives. Jesus described just such a situation in Matthew 5:23–25. Worship is on hold until we release those we need to forgive.

David transformed a tense moment of temptation into an act of worship by sparing Saul's life and publicly announcing his ongoing trust in God. He released Saul to God's judgment by not taking revenge. His was costly worship. David demonstrated that he was a man after God's heart by his persistence in trusting God, even when that trust put his own life at risk.

Forgiveness may not be risky for us, but it will be hard work. We don't forgive easily, especially if our cause is just. But, like David, we demonstrate our understanding of the depth of God's forgiveness of us by the way we go about forgiving others. Worship includes receiving and giving forgiveness. We certainly need God's help to do both. ✤

> **PRAYER**

Lord, help me release those I struggle to forgive ...

HURRY UP AND WAIT

When Saul saw the Philistine army, he was afraid; terror filled his heart. He inquired of the LORD, *but the* LORD *did not answer him by dreams or Urim or prophets.*

1 SAMUEL 28:5–6

No one likes to wait, whether it's in a long line at the grocery store or in traffic. Waiting is tough, but it is especially difficult when it comes to the big issues:

- Waiting for a wayward child to come back.
- Waiting for the results of a medical test.
- Waiting for the outcome of a job interview.
- Waiting to see the results of a company merger.

Often we ask God for patience while we're waiting for an answer to prayer, and then get impatient when the answer doesn't come. Consider Saul's response to waiting. This passage explains that he was waiting for an answer from God. But when he didn't get one, he took matters into his own hands and went to a medium for advice.

God doesn't always answer when we think he should or how we think he should, but he always answers prayer. Our part is to trust him when the answers aren't on our timetable. He doesn't want us to try to address the issue ourselves; he wants us to wait patiently for him.

Have you been praying about something and found God silent? What has your response been? David exclaimed: "I waited patiently for the LORD; he turned to me and heard my cry. He lifted me out of the slimy pit, out of the mud and mire; he set my feet on a rock and gave me a firm place to stand" (Psalm 40:1–2).

Wait for God today. He's going to answer. He promised, and he always keeps his promises. ✤

PRAYER

God, help me to wait on you for . . .

GENEROUS LIVING

David replied, "No, my brothers, you must not do that with what the LORD has given us. He has protected us and delivered into our hands the raiding party that came against us."

1 SAMUEL 30:23

David's men grumbled. They didn't want to share the goods they had recovered from the Amalekites with men who hadn't been a part of David's rescue party. But David showed the generosity of his divine descendant, Jesus Christ, when he told the men that "all will share alike" (1 Samuel 30:24).

What has God given you so that you can share it with others? Perhaps you have resources that could help your church provide for a ministry need. Or you could give a word of encouragement that would enable a struggling friend to keep going. Perhaps you could share the gift of your time so that your neighbor who cares for an elderly loved one can take a break.

Worship in the form of sharing with others doesn't have to wait until you can afford it. Paul says of the believers in Macedonia, "In the midst of a very severe trial, their overflowing joy and their extreme poverty welled up in rich generosity. For I testify that they gave as much as they were able, and even beyond their ability" (2 Corinthians 8:2–3).

Who could use your help? Why not contact that person right now and offer to share what you have as an act of worship to God. ✤

PRAYER

God, thank you for all you have given me. I lift it all up to you now with open hands, asking that you would . . .

LIVING WITH LOSS

Then David and all the men with him took hold of their clothes and tore them. They mourned and wept and fasted till evening for Saul and his son Jonathan, and for the army of the LORD and for the nation of Israel, because they had fallen by the sword.

2 SAMUEL 1:11–12

Loss. Grief. Anguish of soul. Tragedy and disaster take their toll on us. Death is so painful to those left behind. David had lost two people he loved very much, in addition to many men in his army. He openly expressed his grief; he tore his clothes in sorrow.

When loss hits home, it can feel as if you'll never stop aching, that your pain will never stop being a sharp torture.

What loss are you feeling today? The death of a beloved friend, like David's Jonathan? Or the death of a parent, a brother or even your child? The death of your dream of a solid and lasting marriage that ended in divorce? Or the loss of a successful career that disintegrated when your business collapsed?

Even though you may not want to, expressing grief is healthy and necessary if you're ever to heal. It may be a long, slow process, but like David and his men, admit your grief, feel your pain, mourn your losses.

This is the time to grieve and cry (see Ecclesiastes 3:4). God knows how you feel and hurts with you. After all, Jesus was "a man of suffering, and familiar with pain" (Isaiah 53:3). Go to him, ask him to help you bear it, and he will. ✤

> **PRAYER**

God, I offer you my grief . . .

LIVING WITH WILD ABANDON

Wearing a linen ephod, David was dancing before the LORD with all his might, while he and all Israel were bringing up the ark of the LORD with shouts and the sound of trumpets.

2 SAMUEL 6:14–15

In some churches, people clap and lift their hands to God in praise. They don't care what others are thinking or what anyone else is doing. They praise God with abandon.

For others, praise and worship are internal processes with little or no outward sign of celebration, although they're just as thankful and joyful as the more demonstrative believers.

David fell into the first group. He reveled in God's goodness, dancing for all he was worth. While he was later criticized for his exuberance, all that mattered to him was raising his voice and his heart to his wonderful God.

Which type of worshiper are you? Are you a quiet worshiper whose awe and love for God flow out in silent prayer? Or do you raise the roof with your vocal and active worship? Isn't it great to know that God loves both kinds of worship?

Your worship might be enriched by trying something new. If you're quiet, try clapping your hands. If you're a dancer, try standing still and focusing all that energy on God in silent prayer.

David didn't mind actively demonstrating his love for God, and whether we do that in bold witness or uncompromising standards or a particular style of worship—showing our love brings glory to God. ✤

PRAYER

Lord, I worship you . . .

FOR MERCY'S SAKE

Mephibosheth bowed down and said, "What is your servant, that you should notice a dead dog like me?"
2 SAMUEL 9:8

A wayward son, an adulterous wife, a rebellious nation. In the Bible, God's mercy extends to all three and many more who we would consider worthy of judgment. God is lavish—not stingy—with his mercy. He grants it generously to all who are undeserving.

Again and again, David provided a powerful example of God's mercy. He had no legal responsibility to Jonathan's son; he didn't even know the young man was alive. Nor had Mephibosheth come to David asking for help. But in a show of God-like extravagant compassion and grace, David sought out Mephibosheth, called him to himself and gave him a place at his table.

God does the same for us. He draws us to himself with his love and tenderly provides for us, his children. It's only because of his grace that we are saved. It's only because of his love that we are invited to feast at his table. Who might benefit from a lavish display of mercy from you today? Is there someone you haven't thought of in a long time who could use your help? As an act of worship, make a conscious effort to extend God's grace to others today. Instead of judgment, show mercy. Instead of revenge, give forgiveness. Instead of anger, show love. ✤

PRAYER

Lord, I need your help to be merciful to . . .

WHEN THE TRUTH HURTS

Then Nathan said to David, "You are the man! This is what the LORD, the God of Israel, says: 'I anointed you king over Israel, and I delivered you from the hand of Saul. Why did you despise the word of the LORD by doing what is evil in his eyes? You struck down Uriah the Hittite with the sword and took his wife to be your own. You killed him with the sword of the Ammonites.'"   2 SAMUEL 12:7,9

The game comes to an abrupt halt as the referee blows the whistle. "Foul!" he shouts, as he calls out your number and points at you. All eyes are directed at you. Everyone in the crowd knows what you did wrong.

In this passage, David thought he had gotten away with his sins of adultery and murder. But God saw those sins, and Nathan the prophet knew David's secret crimes. Then, like the referee, Nathan blew the whistle on his friend and confronted David with the truth.

The truth hurts. We'd rather hide from it and pretend that everything is okay. Like David, we need to be confronted with the truth of our sins so that we can confess them to God. Perhaps David's greatest strength was his willingness to confess his sins and repent. While David still suffered the consequences of his sins, God forgave him and restored their relationship.

It's hard to admit we did wrong. But the alternative—denial—is much worse. Unconfessed sin separates us from God.

Confession is at the heart of worship. Be honest with God and admit your sins. Remove anything that comes between you and your relationship with God. He already knows, and he stands at the end of your prayer, waiting to forgive. ♣

> **PRAYER**

Lord, I confess my sins to you ...

YOU'RE NOT ALONE

So the king got up and took his seat in the gateway. When the men were told, "The king is sitting in the gateway," they all came before him. Meanwhile, the Israelites had fled to their homes.   2 SAMUEL 19:8

"Your child is dead." Those words crush the spirit, overwhelming a parent with grief. More than once David heard those words. The death of Bathsheba's baby, the murder of Amnon and now the loss of Absalom made the shadowy valley of death an all-too-familiar place for David. He was overwhelmed with sorrow.

We don't know what David was thinking about God in those moments, but Joab confronted David with the need to set his grief alongside his duty to fulfill his God-given role as the king. So David, with tearstained face, walked to the city gate and sat in silent tribute to his men for their courageous defense of his throne. They came to him, not because he was grieving nor because of the great victory, but because they realized he didn't blame them for his grief.

Grief changes life, but it doesn't stop it. Grief itself doesn't even remain the same for long. After the initial blow that turns the world upside down, grief begins to transform into either a series of deep episodes of genuine sorrow over the loss or a series of bouts with self-pity. Grief may affect us in many ways, but one clue that we are not responding to grief in a healthy way can be seen when we try to stop the world and hide away with our pain.

In times of grief we discover just how close we are to God. Death creates a distance that only a vital relationship with God can bridge. Although David was sorrow filled, his grief did not separate him from God.

When you are grieving, keep close to God through worship, prayer and Bible study. Experience God as Lord, so you will know him as your Shepherd when you experience grief. ✤

> **PRAYER**

God, I need you more than ever before because . . .

day78

FUTURE SECURITY

He said: "The LORD is my rock, my fortress and my deliverer; my God is my rock, in whom I take refuge, my shield and the horn of my salvation. He is my stronghold, my refuge and my savior—from violent people you save me. I called to the LORD, who is worthy of praise, and have been saved from my enemies."　　2 SAMUEL 22:2–4

Perhaps your toddler carried a blanket with him wherever he went. Or maybe you found your heartstrings tugged over someone else's small child carrying a favorite stuffed animal that she absolutely could not do without. We smile when we see these youngsters clutching their security symbols. But we adults also cling to "security blankets"—a behavior that's not so cute.

Our security blanket may be a relationship that is unhealthy, but we can't let go of it. Perhaps our security blanket is a job title, the right address, a model of car or the size of a house. Maybe we're clinging to the idea of power or prestige based on our abilities. Whatever our security blanket may be, the truth is that none of these things offer the least bit of security. They can be stolen, lost or taken away.

That's why we need to realize, as David did in this heartfelt song, that our security rests solely on God. Consider the words David used to describe his security: "rock," "fortress," "deliverer," "shield," "stronghold." The words paint a picture of an impenetrable, permanent place of refuge and safety. David knew from experience that God alone could provide a sure security.

Have you experienced God as rock, fortress and stronghold? Bring before him those issues and needs that threaten your security and offer them to him as worship. ♣

PRAYER

Lord, I bring to you this need . . .

A DIVINE BLANK CHECK

So give your servant a discerning heart to govern your people and to distinguish between right and wrong. For who is able to govern this great people of yours? 1 KINGS 3:9

Heaven and earth paused in silence. All creation listened. God had just spoken. "Ask for whatever you want me to give you" (1 Kings 3:5). How would the new king answer? Solomon had just been given a divine blank check. What amount would he write down? What would he ask God to give him?

Given the same opportunity, how would you respond? Solomon paused long enough to review the events that had brought him to this moment. He expressed humble gratitude over the legacy God had preserved through his father, David. He acknowledged God's mighty power in turning Israel into a great nation. And he admitted his awareness of the great task before him. He confessed his ineptness.

Solomon made a God-centered request when he answered God's invitation. He identified God as the source of understanding and discernment. He recognized God's divine ownership over the people he was called to lead. He again acknowledged his inability to govern God's people on his own. He asked for God's provision and participation. God answered with that and much more.

If the wisest king who ever lived bowed in humble adoration to Almighty God, you would be wise to follow his example. Like Solomon, you undoubtedly have aspects of your life that point out your shortcomings and inabilities. You need wisdom you know you don't have. That's not a bad place to be. People who come to God in Solomon's footsteps find that God answers them in the same way he did Solomon. "If any of you lacks wisdom, you should ask God, who gives generously to all without finding fault, and it will be given to you" (James 1:5). ✤

PRAYER

Lord, I ask for wisdom today ...

day80

UP IN THE AIR

"I have provided a place there for the ark, in which is the covenant of the LORD that he made with our ancestors when he brought them out of Egypt."

Then Solomon stood before the altar of the LORD in front of the whole assembly of Israel, spread out his hands toward heaven and said: "LORD, the God of Israel, there is no God like you in heaven above or on earth below." 1 KINGS 8:21–23

There's an old joke that goes like this: Did you hear about the church that couldn't agree whether or not to let worshipers raise their arms during worship? The members reached a compromise. Those who felt the need to lift their hands could only lift one. They signed an "arms limitation treaty."

We may laugh, but sadly, that whole topic of raising hands in worship divides congregations. However, praying with uplifted arms is not a practice that began with the charismatic renewal movement or with modern worship styles. Solomon "spread out his hands toward heaven" when he prayed. This was a tangible way of lifting his heart to the Lord. By raising his arms, the king was reaching for God. It was almost as if he was attempting to hand over his requests as he made contact through prayer.

Solomon's example provides us with a picture of surrender. Can't you feel the drama of this scene? Raising his hands before the Lord was a way of reaching out beyond himself.

The next time you worship, take a lesson from Solomon. Instead of nervously clutching your fingers together as you sometimes do, relax them. Open your palms. Say, "Lord I'm tired of carrying these concerns. I surrender them to you." Allow the Lord to take whatever it is you are holding on to. What could possibly keep you from handing those concerns over to him? Lift your arms to the Lord and remind yourself (and him) that he's all you need today. ✤

PRAYER

Lord, I lift these concerns to you . . .

LESSONS FROM TURNING LEAVES

As Solomon grew old, his wives turned his heart after other gods, and his heart was not fully devoted to the LORD his God, as the heart of David his father had been.

1 KINGS 11:4

Autumn leaves don't turn red, yellow, orange and brown because of peer pressure. To the uninformed observer, it might appear that one solitary green leaf changes its appearance and then soon after those nearby follow suit. But what appears at first blush to be the case is not at all the cause. Rather, leaves are transformed in color because something has stopped. Winter days are short and dry. Trees stop making food in the fall, and the chlorophyll goes away.

You might think that Solomon's willingness to start worshiping pagan gods was simply because of the pressure put on him by his pagan wives. But that explanation would be far too simple. Most likely, as with the leaves of fall, something had begun to slow down within the king's soul. The God-ward flow within his heart had begun to dry up.

It's oh so subtle, but oh so dangerous. The negative influence of other people in your life only starts to take a toll when you have shut off the Holy Spirit's influence. The invitation of friends to join them for sporting events or other activities on Sunday seems more attractive when you haven't prioritized personal worship during the week.

But that isn't what you want, is it? You long for intimacy with your Father. And yet you know how the daily grind so easily leaves you vulnerable to putting everything else first. The Lord longs for you to come into his presence. It breaks his heart when you hold him at arm's length. But it's not too late. You can still run into his arms today. ✤

PRAYER

Lord, draw me to yourself today . . .

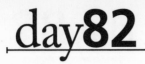

DAFFODILS IN THE DUNG HEAP

Although he did not remove the high places, Asa's heart was fully committed to the LORD all his life. He brought into the temple of the LORD the silver and gold and the articles that he and his father had dedicated.   1 KINGS 15:14–15

The key to accomplishing anything in politics is compromise. Mark Hatfield exemplified this as a United States senator. As a Christian who let his light shine in national politics, Hatfield lobbied for legislation that provided for the poor and oppressed, respected the rights of the individual and reflected Judeo-Christian values. Yet he knew that given the backdrop of a fallen world, you can't expect perfection. You have to give in to what you don't fully endorse in order to hold onto what really matters. That's the nature of compromise.

King Asa understood that. In contrast to the corruption that had characterized Jewish religious life prior to his reign, he was a saint. All the same, he wasn't successful in getting rid of all the garbage that had accumulated in the nation. Certain pagan practices and shrines remained in spite of his influence.

Still, Asa remained faithful to the Lord. He continued to worship God with a pure and undivided heart even when there was proof of heresy around him. He didn't compromise his beliefs, but he recognized that he couldn't legislate others' choices. His life was not without evidence of shortcomings, but he stayed on course.

Does that sound familiar? You can still follow after God and make progress even if you've failed or if others in your life refuse to follow God. Confess to the Lord your desire to stay focused on him in spite of what remains a blur around you. That type of admission is an act of worship. ❖

PRAYER

Lord, give me the determination to do what I can and not be derailed by what I can't . . .

day83

IT'S TIME TO CHOOSE

Elijah went before the people and said, "How long will you waver between two opinions? If the LORD is God, follow him; but if Baal is God, follow him."   I KINGS 18:21

Choices. It's a privilege to be able to express your personal desire and know that it matters. But if you don't know exactly what it is you want, being forced to decide is painful. The worries of uncertainty can cast long shadows in your direction.

The people Elijah addressed had all the facts they needed. They were capable of making the right choice. But they remained silent. They couldn't bring themselves to make a choice. And yet, with their silence they voted. Only after Elijah called on the Lord to demonstrate his power in dramatic ways did his apathetic audience weigh in.

God will not accept the role of default deity. He will not share recognition or position with any other god. The role of God, by definition, fits only One. Those who do not decide *for* God are automatically voting *against* him. The consequences for those who can't commit to choose God are the same as for those who openly choose against him.

As was the case with the Israelites, God has given you adequate proof that he has the right to rule in your life. And every day you're given a chance to affirm his leadership. It's not as difficult as you might think. Submit your agenda to him in prayer. Express your willingness to overrule your own plans. With gratitude in your heart, be proactive in your praise today. There's no need to wait for someone to ask you who you support. ✤

PRAYER

Lord, today I choose ...

WHEN GOD SPEAKS, LISTEN!

When Ahab heard these words, he tore his clothes, put on sackcloth and fasted. He lay in sackcloth and went around meekly.   I KINGS 21:27

Back in the 1970s, E. F. Hutton, a well-known investment firm, took to the airwaves with a successful marketing campaign. It called attention to how investors trusted the advice of the Hutton brokers. The popular tagline to the television ads was this: "When E. F. Hutton speaks, people listen!"

Who's to say how accurate those commercials were? One thing we know for sure is that when our E (Everlasting) F (Father) God speaks, even those who are not accustomed to hearing his voice listen up. Ahab is a case in point. When approached by Elijah with a word from the Lord, this wicked king humbled himself. God's disapproval of his past behavior was obvious. The Lord had succeeded in getting Ahab's attention. Unfortunately for this Machiavellian monarch, his humility was short-lived.

God still speaks. Unwilling to let us wander off into a spiritual wasteland, he holds a mirror to our faces. In lieu of Elijah, he sometimes uses the prophetic voice of a pastor, counselor or friend. But more often than not, we hear him speaking through the pages of the Bible.

Have you heard that familiar voice recently? More than likely it will require silencing the din of daily activities. Easier said than done, right? Babies need to be cuddled and rocked. Kids need to be fed. Deadlines need to be met. But hearing from the God who has your best interests at heart is worth finding the time. Go ahead and listen for your Father's voice. ♣

PRAYER

Lord, as I pause before you in silence, I await the whisper of your presence . . .

US VERSUS THEM

"Don't be afraid," the prophet answered. "Those who are with us are more than those who are with them."   2 KINGS 6:16

Daybreak. The first to rise, the servant goes outside to begin the morning preparations for his master—Elisha, the prophet of Israel. Yet before his startled eyes, he sees an army with chariots and horses surrounding the city. A siege is in progress. How would you have felt if you were that servant?

Elisha is not surprised by the news, however. He seems to have expected it, judging by his reassuring words to his servant. Now imagine yourself in the servant's place once more. How could the prophet be so confident in the presence of an army of enemies?

Elisha is not blind. Indeed, he intercedes for his servant, "Open his eyes, LORD, so that he may see" (2 Kings 6:17). Yes, let him see beyond what his eyes are telling him. Let him see that horses and chariots of fire—the very symbols of power that Elisha saw the Lord use to sweep Elijah to heaven (see 2 Kings 2:11)—have come to fill the hillsides. The enemy army had assembled during the night, but so had God's army.

Enemies, named or unnamed, human or inhuman, surround us at times. The word *outnumbered* scarcely begins to describe how we feel. Do we panic, as Elisha's servant did at first? Or do we ask for a new vision of what's there, for the eyes to see the other army that has assembled during the night?

As you lift your heart in the morning in prayer and praise, may you lift your eyes to see what God has provided. ✣

PRAYER

O Lord, open my eyes that I may see . . .

day86

I CHOOSE YOU!

Jehu got up and went into the house. Then the prophet poured the oil on Jehu's head and declared, "This is what the LORD, the God of Israel, says: 'I anoint you king over the LORD's people Israel.'"
2 KINGS 9:6

The young man lifts the vial over Jehu's head. God has chosen a warrior to be the next king of Israel, one who—if he fulfills the prophecy—will be known for his violence. Elisha even warns the young prophet that he should "open the door and run; don't delay!" (2 Kings 9:3). An unusual anointing, to say the least.

Stop for a moment. An unusual anointing? The passage has another unusual *appointing* as well; not one but two men are set apart by God for a special task. Jehu is called "into an inner room," away from his friends, ultimately away from the litany of kings who did what was evil in the Lord's sight. But the nameless "young prophet" is equally called for a special task. No olive oil is poured from a vial over his head, yet his is an appointing as much from God as Jehu's.

From the beginning, our God has been calling, appointing, setting apart. In Exodus 30:22–33, there is even a special anointing oil, set apart to anoint Aaron and his sons to be priests as well as the tent of meeting and other elements of worship.

The worshipful life of God's people takes many forms, has many roles to fill. Are we attuned to his call? "Know that the LORD has set apart his faithful servant for himself; the LORD hears when I call to him" (Psalm 4:3). As you listen to Jesus' words—"You did not choose me, but I chose you and appointed you so that you might go and bear fruit—fruit that will last" (John 15:16)—take comfort and take action. God has chosen you! ✤

> **PRAYER**

Call me, dear God, for I am listening . . .

day87

SPECIAL PLACES, DIVINE SPACES

Therefore King Joash summoned Jehoiada the priest and the other priests and asked them, "Why aren't you repairing the damage done to the temple? Take no more money from your treasurers, but hand it over for repairing the temple."   2 KINGS 12:7

The people of God had a space dedicated to the worship of God: the temple at Jerusalem. They had priests who were to ensure that the magnificent edifice built by Solomon would stay ready and true to its purpose. But the temple, constructed in every detail to express the worthiness and perfection of the Lord, was now in terrible shape. Its treasures had been plundered and its walls cluttered with the symbols of pagan deities. Beyond the physical damage, however, was the spiritual disarray: The temple's singular purpose had been compromised.

What we see, what we touch, what we hear—it all affects us. We must be aware and responsible lest we, like the Israelites, allow our houses of worship to fall into disrepair or compromise. The result will be the same as in the days of the kings: people pulled away from worship. Do we glory in the new organ, the polished candlesticks, the reupholstered pews? Certainly not. We honor God by honoring the singular purpose of his house.

The Lord is holy, and so must our worship of him be holy. The Lord is wholly divine, and so must our worship places be wholly divine. Set apart a portion of your devotional time specifically for praise and prayer. Perhaps you may want to change locations as a literal "setting apart" time with him. ❖

PRAYER

God, I honor you and praise you . . .

day88

ONLY ONE IS WORTHY

But the LORD, who brought you up out of Egypt with mighty power and outstretched arm, is the one you must worship. To him you shall bow down and to him offer sacrifices.

2 KINGS 17:36

"We need a more modern god for modern times. In fact, things are so complicated, we could probably use several gods."

"Look at the world. It's full of gods. Surely ours isn't that special. When it comes to deities, you can never have too many, can you?"

Is this how the people of Israel thought about worship? It is certainly how they acted. The result? "They followed worthless idols and themselves became worthless" (2 Kings 17:15). Worship moves our character toward the object of our worship. Created in the image of the one true God, the Israelites let their souls be destroyed by the many false gods around them. Caught in the confusion, their worship became a bazaar of the bizarre.

Were the commandments given through Moses not clear enough? Did the Israelites wonder — do we wonder — what did God really mean? Surely he would want us to adapt to new situations, right? No, the words were clear, the meaning transparent: "I am the LORD your God, who brought you out of Egypt, out of the land of slavery. You shall have no other gods before me ... You shall not bow down to them or worship them" (Exodus 20:2 – 3,5). Do not. Never. Ever. So many generations later, "they would not listen and were as stiff-necked as their ancestors, who did not trust in the LORD their God" (2 Kings 17:14).

God is holy, and he is the only God. "Holy, Holy, Holy," a hymn by Reginald Heber, calls us to worship: "Only Thou art holy; there is none beside Thee, / Perfect in power, in love, and purity." To God alone, each day, offer sacrifices of praise. ✤

PRAYER

God, I bow before you, offering you my praise ...

FIRST RESPONSE OR LAST RESORT?

Hezekiah received the letter from the messengers and read it. Then he went up to the temple of the LORD and spread it out before the LORD.   2 KINGS 19:14

The threatening words Hezekiah read in the letter were as bold and as enormous as the literal threat posed by King Sennacherib and his mighty army.

Was Hezekiah tempted to take the deal, to surrender with the promise of a good life for his people? The prophet Isaiah, after the shouted threats, had delivered God's own message: "Do not be afraid of what you have heard—those words with which the underlings of the king of Assyria have blasphemed me. Listen! When he hears a certain report, I will make him want to return to his own country, and there I will have him cut down with the sword" (2 Kings 19:6–7).

But this letter ...

No, Hezekiah did not hesitate, did not meet with his advisers to analyze his options. He showed his faithfulness to the Lord in everything. Hezekiah hurried to the temple. There was only one response. He "spread [the letter] out before the LORD" and then he spread himself out in prayer: "You alone are God over all the kingdoms of the earth. You have made heaven and earth" (2 Kings 19:15).

The result? The Assyrians were indeed defeated, as God alone could accomplish.

We face threats of many kinds. Desperate situations, people offering deals and compromises, problems that redefine the word *hopeless*. What do we do first? Seek human counsel? Construct a chart of pros and cons? Read the latest self-help book? Instead, our first response should be to "spread it out before the LORD" in humble, honest prayer.

As you encounter difficulties or trials during the day, remember Hezekiah, and "spread it out before the LORD." ♣

PRAYER

God, you know the threats I face. I come to you first, not as a last resort ...

BURIED TREASURE

Furthermore, Josiah got rid of the mediums and spiritists, the household gods, the idols and all the other detestable things seen in Judah and Jerusalem. This he did to fulfill the requirements of the law written in the book that Hilkiah the priest had discovered in the temple of the LORD.   2 KINGS 23:24

Imagine a buried treasure. But this treasure is not intentionally hidden for safe-keeping, like a chest concealed by planning and cunning. Its worth is not even known by those who lose it, who push it aside, toss it to the back of the closet and heap other stuff on top of it.

Such was the fate of the Law of God, the very words given through Moses. The scroll containing the Law was buried, lost in the temple, so forgotten by God's people that for centuries they had not even known how to celebrate Passover. Then Hilkiah the priest told the court secretary Shaphan that he had found the Book of the Law (see 2 Kings 22:8). After Shaphan read the incredible words, he knew what to do: Take the book to King Josiah and read it to him.

Josiah's response was to tear his clothes in despair. They had sunk so far—especially under Josiah's father, Amon, and grandfather, Manasseh, one of the most evil kings of Judah. But Josiah aspired to climb to the higher ground of his great-grandfather, Hezekiah. Josiah set out to restore God's Word as treasure in the people's hearts as it once was treasure in the temple.

Where is the treasure that is God's Word today? Where in our churches? Where in our lives? May this treasure be seen in the riches that are our prayers and praises throughout the day. ✤

PRAYER

God, guide me in the truth of your Scripture ...

WHAT'S YOUR PART?

Some of them were in charge of the articles used in the temple service; they counted them when they were brought in and when they were taken out. Others were assigned to take care of the furnishings and all the other articles of the sanctuary, as well as the special flour and wine, and the olive oil, incense and spices. But some of the priests took care of mixing the spices.   1 Chronicles 9:28–30

The division of labor is not a new concept. Optimally, it is practiced on a daily basis within your household — some family member takes out the garbage, another does the food shopping, still another is responsible for the dishes. It is a model that has been handed down through the ages.

God's household is no different. While Jesus suggested that those who follow him are like a family, the apostle Paul compared the mutual ministry of Christians in community to the human body (see 1 Corinthians 12). Every body part and organ is indispensable to the other. Each has a critical part to play.

Division of labor is the picture we have in this passage of Scripture. Although the priests and Levites in the Old Testament were responsible for worship, God did not expect them to carry it off all by themselves. Sure, they were called and set apart. But their holy calling was not disconnected from the rest of the Israelite nation. The priests choreographed a sacred liturgy, the Levites assisted in their duties, and the people of God were very much involved as well. Each had a part to play.

That hasn't changed. When coming before the Lord with a heart of worship, you don't have to wait for Sunday. You don't need a pastor or church staff. God is an audience of one, and he welcomes your soliloquy of praise. In your own inimitable way, you can celebrate his greatness and glory with silence, singing, prayer, a prostrate act of surrender or even a homespun ballet. ✤

PRAYER

Lord, here is my contribution of praise . . .

day92

POUR YOU!

David longed for water and said, "Oh, that someone would get me a drink of water from the well near the gate of Bethlehem!" So the Three broke through the Philistine lines, drew water from the well near the gate of Bethlehem and carried it back to David. But he refused to drink it; instead, he poured it out to the LORD.　1 CHRONICLES 11:17–18

Sacrifice. That's a synonym for worship. When you willingly give up what you'd rather do to spend time in the presence of the Lord, you are worshiping. When you forego what you know is valuable in order to take stock of the priceless worth of God, you are worshiping. That's what the crowned prince David did as he hid from Saul.

While a fugitive, David longed for the cool refreshing water in his hometown. That well-known well would provide him with a tangible connection with family and memories of home. It would connect David to the place where the prophet Samuel had anointed him as the king-elect. It would remind him that God had called him.

His men knew that. Because of their love for their leader, they risked their lives to bring back to David a leather pouch of water. And to their amazement, the future king emptied the contents on the ground in front of them. Recognizing the value of the water, David poured it out as an act of worship to the Lord. He could have drunk it. He could have enjoyed it. But he didn't. David remembered that the source of his call was not his hometown, but the Lord himself. He modeled for his men the costliness of worship.

Three thousand years later, King David reminds us why sacrifice and worship are synonyms. No doubt you're exhausted from projects accomplished and dreading more deadlines to come. The fact that you are still willing to spend time with the Lord instead of doing what you long to do or feel you deserve to do, that's worship. ♣

> **PRAYER**

Lord, I am willing to sacrifice . . .

day93

THE HOLY TWO-STEP

Give praise to the LORD, proclaim his name; make known among the nations what he has done. Sing to him, sing praise to him; tell of all his wonderful acts.

1 CHRONICLES 16:8–9

The graceful movements of dancers as they pirouette to a praise song bring joy to those who watch. Dance can be a wonderful expression of worship. But have you ever thought of worship itself as a dance? In a manner of speaking, that's exactly what it is. It's a holy two-step.

In this passage, David is like a dance-caller. Listen carefully to his instructions and you'll begin to hear the two-directional movement he suggests. "Give praise to the LORD." That's the primary step of worship. With an open heart we move toward the Lord. But it doesn't stop there. David calls us to turn and "proclaim his name." That's another step in which with open mouths we move toward those around us who may not understand just how awesome our great God is.

The dance continues. "Make known among the nations what he has done." Again we step toward people around us, proclaiming the incredible works that God has done in our lives. Then it's back to the first step in which we move toward God. "Sing to him, sing praise to him." But we don't stop there. David, the dance-caller, reminds us to "tell of all his wonderful acts."

Toward the Lord, then toward our neighbors. Gratefully singing to God, then confidently bragging about him to people around us. One step. Two step. Repeat. One step. Two step. Feel the rhythm? Wherever you are, whatever you are doing, the cadence of worship is all-encompassing. ♣

PRAYER

Heavenly Father, when I think of all you have done for me, I want to . . .

PROMISES, PROMISES

And now, LORD, let the promise you have made concerning your servant and his house be established forever. Do as you promised, so that it will be established and that your name will be great forever. Then people will say, "The LORD Almighty, the God over Israel, is Israel's God!" And the house of your servant David will be established before you.

1 CHRONICLES 17:23–24

Margaret had been raised in the Blue Ridge Mountains of Virginia. When her mother died, she had to drop out of school to care for her grieving father and her two brothers. As a result, she never had the opportunity to go to college. With the Lord's help, she did the best she could to teach herself.

Although she loved to read, Margaret never outgrew her insecurity when carrying on conversations with highly educated people. But when it came to carrying on conversations with the Lord, she knew what she was talking about ... and to whom.

In addition to reading each morning from a dog-eared, leather-bound Bible, Margaret would also pull a Scripture card from a little wooden box on her kitchen table. She called it her "box of promises." It was filled with verses from the Bible documenting the myriad ways God had guaranteed to intervene on behalf of his people. Margaret would remember the promises of God to his people, including herself, her husband and her children.

Like Margaret, King David took God at his word each day. Living with the assurance of God's involvement in his life was the way David coped with his stress as Israel's ruler.

When you face challenges, how do you handle them? When you identify one of God's promises, you are falling at his feet in joyful—and expectant—dependence. ✤

PRAYER

O Jesus, today, I think of this promise ...

MUSICAL MEMORIES

David, together with the commanders of the army, set apart some of the sons of Asaph, Heman and Jeduthun for the ministry of prophesying, accompanied by harps, lyres and cymbals.
1 CHRONICLES 25:1

Forgetfulness—it plagues us all. We struggle to recall names, passwords and phone numbers. But more than that, we tend to forget things we value as significant while remembering events or thoughts we'd rather forget.

Perhaps that's why memorizing God's Word is so difficult. Try as you will, you can't seem to hide it in your heart. What causes you to keep trying, however, is the joy you've experienced in the past when you quoted a verse from memory to someone who wanted to know what God had to say on a certain topic. Being able to recite a passage of Scripture when the truth it celebrates describes a given life situation is wonderfully freeing. But lest you think it impossible, try adding music.

When David and the army commanders instructed certain families to put a musical accompaniment to the words of God, they were doing us a big favor. Putting Scripture to music makes memorizing it easier. That's been tested and proven. In fact, you probably already have memorized Scripture without even knowing it because some songs you sing come straight out of the Bible.

By listening to worship music as you work around the house or drive back and forth to your place of employment, you will sing those lyrics over and over until they become part of you. And guess what? In the process of listening, singing and memorizing the Word of God, you'll be worshiping him. Sing a different tune today, and hide God's Word in your heart. ✤

PRAYER

Lord, when it comes to your Word, I remember . . .

day96 april 6

PASSING THE BATON OF FAITH

And you, my son Solomon, acknowledge the God of your father, and serve him with wholehearted devotion and with a willing mind, for the LORD searches every heart and understands every desire and every thought. If you seek him, he will be found by you; but if you forsake him, he will reject you forever. 1 CHRONICLES 28:9

Harold Barnes didn't always have a knack for memorizing the Bible, and for good reason. Hal was over 40 when he became a Christian. Once he trusted Christ as his Savior, Hal developed an insatiable hunger for God's Word. He loved to read and meditate on Scripture. This traveling salesman carried a pocket-sized version of the Bible wherever he went. As he drove several hundred miles between clients, Hal would read and audibly recite long passages.

By the time he turned 80, Harold Barnes had memorized over 170 chapters of the Bible. The amount of truth he hid in his mind and heart was the by-product of spending time in worship. Just as David hoped Solomon would do, Hal worshiped and served the Lord with his whole heart and a willing mind. Because he did, Hal shared his joy and inner peace with his clients, his neighbors and his family.

In fact, when his grandson Jacob turned 13, Grandpa Hal was invited to speak at the birthday celebration. As he stood up in front of a roomful of invited guests, the elderly man challenged the boy to seek the Lord and spend time in his Word. More than anything, Hal wanted the faith he had found in midlife to be passed on to family members who would come after him.

Essentially that's what David was saying to his son when he challenged him to "acknowledge the God of your father." It's what the Lord longs for for you. ✤

PRAYER

Lord, I acknowledge that you . . .

AWESOME ARCHITECTURE

"The temple I am going to build will be great, because our God is greater than all other gods."   2 CHRONICLES 2:5

Finally. A temple worthy of God was going to be built. Cedar, gold, bronze, purple cloth. The house for God that David had envisioned so long ago was finally under way.

David had desperately wanted to construct a true temple, saying to the prophet Nathan, "Here I am, living in a house of cedar, while the ark of God remains in a tent" (2 Samuel 7:2). Although his heart was "after [God's] own heart" (Acts 13:22), David's hands were those of the battlefield. God said to him, "You are not to build a house for my Name, because you are a warrior and have shed blood" (1 Chronicles 28:3).

Solomon, granted extraordinary wisdom, was entrusted with the extraordinary task. Demonstrating his God-given wisdom, he acknowledged his limitations. What if this temple was but a paltry reflection of a God "greater than all other gods," whom the very heavens cannot contain? He wondered, "Who then am I to build a temple for him, except as a place to burn sacrifices before him?" (2 Chronicles 2:6). So, in addition to the exquisite supplies and the enormous work force, Solomon sought and found a master craftsman who could work with his craftsmen to turn all these fine materials into the temple. Only the best of the best, shaping the best of the best, could make it truly magnificent.

Awesome architecture for an awesome God. Believer, whatever gifts, abilities or talents you possess, give your all, that your life of praise will honor him to the fullest. ✤

PRAYER

O Lord, I offer these abilities you have given me ...

HEAR AND HEAL

If my people, who are called by my name, will humble themselves and pray and seek my face and turn from their wicked ways, then I will hear from heaven, and I will forgive their sin and will heal their land.
2 CHRONICLES 7:14

He stood on a platform before the entire assembly. Then he knelt, lifting his hands high toward heaven. King Solomon prayed, with eloquence and passion, dedicating the temple. Now—months later, maybe years later—the Lord appeared to Solomon at night. He assured Solomon, "I have heard your prayer and have chosen this place for myself as a temple for sacrifices" (2 Chronicles 7:12).

Does God think that, from this point on, his people will never stray? That they will continually offer sacrifices with clean hearts and hands? No, he knows them too well, these people called by his name. Their wicked ways will return, and with them droughts and locusts and plagues. Still, there will be mercy and healing if the people humble themselves, pray, seek God's face and repent. "Now my eyes will be open and my ears attentive to the prayers offered in this place. I have chosen and consecrated this temple so that my Name may be there forever" (2 Chronicles 7:15–16).

But what of us? The great temple at Jerusalem is no more. Yet God still hears us from heaven, still calls us to the same humility, prayer, seeking of his face and repentance. The early Christians could be certain of this, and so can we: "Submit yourselves, then, to God ... Come near to God and he will come near to you ... Grieve, mourn and wail. Change your laughter to mourning and your joy to gloom. Humble yourselves before the Lord, and he will lift you up" (James 4:7–10).

Bow down before the Lord; humble yourself even to tears. As you rise and move through the day, still your heart before him, continually confessing. He will draw near to you. ✤

PRAYER

O Lord, hear me from heaven ...

THE PRICE WE PAY

When the LORD saw that they humbled themselves, this word of the LORD came to Shemaiah: "Since they have humbled themselves, I will not destroy them but will soon give them deliverance. My wrath will not be poured out on Jerusalem through Shishak. They will, however, become subject to him, so that they may learn the difference between serving me and serving the kings of other lands." 2 CHRONICLES 12:7–8

The people had clamored for a king long ago — way back, in the days before Saul, in the days of the judges. "Give us a king to lead us," they had said to Samuel (1 Samuel 8:6). Although they had grieved Samuel, the Lord knew their true motives: "It is not you they have rejected, but they have rejected me as their king" (1 Samuel 8:7). And so God had given the Israelites kings, but not all of the kings followed the Lord.

Now it was happening again. King Rehoboam, Solomon's son, was firmly established. Although he had started out following God's ways, he soon abandoned the law of the Lord. All God's people followed him in sin, and consequently, God allowed the king of Egypt, Shishak, to attack Jerusalem. But since God did not let the Egyptians completely destroy Judah, one could say, "It could have been worse."

In reality, it could have been so much better. The people could have been following wholeheartedly the one true God. We too swerve in our loyalties, sometimes following after this political leader or that cultural guru despite their lack of faith in God. Only One deserves to be followed, and only One deserves the homage of his people.

In today's passage God gave the message through the prophet Shemaiah that becoming Shishak's subjects could teach the people of Israel something. Did the people of God learn to whom they should ultimately swear allegiance? Do we? How much better it is to serve God than earthly rulers. How much better it is to revere God, to come into his courts with praise today. ✤

PRAYER

King of kings, I pledge to you my honor and my loyalty . . .

FULLY COMMITTED OR FOOLISHLY CLEVER?

For the eyes of the LORD range throughout the earth to strengthen those whose hearts are fully committed to him. You have done a foolish thing, and from now on you will be at war.   2 CHRONICLES 16:9

It had seemed like a prudent move. Strategic diplomacy, some might say. "Let there be a treaty between me and you," [Asa] said, "as there was between my father and your father" (2 Chronicles 16:3)—what could be better than such negotiations?

What could be better? A lot, said the Lord to King Asa, through Hanani the seer. "Because you relied on the king of Aram and not on the LORD your God, the army of the king of Aram has escaped from your hand" (2 Chronicles 16:7). And after years of trusting God against the Cushites and the Libyans, the idols and the Asherah poles, Asa made a poor choice. "You have done a foolish thing," said Hanani.

Having trusted in the Lord in the past, Asa now was trusting in a foreign ruler to bring peace and, later, would be relying only on his physicians to heal his foot disease.

We shake our heads. Having trusted in God and found him trustworthy, how could Asa place that trust in anything or anybody else? Then we remember our own temptation to do for ourselves. We say, "God would have done something by now if he were going to." Or perhaps we cloak our misplaced trust in words such as, "Maybe I'll just try this too. The Lord helps those who help themselves, right?"

In what areas of your life are you trusting something or someone other than the Lord? Turn over those situations to God. He willingly helps all who come to him, fully committed, worshiping him. ✤

> **PRAYER**

O God, I trust you to . . .

POWERFUL PRAISE!

After consulting the people, Jehoshaphat appointed men to sing to the LORD and to praise him for the splendor of his holiness as they went out at the head of the army, saying: "Give thanks to the LORD, for his love endures forever." 2 CHRONICLES 20:21

What an unusual way to start a battle! The people of Judah were facing three armies determined to wipe their nation from the earth—and they put a choir in the front lines! In this wonderful story, God promised to deliver the people of Judah from their enemies, and the people believed his word. The singers were not asking God to protect them and give them victory. They simply praised him for his faithful love to them. But notice the significance of the sequence of events in this battle. The people praised God based on their knowledge of his character—not the outcome of their circumstance.

It's easy to thank God when we receive the promotion, or the test results come back negative, or our prayer is answered in the way we imagined. But thanking God before we know the outcome? That requires putting our faith and trust in the One who is in control.

What battle are you facing right now? Perhaps you are waiting to hear back from a recent job interview. Or maybe you are in a broken relationship that you are trying desperately to reconcile. Perhaps you are battling a life-threatening illness or an addiction or a sinful habit that just seems to defeat your best efforts. Whatever it is, praise God right now. Offer your thanksgiving to him for his holy splendor and for his faithful love. ❖

PRAYER

Lord, in the midst of this battle, I offer you this praise ...

day102

COURAGEOUS WORSHIP

In the seventh year Jehoiada showed his strength. He made a covenant with the commanders of units of a hundred: Azariah son of Jeroham, Ishmael son of Jehohanan, Azariah son of Obed, Maaseiah son of Adaiah, and Elishaphat son of Zikri ... Jehoiada then made a covenant that he, the people and the king would be the LORD's people. All the people went to the temple of Baal and tore it down. They smashed the altars and idols and killed Mattan the priest of Baal in front of the altars. 2 CHRONICLES 23:1,16–17

Ask the typical churchgoer to describe what worship involves, and you most likely will receive answers that go something like this—singing, confession, praying, thanksgiving, praising, celebrating, dancing and maybe teaching and preaching. But would you include *the courage to take a stand* as part of worship? Perhaps not, but sometimes our worship requires just that.

Jehoiada the priest decided it was time to act to restore the throne to a descendant of David, according to God's promise to his people. God used Jehoiada's courage and willingness to act to bring about his purposes. After Joash became king, Jehoiada continued to demonstrate worship through action, making a covenant with the king and the people that they would be the Lord's people. Because of Jehoiada's actions, the temple of God was restored during Joash's reign and the people lived in peace.

What action is God asking of you today as part of your worship? God treasures the private time you spend with him reading his Word, praying to him and honoring his power and greatness. Yet, he also desires your active participation in extending his kingdom. Have the courage to ask him what he wants you to do to demonstrate your love for him. Perhaps an estranged relationship needs forgiveness and healing, or a new person in your church or your neighborhood needs your friendship. Take courage and choose to act. ❖

PRAYER

Help me worship you with my actions, Lord ...

day103

PRIDE AND POWER

But after Uzziah became powerful, his pride led to his downfall. He was unfaithful to the LORD his God, and entered the temple of the LORD to burn incense on the altar of incense.

2 CHRONICLES 26:16

"I'm so proud of you," we say when our child masters a difficult task or earns a college degree. "I'm proud of you," we say to our spouse or friends who have accomplished something significant. So what's wrong with pride? When those we love are proud of us, it gives us a sense of dignity, value and self-respect.

The danger in pride comes when we take our eyes off God and begin to think we are in charge of our lives. We become arrogant, haughty and disdainful of others. Uzziah's pride led him to believe he did not need a priest to offer sacrifices on his behalf.

Is pride a problem for you? Have you become self-sufficient and even a bit arrogant? If you continually seek the Lord and allow yourself to be instructed by him, pride will not overtake you.

But it's also easy to be guilty of pride about our spirituality, to think we are better than others who may not feel as close to God as we do, who may not have the gifts that we do or who may have struggles that we do not.

If we seek him, God promises to be with us. With his presence, we have his power to praise him, to claim victory over sin and circumstances, to use the talents and gifts he has given us for his glory, to love others as he has loved us, and to transform our pride into praise. Worship God today for his awesomeness, not yours. ✣

PRAYER

God, I sometimes fall into this pride trap ...

CAN YOU HEAR ME NOW?

And the LORD heard Hezekiah and healed the people . . . Hezekiah spoke encouragingly to all the Levites, who showed good understanding of the service of the LORD. For the seven days they ate their assigned portion and offered fellowship offerings and praised the LORD, the God of their ancestors . . . The priests and the Levites stood to bless the people, and God heard them, for their prayer reached heaven, his holy dwelling place.

2 CHRONICLES 30:20,22,27

Do you ever feel like your prayers and praise get no higher than the ceiling? Sometimes God seems distant. You can't imagine the Lord of the universe paying attention to you, let alone listening to your concerns. But the Bible tells another story. *God heard them from his holy dwelling in heaven.* He hears you too.

Some of the Israelites joining in the Passover celebration had not completed the purification rituals required by Jewish law, but God heard Hezekiah's prayer on their behalf and healed the people.

Today, Jesus' death and resurrection have torn down the veil that separated the people from God. Even when our prayers are inadequate or faulty, "the Spirit helps us in our weakness. We do not know what we ought to pray for, but the Spirit himself intercedes for us through wordless groans" (Romans 8:26).

As you follow the Lord, you can be confident he hears your prayers. Do you need his healing and forgiveness today? Do you need his purifying power to heal you before you can worship him? He is as near as your next breath. He will hear your confession and restore your soul. "Because he turned his ear to me, I will call on him as long as I live" (Psalm 116:2).

Today, picture God bending down to catch every word you say, every thought directed to honoring him. Imagine God paying attention to just you. He's listening! ✤

PRAYER

Lord, I am so grateful you listen . . .

day105

OUR EMOTIONAL GOD

In his distress he sought the favor of the LORD his God and humbled himself greatly before the God of his ancestors. And when he prayed to him, the LORD was moved by his entreaty and listened to his plea; so he brought him back to Jerusalem and to his kingdom. Then Manasseh knew that the LORD is God.　　　　　2 CHRONICLES 33:12–13

Manasseh paid a heavy price for his unfaithfulness to God. He lost his throne and was imprisoned in a foreign land. Manasseh deserved his punishment—and worse. He did terrible things, even sacrificing his own sons to a heathen god. But Manasseh's story includes more than punishment. When he humbled himself before God, the Lord was moved by his request for help. God forgave Manasseh and restored his kingdom.

God is moved by our prayers of confession. But that's not an easy concept for us to accept. Because we know that God is the all-powerful Creator, we may assume that he is aloof and disinterested. Even if we acknowledge that he loves us, we often have trouble believing that he really does care about us personally. God grieves when we disobey him, burns with anger at our sin, but is moved with compassion when we humbly confess our wrongs.

Jesus offers us a glimpse of the Father's delight with us through the parable of the lost coin (see Luke 15:8–10). He relates the joyous celebration that the heavenly angels throw "over one sinner who repents" (Luke 15:10). Every individual is precious before God, and he is moved as we come to him in total dependence and repentance.

Today, remember that you are created in God's image, and that image includes God's emotions. Your actions affect him. Confess any disobedience, and ask him to forgive you. Know that he will respond to your request for help. ❖

PRAYER

God, by your grace, I will act ...

day106

GOD WORKS OUTSIDE THE BOX

In the first year of Cyrus king of Persia, in order to fulfill the word of the LORD spoken by Jeremiah, the LORD moved the heart of Cyrus king of Persia to make a proclamation throughout his realm and also to put it in writing. EZRA 1:1

It's not hard for us to comprehend that God would use other Christians to work in our lives and in our circumstances. What we don't expect, however, is for God to use our unbelieving friends or an evil ruler or government to accomplish his plans.

The book of Ezra shows us that God's plans encompass it all—what we often think of as the secular and the sacred—and he will use whatever he chooses to move his story forward. God stirred the pagan heart of King Cyrus to issue a decree for the Jews to return home to Jerusalem to rebuild their temple. As Proverbs 21:1 reminds us, "In the LORD's hand the king's heart is a stream of water that he channels toward all who please him."

God is always taking the initiative to call his people to himself, and he will work through whatever he chooses to do so. Nothing is outside God's power to control. He can stir the hearts of people who don't know him. He can use their misguided desires and work through their worldly roles. We can be glad that whenever we think we know how God works, he breaks out of our box. His boundless love uses anything to move his people one step closer to his plans for them.

Think about the people in your own life—believers and nonbelievers. How is God using them to work in your life? Take time to thank him that he is not bound by your preconceived ideas about who is "worthy" or not to be his instruments. ✤

> **PRAYER**

Lord God, I see you working through . . .

HOW MUCH DO YOU WANT IT?

For seven days they celebrated with joy the Festival of Unleavened Bread, because the LORD had filled them with joy by changing the attitude of the king of Assyria so that he assisted them in the work on the house of God, the God of Israel. EZRA 6:22

Real worship can be quite a challenge. The whole house may be quiet until you pick up your Bible or sit down to pray. That's when the kids start arguing, the dog needs to go out, you remember the phone calls you haven't returned ... and you begin to feel guilty for ignoring it all to worship God.

The scene Ezra describes is no different. The flesh, the devil and the world all worked against God's people rebuilding the temple. Their desire to put God first met with opposition from within and without.

First, enemies approached, deceitfully claiming their allegiance to God (see Ezra 4:1–3). What a picture of our lives. If we look closely inside, despite our soul's longing for God, parts of us still want to rebel. Our flesh values self-inflation, blessings and ease above relationship with God.

Second, Satan incited others to try to defeat God's people with bribes and frustration (see Ezra 4:4–5). Similarly, he bribes us with promises of more time if we'll just push worship aside.

Third, the peoples around them accused the Jews of disloyalty (see Ezra 4:13–14) in an effort to prohibit their progress. Still today, when we spend time focusing on God, the world competes for our loyalty with its many worries and concerns.

Thankfully, God's people pushed through the obstacles and pursued God's plan to complete the temple. God rewarded their perseverance with great joy. As they did what they could, God did what only he could, and changed the king's attitude to grant them success. When nothing can stop our desire to put God first, he takes care of the rest. ✜

PRAYER

Lord, these are the distractions that keep me from you ...

day108

MY STUPID SINS

Then, at the evening sacrifice, I rose from my self-abasement, with my tunic and cloak torn, and fell on my knees with my hands spread out to the LORD my God and prayed: "I am too ashamed and disgraced, my God, to lift up my face to you, because our sins are higher than our heads and our guilt has reached to the heavens." EZRA 9:5 – 6

Where do we get the strength to stand against sin? How can we live in a society that compromises continually without desiring to do the same? What keeps us from giving in to the enticement of sin? Ezra knew the answer to all of these troubling questions was to worship God.

Ezra shines like a star among the darkened hearts of his people. They had disobeyed God by marrying unbelievers and accepting their pagan ways. Brokenhearted, Ezra mourned over such sin. He saw it so clearly and refused it so easily because he practiced three key elements of worship—he understood God's laws, experienced God's favor and accepted his need for God.

In worship we affirm that everything God says and does is right. We see his laws not as restrictive prohibitions against enjoyment but as protective guidelines for abundant living. This leads us to abandon ourselves more and more as we consider God's care for us. We're able to relax our sinful grasping and rest in his favor. Worship changes our demanding nature to one that acknowledges God.

Ezra was living proof that when we know God's Word (see Ezra 7:6), experience God's favor (see 7:28) and accept our dependence on God (see 9:15), nothing can entice us to return to life without him.

As you go through your daily activities, consider which of these three areas you need to focus on in order to remain in constant worship with God. ✤

PRAYER

Dear God, search me and show me the things that block my wholehearted worship...

HOMESICK

They said to me, "Those who survived the exile and are back in the province are in great trouble and disgrace. The wall of Jerusalem is broken down, and its gates have been burned with fire." When I heard these things, I sat down and wept. For some days I mourned and fasted and prayed before the God of heaven. NEHEMIAH 1:3–4

The opening verses of Nehemiah may strike you as simply a factual account of the setting for the book and the reason for its being written. That is true; but something else about this passage is equally important, something easy to overlook.

Nehemiah was a Jew living in exile in Susa, the capital city of Persia, on the Persian Gulf, in service to King Artaxerxes. Nehemiah had likely never lived in Jerusalem. It's possible he had never even been there. Yet his heart turns to Jerusalem, the city of his ancestors, longing for it as his true home.

Is there a place like that in your life? A place where life seemed happier, simpler or at least less hectic? A place that you think of as home? Most would say yes, but even if earth holds no place like that for you, heaven does. In heaven our Father waits to greet us as beloved children who have been away on a long journey, to welcome us home with the words, "Well done."

Worship, whether corporate or individual, evokes in us a longing for a better world, a world where God himself will be with us, where he will remove all of our sadness, and there will be no more death or sorrow or crying or pain, "for the old order of things has passed away" (Revelation 21:4).

Nehemiah was homesick for a place he had never been before, but was longing to go to. Worshiping God will have the same effect on us. ❖

PRAYER

Father, thank you for preparing my place in heaven ...

113

A JOB WELL DONE

So the wall was completed on the twenty-fifth of Elul, in fifty-two days. When all our enemies heard about this, all the surrounding nations were afraid and lost their self-confidence, because they realized that this work had been done with the help of our God.
NEHEMIAH 6:15–16

The boy was so slow to talk that his parents were concerned. He failed his first college entrance exam at a college in Zurich, Switzerland. A year later he tried again. In time he became world famous. His name? Albert Einstein.

Perhaps you can relate to the pride of overcoming active opposition. That's a normal reaction. And that's not all wrong—as C. S. Lewis once observed, there are two kinds of pride. One is the opposite of humility, and that's bad; the other is the opposite of shame, and that's good. Taking pride in doing a job well is acceptable.

Nehemiah undoubtedly felt some of that pride when he and his fellow workers finished rebuilding the wall around Jerusalem in just 52 days. His opponents had mocked and scoffed, but Nehemiah's team had persevered and overcame. Even so, he eschewed taking the credit himself, giving the accolades to God.

When we serve God faithfully, using our spiritual gifts, we have a sense of fulfillment and satisfaction, a sense of connectedness to him that we find nowhere else. This is true in our everyday lives and it is especially true in worship. When we offer praise and tribute to God for his goodness to us, we experience the completeness of "This is what I was born to do."

Like Nehemiah surveying that improbable wall, take pride—the right kind of pride—in offering up to the Lord your accomplishments and abilities today. ✤

PRAYER

Father, today, I take pride in . . .

LOOK UP!

You alone are the Lord. *You made the heavens, even the highest heavens, and all their starry host, the earth and all that is on it, the seas and all that is in them. You give life to everything, and the multitudes of heaven worship you.* Nehemiah 9:6

What natural phenomenon fills you most with awe and wonder? A beautiful sunrise or sunset? Waves crashing on a beach? A majestic, snow-capped mountain peak? Whales breaching and spraying water in a foaming frenzy? The night sky splashed with stars, glittering like diamonds on black velvet? Your newborn child?

As you stand awed and amazed, remember the One who ordained that the cosmos and our planet should work in such a marvelous fashion, who formed us in his own image and who holds it all together by his will (see Colossians 1:15–17).

Most of our early scientists were driven to discover the great truths about the laws of nature by their logical convictions that creation must have a Creator and that natural laws must have been given by a Lawgiver. They were convinced that such a beautiful and well-ordered universe and planet could not be the result of accidents and chance, but were engineered by an intelligent Designer.

The Levites—Israel's worship leaders—expressed similar ideas as they exhorted the people to worship the Lord, the creator and sustainer of the universe. That must have been some worship service! But they didn't know what we know: how the first creation points toward the new creation, when all things are made new in Christ (see Revelation 21:5).

The next time you have the opportunity to watch the sunrise in all its gold-orange-red-blue glory or hold a baby, give thanks to the Creator. ✤

PRAYER

Lord, I marvel at . . .

day112

NOT A SPECTATOR SPORT

These were the priests and Levites who returned with Zerubbabel son of Shealtiel and with Joshua: Seraiah, Jeremiah, Ezra . . . NEHEMIAH 12:1

Most people tend to skip this kind of chapter in their devotional reading. What could be duller than a list of people who attended a religious ceremony in Jerusalem in 444 BC? These men, women and young people are—except for Nehemiah, Ezra and maybe Asaph—total unknowns. Yet they have something important to teach us about worship.

For one thing, *Biblical worship is not a spectator sport.* Judging from the names included here in chapter 12, it would have been easier to name the people who were *not* involved in this worship service. The people who participated included priests, Levites, singers, trumpet players, choirs, scribes and the governor himself—and those are just the people on the wall. Worship is meant to involve everyone, not just the "professionals."

Biblical worship also places great emphasis on holiness. In Nehemiah 12:30, we read that after the priests "purified themselves ceremonially, they purified the people, the gates and the wall." Their example shows that we should not come into the presence of a holy God in a slovenly, disrespectful way, but with our best and noblest efforts.

We also learn that Biblical worship places a premium on joy. Verse 43 alone uses the root word for *joy* five times. Worship must be reverent, of course, but it should also be joyful.

Participation, holiness, joy—are these present in your worship? Have you experienced the fullness and richness of true worship? If not, ask God to help you grow in these areas. ✤

PRAYER

Father, give me a hunger for your holiness . . .

EMBRACE WHAT HE HAS GIVEN YOU

Go, gather together all the Jews who are in Susa, and fast for me. Do not eat or drink for three days, night or day. I and my attendants will fast as you do. When this is done, I will go to the king, even though it is against the law. And if I perish, I perish. ESTHER 4:16

What might God want to do through us? It may be bigger than we expect. We wait. We hope. We pray. But often underneath it all, we are thinking: "I can't do that" or "That's not allowed" or "Things will turn around without me." Esther is the story of a young woman who overcame those inhibiting thoughts, put her life on the line and fulfilled God's purposes through her actions.

What gave Esther the courage to step out? Certainly, prompting by Mordecai played a role. Undoubtedly, the support of people fasting and praying boosted her boldness. But most importantly, Esther knew that King Xerxes wasn't her ultimate authority. Her Jewish faith reminded her that she answered to God, the King of kings. Esther's belief in God changed her from a powerless victim into a proactive player.

What is making you feel helpless? Psalm 23 reminds us that because the Lord is our shepherd, we have everything we need to live the life he wants us to live. Our passions, desires, resources, ideas, creativity, connections, energy and gifts aren't accidental. They're within our reach so we can accomplish the purposeful plans of a sovereign God. As we spend time in God's presence, we see, as did Mordecai and Esther, the bigger story, and we can develop the confidence to step out.

The story of Esther encourages us to embrace what God has given us—whether beauty, talent, favor or position—for his purposes. Instead of letting the "what ifs" of life control us, we can let God control us. In the process, we may just change the course of history. ❖

PRAYER

Lord, give me a bigger picture of what you can do through my life ...

GOD BETWEEN THE LINES

Mordecai recorded these events ... to have them celebrate annually the fourteenth and fifteenth days of the month of Adar as the time when the Jews got relief from their enemies, and as the month when their sorrow was turned into joy and their mourning into a day of celebration. He wrote them to observe the days as days of feasting and joy and giving presents of food to one another and gifts to the poor. ESTHER 9:20–22

If you want to find God in the book of Esther, you'll have to read between the lines. The plot reveals a hotheaded king, a beautiful, orphaned Jewish young woman, a murderous small-minded official and a wise older cousin. God is never mentioned by name throughout this book, yet he is behind the scenes, actively working to turn a nation's mourning into joy.

What a powerful lesson! We may only see an overbearing boss, a crippling grief or a spiteful enemy. To find God's prevailing goodness requires that we read between the lines of our lives. That happens when we worship. Worship shifts our focus off the action of our lives onto the director of it. Rather than giving in to the worries and fears clamoring for our attention, we focus on our center, our real life. In God's presence we come to trust his goodness even when we can't see his hand.

In the book of Esther we find God working effectively even without anyone's conscious knowledge of it. He is between the lines of your story too—between any plots against you, between any fears about your future, even between the glimpses of your understanding and your perceptions of his presence. Always active. Always loving. His ever-present, transcendent caring fills every space. Trusting in God's presence changes our sorrows into gladness and our mourning into joy.

Look between the lines of your life. God is there. ❖

PRAYER

God, tune my heart to how you are working ...

INDEXING YOUR SORROW

At this, Job got up and tore his robe and shaved his head. Then he fell to the ground in worship and said: "Naked I came from my mother's womb, and naked I will depart. The LORD gave and the LORD has taken away; may the name of the LORD be praised." In all this, Job did not sin by charging God with wrongdoing. JOB 1:20–22

Try this exercise ... Take five index cards. On the top of each one, write one of the five most important things in your life, including people. Now consider this ... A hurricane (or tornado, earthquake, fire or mudslide—whatever natural disaster you have where you live) hits your home. You lose all your possessions. If you had any material possessions written on any of your index cards, tear them up.

Your family is in a car accident. Only your spouse and you survive. If you have anyone else in your family written down on one of those cards, tear up those cards too.

The doctor calls you in, looking very grim. "I have your test results and they're not good." If your health was one of your top five, throw that card out too.

What do you have left?

This depressing scenario is a thinly veiled retelling of what happened to Job long, long ago. How did he respond to such overwhelming loss and sorrow? Unbelievably, by worshiping God. Job refused to give in to the grief and pain he undoubtedly felt, instead choosing to let God be God.

This is not to suggest in any way that if any of these things happens to you that you are not to feel angry, sad, hurt, confused or depressed. God understands; he gave you the capacity to feel all those things. But in the midst of your troubles or stressful circumstances, turn to God. Allow him to carry your sorrows. ❖

PRAYER

Lord, I offer you the burden of my sorrow ...

day116

LET'S BE REAL

"I loathe my very life; therefore I will give free rein to my complaint and speak out in the bitterness of my soul. I say to God: Do not declare me guilty, but tell me what charges you have against me. Does it please you to oppress me, to spurn the work of your hands, while you smile on the plans of the wicked? Do you have eyes of flesh? Do you see as a mortal sees?" JOB 10:1–4

Wait a minute—is this the same person who refused to become bitter and turn away from God? He's changed his tune pretty radically, hasn't he? Yes, it is, and no, he hasn't. How's that?

When we read Job's words in 1:21–22, we saw his faithfulness and refusal to sin against God in spite of his unspeakable loss. Now, here he is, freely and openly acknowledging his bitterness and disillusionment with his Maker. Yes, Job is expressing his hurt and frustration now—after all, it's been quite some time since his troubles began and still no relief in sight—but don't miss the key aspect of his lament. He's still pouring his heart out to God, not turning away from him.

It's all right to be honest with God about your feelings, even the dark, negative ones you don't want anyone else to see. Do you think God will be surprised or disappointed? He already knows how you feel, and he isn't the least bit threatened by it. What parent doesn't want their child to come to them when the child is hurt?

You can be completely honest with God. If not with him, then who? He is the one you can count on to never leave you or abandon you, even when you are in your darkest times.

Be honest with him now. Tell him what's on your heart. ✤

PRAYER

Father, this is how I really feel . . .

day117

WHAT DO YOU KNOW?

I know that my redeemer lives, and that in the end he will stand on the earth. And after my skin has been destroyed, yet in my flesh I will see God; I myself will see him with my own eyes—I, and not another. How my heart yearns within me! JOB 19:25–27

Eat health food—jog daily—die anyway. You may remember that bumper sticker from some years back. The point it makes, rather darkly, is that our bodies are not designed to last forever in their current condition. No matter how well—or how poorly—we maintain them, they will wear out sooner or later. The question confronts us all: What then?

The Bible makes it clear: "People are destined to die once, and after that to face judgment" (Hebrews 9:27). Does that thought fill you with anticipation or dread? For the man or woman who does not know the atoning power of Christ's death on the cross, the thought of appearing before a holy God is terrifying.

But for those who have accepted the payment Jesus made on their behalf, there need be no fear or apprehension. We stand justified—made right—before God. Paul puts it this way in Romans 8:1: "There is now no condemnation for those who are in Christ Jesus." No condemnation—only love, forgiveness, mercy and grace.

The Old Testament addresses life after death in only a handful of places, and nowhere more compellingly than here in Job 19:25–27. In spite of his great suffering, or perhaps because of it, Job lifts his eyes and his thoughts to eternity and finds great comfort there. As we grow older, and the prospect of our mortality becomes more real with each birthday, let us set our gaze in that same place, find that same comfort and assurance. He's our Redeemer too. ✣

PRAYER

Lord Jesus, I know that you are . . .

day118

April 28 appears as:

IT'S A MYSTERY TO ME

God understands the way to it and he alone knows where it dwells, for he views the ends of the earth and sees everything under the heavens ... He said to the human race, "The fear of the Lord—that is wisdom, and to shun evil is understanding." JOB 28:23–24,28

When we suffer—and everyone does, at some level, from the princess in the palace who is subject to her position to the Jobs of the world who suffer unbelievable pain and hardship—it is almost reflexive that our first reaction is to raise our voice to heaven and ask, "Why me? Did I do something to deserve this? Is God angry with me, punishing me for some sin I've committed? Is God involved in my pain at all?"

"Why" is a question we are free to ask God. Job certainly did, over and over, but God is not bound to answer. He sometimes gives us glimpses into his purposes in our pain but not always. Often the reason for our suffering remains a mystery to us. In those times it is good to focus on what we do know—the character of our God.

Job acknowledged that, even though he could not penetrate the veil of mystery surrounding God's plan for his trials, wisdom begins with, resides in and ends with God. We may not understand God's ways, but God knows what he is doing, and he understands what we are going through. Our lives, including the dark parts, the parts where all we see is blackness all around us and every sensation is pain, are part of the great tapestry of God's unfolding plan of redemption. We may not know what his purpose is, but knowing that he has a purpose is what keeps us from giving in to despair.

Trust him with your unanswered questions. ❖

PRAYER

Father, help me to trust you even when I do not understand you ...

UNJUST DESSERTS

The Almighty is beyond our reach and exalted in power; in his justice and great righteousness, he does not oppress. Therefore, people revere him, for does he not have regard for all the wise in heart?   JOB 37:23–24

If you were a dictator with unchallengeable power over your domain, how would you deal with rebels, with those who chafed at being under your rule?

God rules his creation by his unlimited, sovereign power. He can control this planet and its inhabitants any way he sees fit, and the Bible makes it clear that the inhabitants are all guilty of revolting against him (see Romans 3). How would you expect a just God to deal with such rebels?

He could deal with us harshly, pouring out the penalties our sins deserve. Who could blame him or say he was being unfair? And yet he chooses to be merciful, extending to us forgiveness, compassion and grace. His very nature is to be merciful and compassionate: When God passed before Moses, he said, "The LORD, the LORD, the compassionate and gracious God, slow to anger, abounding in love and faithfulness, maintaining love to thousands, and forgiving wickedness, rebellion and sin. Yet he does not leave the guilty unpunished; he punishes the children and their children for the sin of the parents to the third and fourth generation" (Exodus 34:6–7).

Do you need a reason to worship God? Thank him for his power, his majesty and his sovereignty. Thank him that he poured out the wrath our sins deserve on his Son, Jesus. And thank him that he gives out mercy instead of justice. ✤

PRAYER

Father, I thank you for …

HIS HOPE LEAVES ME SPEECHLESS

Then Job answered the LORD: "I am unworthy—how can I reply to you? I put my hand over my mouth. I spoke once, but I have no answer—twice, but I will say no more."

JOB 40:3–5

Job, as most everyone knows, was the man who found himself at the center of a cosmic drama. Satan charged that Job's "faith" was a thin veneer, built solely on the blessings of God. "Stretch out your hand and strike everything he has, and he will surely curse you to your face," the evil one snarled at God (Job 1:11).

God allowed Satan to assault his servant with a malevolence rarely seen on earth. Job was devastated in every conceivable way. He poured out his shattered soul to God, even as he doggedly hung on to his flagging faith.

For most of the book, God says nothing as Job cries out in his confusion. And heaven remains silent, even when Job's advisers offer their multiple theories on suffering.

At last, God speaks. He thunders forth with an avalanche of questions that leave Job dumbfounded. God's point? That he is in control. Humbled, Job realizes that sometimes the most appropriate form of worship is simply to be silent before the Almighty.

Today as you go about your routine, make it your goal to talk less and listen more. Focus on the fact that the God of the universe has a personal interest in you and wants a relationship with *you*. Then allow his love to leave you speechless. ✤

PRAYER

Lord God, do whatever it takes to leave me speechless . . .

day121

WIDE AWAKE AND WIDE ALIVE!

In peace I will lie down and sleep, for you alone, LORD, make me dwell in safety.

PSALM 4:8

Doesn't that sound wonderful—to lie down in peace and sleep restfully, completely? For many of us, though, a peaceful night's sleep is more a dream than a reality. In fact, one of the most widely prescribed classes of pharmaceuticals is sleep aids. Insomnia is at epidemic levels as people pack their days with busyness and then stay up half the night worrying about what they didn't get done, what they didn't do well and what they must accomplish tomorrow.

Sweet sleep can come, however, when we sense—bone deep—that God is in control. That means spending our days not in a heightened state of activity, but in a heightened state of being attuned toward God. Sleeping well at night, we might say, is a by-product of being more than wide awake—rather, being wide alive—during the day.

What does it mean to be "wide alive"? You may be familiar with the quote by Irenaeus that says, "The glory of God is a man fully alive." But do you know how the whole quote runs? "The glory of God is a man fully alive, and the life of man consists in beholding God." Wide-aliveness, then, is living with a God-focus.

Living with a God-focus does not imply inactivity. We may, in fact, have a rather full schedule. But at the same time, we're always testing the wind to see where the Spirit is blowing. We're living in purest freedom, because we know his eagle eye is searching the skies to guard us from the circling raptors.

Everything is going to be all right. Keep your focus and worship on the One who will keep you safe, and rest assured. ❖

PRAYER

In the day, Lord, and in the night, let me sense your presence ...

STARRY, STARRY NIGHT

When I consider your heavens, the work of your fingers, the moon and the stars, which you have set in place, what is mankind that you are mindful of them, human beings that you care for them? PSALM 8:3–4

David gazed into the night sky and was overwhelmed by the greatness of God displayed before him. He was not the first.

When Abraham stepped outside his tent one night and was awed to learn that his descendants would be vast in number like the stars (see Genesis 15:5–6), how many stars did he actually see? About two thousand, if he had average eyesight. Yet astronomers tell us that our galaxy alone contains hundreds of billions of stars—and the Milky Way is just one of hundreds of millions of galaxies.

Another stargazer, Job, identified God as the one responsible for placing the constellation Orion in the sky (see Job 9:9). Little did he dream, however, that Betelgeuse—the star forming the right shoulder of Orion—is so big that if you were to put it where our sun is, it would engulf the planets Mercury, Venus, Earth and Mars.

And then Solomon, in his guise as the teacher, assured us that there is nothing new under the sun (see Ecclesiastes 1:9). But he could not know that if we were to drive a car 60 miles per hour for 24 hours a day, it would take us more than three years to reach the sun.

Astronomy keeps expanding our vision of what the universe is and how great the Creator of the universe is. As you observe a sunrise or a sunset or gaze into the starry night, join Abraham, Job, Solomon and David in worshiping the awesome splendor of our God. ✤

PRAYER

Lord, your creation reminds me . . .

FURTHER UP AND FURTHER IN

Those who know your name trust in you, for you, LORD, have never forsaken those who seek you.   PSALM 9:10

In *The Last Battle*, the concluding volume in his Narnia series, C. S. Lewis describes his characters' first encounter with the "new Narnia"—a picture of heaven. The call that goes out to them again and again from Aslan is "Further up and further in!" The children find themselves in a land that is not only more wonderful—and somehow more right—than any other they have ever known but also infinite in its variety and scope. Racing effortlessly across the landscape, they find they can explore deeper into the new Narnia without ever exhausting its possibilities.

As is heaven, so is her Master. In eternity, we will discover more and ever more of the excellences of our Lord. But why wait until then? In this life—in the "old Narnia," so to speak—we can be busy with a discovery process that has knowing God as its objective. Those who think they have arrived at a destination and can stop moving, who have lost their sense of wonder and adventure, who think they know all there is to know of God—those are the ones who know least of all.

Unbelievers are not the only ones who can be spiritual seekers. As today's passage informs us, we who know God's name and trust in him search for him too. We seek to understand better his nature and his will for us.

Renew your resolve—like David—to know and worship the name of the One you trust and to continue searching for him "further up and further in." ♣

PRAYER

Inexhaustible God, show me a new vista of your holiness . . .

SING HIS PRAISES

I will sing the LORD's praise, for he has been good to me.   PSALM 13:6

The Bible tells us that King David loved music. David first came to royal notice as a man "who knows how to play the lyre" and so was called in to soothe King Saul (1 Samuel 16:18). Ironically, a song sung by women ("Saul has slain his thousands, and David his tens of thousands" [1 Samuel 18:7]), almost doomed David by arousing the jealousy of Saul. David later sang a funeral song for Saul and Jonathan—and another for Abner (see 2 Samuel 1:17–27; 3:33–34). Even in the short psalm above, while David cried out to God from the depths of his despair, he still found reason to sing to the Lord "for he has been good to me."

David refused to squelch his musical inclinations when he was king. As the ark was brought to Jerusalem, "David and all Israel were celebrating with all their might before the LORD, with castanets, harps, lyres, timbrels, sistrums and cymbals" (2 Samuel 6:5). And later David gave orders for the establishment of a Levite choir and appointed men "to make a joyful sound with musical instruments: lyres, harps and cymbals" (1 Chronicles 15:16). David was responsible for a large portion of Israel's hymnbook, the Psalms.

Music has a power to inspire emotion and to express it. What song can you sing today to God? Like David, "sing the LORD's praise" because he has been so good to you. ✤

> **PRAYER**

When I think of what you've done, O God, I can't help singing . . .

HIDING IN THE SHADOWS

Keep me as the apple of your eye; hide me in the shadow of your wings from the wicked who are out to destroy me, from my mortal enemies who surround me.   Psalm 17:8–9

While being persecuted by King Saul, David wrote this psalm as a plea for justice in the face of false accusations. David offered up this entreaty with the confidence of someone who knows that his prayer will be answered and that he is praying to the One who can protect him and hide him.

Christians throughout the centuries have encountered harsh opposition. Yet they have prevailed because of their confidence in the One who has overcome the world and who has promised a secure future to all who trust in him. We see this unassailable faith in a portion of the second-century *Letter to Diognetus.*

[The Christians] pass their days on earth, but they are citizens of heaven. They obey the prescribed laws and at the same time surpass the laws by their lives. They love all men and are persecuted by all. They are poor yet make many rich. They are dishonored and yet in their very dishonor are glorified. They are evilly spoken of and yet are justified. They are insulted and repay the insult with honor. They do good yet are punished as evildoers. When punished, they rejoice as if quickened into life. They are assailed by the Jews as foreigners and are persecuted by the Greeks, yet those who hate them are unable to assign any reason for their hatred.

Christ said, "In this world you will have trouble. But take heart! I have overcome the world" (John 16:33). Are you ready to trust that God will be with you in the midst of persecution? ❖

PRAYER

Lord, spread your sheltering wings over me . . .

TAKE A BREAK

He makes me lie down in green pastures, he leads me beside quiet waters.   PSALM 23:2

Daytime and nighttime, wakefulness and sleep, workday and weekend, motion and stillness, labor and rest—life has a rhythm, impressed into earthly existence when the clay was still wet. God himself rested after laboring six days to make the world, and he declared a Sabbath for his people.

Still, sometimes we dismiss the restful side of the equation. "If I just skip lunch, go to bed later and work through the weekend, I can get so much more done." It doesn't work, or at least not for long. The always-on lifestyle is likely to be switched off prematurely.

Nothing is wrong with hard work, of course. After all, Jesus pushed himself pretty hard to meet the needs of the people who came to him. But he also made time to get away for prayer and escape the press of the crowds.

Rest times can become special times of worship. In our leisure we can turn our focus on God with a concentration not possible amid the distractions of our busy days. Worship, in fact, can become an aid in our resting.

Times are coming when we will walk through the valley of the shadow of death. Let us settle gratefully in the meadows while we have them.

As you go through your daily routines, find ways to schedule mini-Sabbath times with the Lord. Take a break to sit and reflect upon God. Let this time renew and refresh you. ✤

PRAYER

Shepherd of my soul, I come to you for rest . . .

IN GOD'S WAITING ROOM

Wait for the LORD; be strong and take heart and wait for the LORD. PSALM 27:14

In a world that honors assertive action, it is something of a shock to realize how many of the great heroes of faith spent some of the best years of their lives in what must have seemed unendurable waiting. Sarah's hope ran out as she waited decades to conceive her promised son. Moses had to stay in the wilderness for 40 years before he could move his crowd toward the promised land.

David was no stranger to God's waiting room. He had been anointed king at age 16, but didn't take the throne until he was 30. In the intervening 14 years, David was chased through the wilderness by the jealous Saul. Waiting on God's timing was not easy.

What is God thinking when he lets his servants languish in inactivity? And what are we supposed to do in our stymied times?

Let's be honest. Waiting is never easy. It is not only the soldiers on the brink of war who need a reminder to be brave; those who wait need courage like iron forged in their souls. They also need to know that waiting is a something and not a nothing, for it is a time when God is working on *who we are* more than on *what we do.* And it is a time when we can learn to worship God for who he is rather than for immediate benefits we receive when we act.

For what are you waiting today? While you are in God's waiting room, thank him now for the molding and refining he is doing in you. ✣

PRAYER

Lord, have mercy on me as I wait for . . .

HEAVEN ON EARTH

Blessed is the one whose transgressions are forgiven, whose sins are covered.

PSALM 32:1

Knowing in the summer of AD 430 that his illness must surely prove fatal, what did the great churchman and theologian Augustine request as a singular favor? He asked for the words of Psalm 32 to be painted on the walls of his bedroom where he could view them for as long as his eyes held sight.

Somehow, it seems appropriate that the writer who gave us an autobiography titled *Confessions* wanted to meditate until the end upon a psalm about confessing sin.

Augustine was 75 at the time of his death. Unless something goes seriously askew in our spirits, we never outgrow our awe of God's forgiveness. As David did in this passage from Psalms, we experience indescribable joy that comes when God has put our sin out of sight. Divine grace for sinners is a perennial theme of worship.

Refusing to confess sin produces a kind of pent-up internal pressure that builds and builds, resulting in every manner of misery for body and spirit. Psalm 32 speaks of this effect as well as the joy of forgiveness. But, oh, the relief of confession as the pressure flows out with the penitent's tears! Praise then becomes as natural and as necessary as breathing. Confession renews worship.

Eternal life begins at salvation. Surely the joy of the forgiven sinner, then, is the natural reaction when what was dead comes to life. And it's a joy we can know in a new way every time we repent.

What do you need to confess before God? Tell him what's burdening your heart, then rejoice in a life lived in complete honesty and forgiveness. ✤

PRAYER

Lord, here's what's on my heart . . .

day129

RECOVERING YOUR "OH!"

They feast on the abundance of your house; you give them drink from your river of delights.
PSALM 36:8

What a contrast David paints in this passage between those who are blinded to their sin and those who truly see the knee-bending, heart-stopping "oh!" of God's unfailing love and righteousness. The truth is that we can lose our "oh!" when we allow our relationship with God to become dry and predictable. We no longer experience the "river of delights" because we are slogging through the mud of daily existence.

Not only God himself but also his gifts are greater than we can express. Seen aright, so-called "ordinary," everyday events and scenes are, in fact, rivers of delight gushing from heaven.

In *Pilgrim at Tinker Creek*, Annie Dillard writes of trying to see the world like someone who has been blind all her life but can suddenly see. "I saw the backyard cedar where the mourning doves roost charged and transfigured, each cell buzzing with flame. I stood on the grass with the lights in it, grass that was wholly fire, utterly focused and utterly dreamed."

The good news is that you can regain your "oh!" if you find yourself bogged down in a spiritual rut. Begin by looking for the "oh!" in your familiar routine—as you drive to work, as you carpool and run errands and as you walk through all the events of your day. ❖

PRAYER

Lord, oh the wonders of your creation . . .

UNCONDITIONAL SURRENDER

Commit your way to the LORD; trust in him and he will do this.   PSALM 37:5

Like many artists, Judson W. Van DeVenter was good, but not good enough to survive solely on what he earned from selling his paintings. So to pay his bills, Judson taught school. His income as a schoolteacher allowed him to pursue his art, a passion that filled his heart with great joy. *But will I ever be able to fully devote myself to what I love?* Judson wondered.

When a series of evangelistic services was held in the church he attended, the artistically inclined teacher volunteered to help. As individuals came forward to acknowledge their need for Christ, Judson would counsel them at the front of the church. His gifts in working with people were obvious to his friends; it was clear to them he had the gift of an evangelist.

For five years Judson's focus vacillated between his abilities as an artist and an increasingly apparent giftedness for ministry. Finally, he understood the truth of the psalm writer who committed everything he did to the Lord. When he finally surrendered to God's call on his life, Judson wrote lyrics to a hymn of consecration we continue to sing more than a century after it was first published.

"I Surrender All" begins, "All to Jesus I surrender; / All to Him I freely give." But those aren't just the lyricist's words. They can be your words as well. Examine your gifts and abilities in light of Judson Van DeVenter's song. What do you need to surrender to God, to freely give him today? ✤

PRAYER

Lord, I freely give you . . .

MOONLIT MELODIES

By day the LORD *directs his love, at night his song is with me — a prayer to the God of my life.*
PSALM 42:8

In 1943, a young Wheaton College graduate named Billy Graham became pastor of Western Springs Baptist Church near Chicago. Billy and his new wife, Ruth, had barely settled into life in the pastorate when a well-known radio evangelist named Torrey Johnson challenged the young pastor with an opportunity.

Torrey wondered if — in addition to being a local church pastor — Billy would like to broaden the influence of his new ministry by becoming the regular speaker on a Sunday evening radio broadcast called *Songs in the Night*. Graham nervously accepted and proceeded to seek out a popular staff announcer at WMBI radio at Moody Bible Institute in Chicago to work with him. So began the ministry partnership of George Beverly Shea and Billy Graham.

Each week Billy would relate Biblical promises to current events and Shea would sing hymns that celebrated God's faithfulness. *Songs in the Night* provided a vocabulary of praise with which listeners could close out the Lord's Day in preparation for the challenges of a new week. Although Billy only hosted the program for a brief time, its popularity continued. Nearly 70 years later, the program continues to guide late-night reflections to those who drift off to sleep mindful of the Lord's goodness.

Millennia before radio, the psalm writer recognized the importance of reflection and singing at the end of the day. For him it was a natural expression of faith and a means to focus on God as he laid his head down to sleep. Can you relate to that? ✤

PRAYER

Lord Jesus, this is my song to you in the night . . .

THE SOUNDS OF SILENCE

He says, "Be still, and know that I am God; I will be exalted among the nations, I will be exalted in the earth."   PSALM 46:10

Is it possible to hear anything in silence? The popular folk/rock singing duo of Simon and Garfunkel thought so. In a classic folk ballad of the sixties, they challenged a superficial generation with the haunting lyrics of "The Sounds of Silence." With prophetic voices they invoked a nation to listen to what life had to say in the empty sounds of a shallow world.

When the Sovereign Lord insists that we "be still," he wants us to press the mute button on life. He knows—and we can discover—that only in a quiet place can we truly hear his inaudible whispers. In God's book, the sounds of silence have nothing to do with analyzing meaningless cultural chatter. Rather they have to do with the space we alone can create, a carved-out space distanced from the hue and cry of a too-fast and too-noisy world where we can contemplate the awesomeness of God without distraction.

Sound inviting? You bet it does. But where will you most likely create such a cocoon of quiet? In a hot bath? On a long walk through the woods? In an easy chair by the fire after everyone is in bed (and the TV is finally off)? Wherever it is for you, it's a space worth finding. ✤

PRAYER

Lord, I will be still before you today . . .

A CHILDLIKE HEART

My sacrifice, O God, is a broken spirit; a broken and contrite heart you, God, will not despise.   PSALM 51:17

Jesus is the One who taught us that we have a lot to learn from children. In their wide-eyed curiosity, innocent trust and unvarnished honesty, we are given a picture of what God hopes we will be like when we grow up. Children also mirror the tenderness of heart our heavenly Father desires when we have been justly disciplined.

Broken and repentant hearts beat within the breasts of pint-sized humans. If you have ever been in the presence of a child who has been caught in an act of disobedience, you probably have witnessed an example of the psalm writer's "broken and contrite heart." Caught with the proverbial hand in the cookie jar, or clasping the forbidden bat that just sent the ball careening through the neighbor's window, the child stands before the parent with the sounds of uncontrollable sobbing, interrupted only by a whispered admission of guilt and declaration of sorrow. With tears rolling down a crestfallen face, arms are extended in search of a forgiving embrace that will soon follow.

These evidences of remorse are good indicators that the perpetrator is genuinely sorry. No reasonable parent would withhold love, acceptance and forgiveness from one so broken. And neither does a loving God distance himself from "older children" who own up to their sin and humbly cast themselves on his mercy.

Doesn't the image of a child's acknowledgment of wrongdoing bring this passage to life? You can feel the emotion. You can sense the humility. You are that child. So don't delay. The authentic worship you desire to offer a holy and approachable God is fueled by childlike repentance.

Come before your Father right now, and tell him what is breaking your heart. ✤

PRAYER

Loving God, this breaks my heart . . .

FIGHTING OUR FEARS

When I am afraid, I put my trust in you. In God, whose word I praise — in God I trust and am not afraid. What can mere mortals do to me? PSALM 56:3–4

David's fears were very real. He had enemy troops pressing in on him and slanderers hounding him constantly. Today, the causes of our fears often are not as imminent or life-threatening, though there is a named phobia for nearly every part of life. *Arachnophobia*: fear of spiders. *Ophidiophobia*: fear of snakes. *Musophobia*: fear of mice and rats. The list goes on and on.

Evidently young Timothy, Paul's young disciple, was prone to getting sweaty palms. No wonder Paul encouraged his protégé with these words in 2 Timothy 1:7: "For the Spirit God gave us does not make us timid, but gives us power, love and self-discipline."

But being told that the fear factor doesn't have divine origin doesn't mean that anxiety evaporates. A relationship with God doesn't vaccinate a person from being afraid. David certainly was in tune with God, and yet fear tracked him down on occasion. But when confronted with fear, David knew where to turn. He dropped to his knees and called on the name of the Lord. Acknowledging his need of God in a time of anxiety was an expression of worship. And it can be for you too.

What grips your heart or leaves you feeling faint? Don't pretend you're unflappable; admit your fear in the presence of God. Such an admission is a type of praise the Lord loves to hear. He longs to wrap his arms around you and comfort you. He wants to be your protector.

Kneel before him now. Tell him the fears that loom ahead of you this day. Allow him to hold and protect you. ✤

PRAYER

Father, I fear …

day135

A SONG FOR ALL NATIONS

I will praise you, Lord, among the nations; I will sing of you among the peoples.

PSALM 57:9

In 1984, an ordained minister named Ray Barnett heard a BBC news report from Africa that disturbed him greatly. It described the plight of thousands of children in Uganda who were victims of the oppressive reign of dictator Idi Amin. Barnett, himself an orphan, was moved to help the suffering children robbed of parents and hope.

While traveling through Africa, he picked up a young African boy who was hitchhiking between two cities. During the journey the boy sang simple melodies that inspired Barnett. He began to picture an entire choir of African children filled with the love of Jesus and touring the world. Not only would the choir provide a practical means to raise money to feed, clothe and educate countless orphans, but the children also would bear witness to God's faithfulness.

Within a short period of time the African Children's Choir was formed. Since then, more than six thousand children from Uganda, Kenya, Rwanda, Nigeria and Ghana have brought the words of David's psalm to life: "I will praise you, Lord, among the nations; I will sing of you among the peoples." Grateful children have traveled the world giving public praise to God as they sing from the depths of grateful hearts.

The response of the nations has been humbling. Not only are needy children being cared for, but, amazingly, the praise of children provides a practical means to enrich their lives. But you would expect that, right? Haven't you discovered the same?

When you grieve a loved one's death or you struggle with health issues, you choose between sulking and singing. A life of praise pays big dividends. Sing his praises throughout the day! ❖

PRAYER

Lord, here is my offering of praise . . .

AN OPEN DOOR

Hear my cry, O God; listen to my prayer. From the ends of the earth I call to you, I call as my heart grows faint; lead me to the rock that is higher than I. PSALM 61:1–2

It's a scenario many a young mom can relate to. Opening the door and flipping on the light in his room, she sees her preschool-age son clutching his favorite blanket and sitting upright on his bed. With knees pulled up to his quivering chin, his thumb is inserted into his mouth and his eyes are puddled with fresh tears.

Sitting down on the edge of the bed, the mother pulls her little guy close and embraces him. "Don't be frightened, sweetheart," she says calmly. "Daddy and I are just down the hall. Everything is okay." As the comforted child lies back down on his bed and watches his mother walk toward the hallway, he calls out, "Leave my door open and the light on in the hallway, okay, Mommy? It helps me know you're not far away."

David experienced fear. In this psalm, most likely written after he had narrowly escaped Saul's effort to kill him, David cried for God's security and assurance of his presence.

Most likely you can relate to being overwhelmed by the thought of isolation. And, yet, just as that mother eased the panic in her child's heart by providing the reality check that she was indeed present in the house, so God wants to do the same in your anxious heart. He hears your frantic cries for help. Just ask David. Revealing his love and promises in the Bible is God's way of leaving the door open. ❖

PRAYER

Lord God, I cry out to you today because . . .

IN THE ARMS OF GOD

Praise be to the Lord, to God our Savior, who daily bears our burdens.   PSALM 68:19

On a hot July day in 1967, Joni Eareckson Tada's life changed forever. This athletic teenager dove into a shallow lake, breaking her neck and fracturing her spinal cord. She instantly became a quadriplegic.

The next two years of hospitalization and therapy were excruciating, but Joni persevered. Eventually, she learned to paint with a brush between her teeth. Through a friend's witness, she also discovered a personal relationship with Jesus and a faith that enabled her to rely on God's everlasting arms. Remarkably, Joni has not just experienced what it's like to be carried by the Lord through the predictable dark days; she has experienced it *every* day.

The psalm writer here claims that our daily burdens are no match for the power of God. In fact, he is a God who saves (see verse 20). In light of his power, our daily struggles are easy for him to carry.

Isn't that good news? What has happened today that has left you feeling weak? You don't have to be confined to a wheelchair to attest to the reality of God's care. When life cuts you off at the knees, God is there reaching out to help you stand up. Use those moments of weakness to celebrate and rejoice in his strong arms! ❖

PRAYER

O God, give me the faith to lean on you ...

RUN FOR YOUR LIFE!

Since my youth, God, you have taught me, and to this day I declare your marvelous deeds. Even when I am old and gray, do not forsake me, my God, till I declare your power to the next generation, your mighty acts to all who are to come.   PSALM 71:17–18

On January 21, 1925, the lives of countless children in Nome, Alaska, were at stake. An epidemic of diphtheria had broken out in the gold rush city, and they didn't have enough antitoxin to treat the sick. Dr. Curtis Welch telegraphed Fairbanks, Anchorage, Seward and Juneau, asking for help. The only serum in the entire Alaska Territory was found in Anchorage. The challenge was how to get the needed medicine to Nome in the shortest time possible.

With the Bering Sea frozen and no railroad or roads extending to Nome's remote location, dog teams were the only solution. A doctor in Anchorage placed the serum on an overnight train to Nenana. From there, 20 dog sled mushers took turns transporting the precious medicine over 674 miles. The relay ended in Nome on February 2. In only 127½ hours the lifesaving serum arrived in time to save the next generation of Nome's future leaders.

According to the psalm writer, passing the faith from one generation to the next is like passing the baton in a relay race or completing a serum run. What God had taught him is precious truth. He felt an obligation to pass it on to those who came after him.

What a challenge for every believer. What we have received we can't just keep to ourselves. Our children need to know. So do our neighbor's children. Think about it. That's the way it is with worship. We catch a glimpse of God and then we help others focus on what we've seen. ✣

> **PRAYER**

Lord, I want to pass on this truth . . .

day139

THE SINGLE-MINDED LIFE

Whom have I in heaven but you? And earth has nothing I desire besides you. My flesh and my heart may fail, but God is the strength of my heart and my portion forever.

PSALM 73:25–26

In the 2002 movie *The Emperor's Club*, Kevin Klein plays William Hundert, a history teacher at St. Benedict's Academy for Boys. He sees his role as a teacher as far more than just a job. It is a calling. Early in the film, Mr. Hundert makes the statement that a person's character determines his future. If every person's life is a book, the end of the story is known long before the last chapter has been written. In other words, what men and women value will filter their choices and brand their reputations.

That certainly is true of the psalm writer. Worshiping God was his sole focus. As a result it was his soul's focus too. His desire was to grow a relationship with the living God, and that focused goal remained throughout his long life. To use Mr. Hundert's analogy, those who knew the writer as a young man would not have been surprised to see him die with praises on his lips. His passion defined his life, so at the end of his life, that one overriding passion sustained him.

What a beautiful picture. Doesn't that motivate you to spend more time with the Lord? As you read your Bible and listen to praise music, why not let the complicated issues that divide your loyalties fall by the wayside? Look to the Lord as the one worthy object of your affection—and attention. ✤

PRAYER

Jesus, I want to start today by lingering in your presence...

REMEMBER THE GOOD OLD DAYS?

Your ways, God, are holy. What god is as great as our God? You are the God who performs miracles; you display your power among the peoples. With your mighty arm you redeemed your people, the descendants of Jacob and Joseph.   PSALM 77:13–15

The night seems endless. The trouble is overwhelming. You have never been so sad or worried. You toss, you turn, but sleep eludes you. You cry out to God in anguish, but hear no answer. Is God even listening?

The author of Psalm 77 experienced such a night. With hands lifted up to heaven, he pleaded for mercy. He yearned for God's help but heard no answer. Had the Lord slammed the door on compassion? Had the Lord rejected him forever?

Then he remembered the "the former days, the years of long ago; I remembered my songs in the night" (Psalm 77:5–6). He recalled the wonderful deeds of long ago, when the Lord parted the Red Sea and led his people out of Egypt. Soon his thoughts were filled with the miracles of the Lord.

At times, you may think your situation is hopeless, that the problems you face have no solutions or end in sight. At those times, remember, your God is "the God who performs miracles" (Psalm 77:14). Trapped between the Egyptians and the Red Sea, the nation of Israel faced certain destruction. But in one creative and unexpected act, the God of miracles parted the waters and redeemed his people. Surely he can be trusted to redeem your life as well.

Do you remember the good old days of your life? Starting with the miracle of your birth, think of the many wonders God has performed. Reflect on the blessings of health, family and home. Recall his faithfulness in your darkest hours. Trust in the goodness of those days to see you through your current situation. ✤

PRAYER

Mighty God, I praise you for . . .

A PLACE CALLED HOME

How lovely is your dwelling place, LORD Almighty! My soul yearns, even faints, for the courts of the LORD; my heart and my flesh cry out for the living God. PSALM 84:1–2

A soldier sits in a camp chair in a country far away and dreams of home. Home, where family and friends gather. Home, with comfortable chairs and familiar food. Home, where he is safe and secure.

In much the same way, the psalm writer longed for home—to get away from the bustle and cares of this world and to be in the presence of his Lord. For the writer, being home with God meant physically being in God's dwelling place, his holy temple. Just as the solider yearned for the physical presence of his home, the psalmist wrote with urgency about "the courts of the LORD" (Psalm 84:2).

The truth is, God's dwelling place can be felt anywhere. He is at home in the quiet sanctuary of a stained-glass cathedral, or as we sit in our cozy chair in the corner of a room, or walk outdoors under the leafy canopy of the woods. Wherever we go, God's presence is with us.

It is equally true that entering a church building provides a special place where we can, if only for a few hours, escape the busyness of our lives and find the solitude to meditate and pray. There we can refresh and refocus through the music, the prayers and the lessons taught.

No wonder the psalm writer faints with longing to enter God's presence. It is the very place where he feels most at home. With his whole being he shouts praises to the living God. "Blessed are those who dwell in your house; they are ever praising you" (Psalm 84:4). ✤

PRAYER

Almighty God, I long to be in your dwelling place ...

LOVE ME FOREVER

I will sing of the LORD's great love forever; with my mouth I will make your faithfulness known through all generations. I will declare that your love stands firm forever, that you have established your faithfulness in heaven itself. PSALM 89:1–2

The young father gazes upon the face of his newborn son and his heart fills with love. He delights in the child's first word, his first step, his first day of school. He celebrates his son's victories and comforts him in defeat. As his son grows in stature, so grows the love in the father's heart. "I will love you forever," he sings.

Then one day a police officer knocks at his door. His son is in trouble with the law. The problems are devastating, the father's sorrow overwhelming. Though family and friends abandon him, the father stands by his son. His love never fails.

As the father loves his son, how much more does our heavenly Father love his children? David, the man after God's own heart, sinned grievously. Yet God forgave him and promised, "I will maintain my love to him forever, and my covenant with him will never fail" (Psalm 89:28). God's love for David reached beyond the grave, for he also promised to love and bless David's heirs. "His line will continue forever and his throne endure before me like the sun" (Psalm 89:36).

No matter how great our trouble, God's love is greater still. The Scriptures are filled with testimonies to his unfathomable love for us. No ocean is deeper, no mountain higher than the love our Father has for us. Human relationships may falter, but God's love never fails. Heaven and earth will pass away, but God's love will remain. His love endures forever.

Join David in song, praising God for his unfailing love. ✤

PRAYER

With my lips I will glorify you, Lord...

UNDER HIS WINGS

He will cover you with his feathers, and under his wings you will find refuge; his faithfulness will be your shield and rampart. PSALM 91:4

The bird huddles over its young as the storm rages on. The tree sways crazily in the wind, but the nest holds fast. Sheets of rain pour over the bird, but the nestlings stay warm and dry. Lightning flashes, thunder booms, but the little birds are not afraid. They are safe and secure under the wings of their protector.

Likewise, the psalm writer recognized that when life's storms hit, there is only one place to turn: "He is my refuge and my fortress, my God, in whom I trust" (Psalm 91:2). In the midst of turmoil and danger, he was confident that God would shelter him "with his feathers" and protect him with "his faithfulness."

Do the storms of life threaten to overpower you? Is your life swaying crazily out of control? Is trouble pouring down on your head? Find shelter and rest in the shadow of the Lord Almighty. Take refuge under the wings of the Most High. Draw close to him and he will shield you from the storm.

In medieval times a soldier wore pounds of metal to deflect the arrows of the enemy, but we wear the promises of God. The Lord promises, "I will rescue him; I will protect him, for he acknowledges my name. He will call on me, and I will answer him ... With long life I will satisfy him and show him my salvation" (Psalm 91:14–16). Put on the armor of God's promises and stand against the enemy.

What protection do you need today? Look to God's promises and claim them as your own. In each battle, worship the One who helps you overcome. ♣

PRAYER

Lord, please shield me from ...

SHOUT IT OUT!

Shout for joy to the LORD, all the earth. Worship the LORD with gladness; come before him with joyful songs.   PSALM 100:1–2

It's called March Madness. Every year the top 64 teams in college basketball battle it out for the right to be called champions. As the field is whittled down from 64 to 16 to 8 to the "Final Four," we are witnesses to runaway victories, last-second thrillers, overtime nail-biters and incredible come-from-behind wins. At last the final two teams compete—and only one emerges as the victor. As those last seconds tick off, the fans stream onto the court with shouts and cheers, celebrating the victory.

Do the mighty deeds of the Lord generate that kind of enthusiasm in you? Do you shout with joy when you recall the wondrous things he has done? Or do you calmly go about your business, barely giving him a thought?

Maybe you think you don't have much to shout about. What about the Lord's return? For he is coming soon. Tell everyone you meet about his amazing wonders. Proclaim the good news of his salvation every day. Make his name known to the nations, so they can bow down and worship him. "He comes, he comes to judge the earth. He will judge the world in righteousness and the peoples in his faithfulness" (Psalm 96:13).

Now is the time to sing a new song to the Lord. Leave behind the songs of bitterness and complaint. Bring out songs of glory and praise. Worship him for all of his splendor. Praise him for the wonders of his creation. Exalt his holy name to all the earth. Laugh and shout and sing, for he is coming soon. Rejoice! ♣

PRAYER

Lord, you are my King. I praise you for . . .

THE PERFECT DAD

As a father has compassion on his children, so the LORD has compassion on those who fear him.
PSALM 103:13

David knew. He had felt the pain and experienced the shame of going so far astray that he feared he would never get home again. He knew what it was like to admit all this to God the Father.

But he also knew what manner of father his God was. The bellowing kind, determined to make an example of David for his other children? The sullen kind, who is so hurt, so wounded in pride that one of his sons could do wrong that he withdraws his love into angry silence? The preoccupied "boys will be boys" style that barely acknowledges, much less punishes, a wayward child?

The great Lord of heaven—the One who had the power to bellow, the reason to withdraw and a universe occupying his attention—was none of those. He was a perfect father, tender and compassionate. Why? "For he knows how we are formed, he remembers that we are dust" (Psalm 103:14). David ran like the shepherd boy he was to such a father.

David ran to worship as well, calling to himself and other children of God to "Praise the LORD, my soul ... Praise the LORD, my soul ... Praise the LORD, my soul" (Psalm 103:1–2; 104:1). Do we, children of God just as dear to the Father as the great King David, respond in praise?

As you go through the day, remember your tender, compassionate Father who stands ready to tend you, spare you, rescue you and care for you. Tell yourself to praise him! ✤

PRAYER

Father, I am grateful for your compassion because ...

TELL ME A STORY

Give thanks to the LORD, for he is good; his love endures forever. Let the one who is wise heed these things and ponder the loving deeds of the LORD.   PSALM 107:1,43

Telling and retelling stories is one of the most basic ways people communicate. From the birth of language, humans have remembered and shared.

For the people of God, storytelling is more than a mere accounting; the telling of stories is the telling of *the* story, of God's relationship with his people. From the song recounting God's deliverance of his people out of Egypt (see Exodus 15:1–18) through Peter's and Paul's testimonies about the reality of Jesus' life and purpose, we can see "the loving deeds of the LORD."

The anonymous writers of some of the psalms richly recount God's deeds through the centuries. What moves them to move others, to remember together? It is the pull of worship. "Give praise to the LORD, proclaim his name" (Psalm 105:1). "Give thanks to the LORD, for he is good; his love endures forever" (Psalm 106:1; 107:1).

But listen. Centuries later, having come down through the years to us, is a quiet recounting. A young woman speaks of the Lord's faithful love, how he has blessed her, how he has blessed his people, how he has revealed his goodness. Yet the quiet recounting, found in Luke 1:46–55, is known by a grand name: the Magnificat.

"My soul glorifies the Lord and my spirit rejoices in God my Savior," Mary begins. "For the Mighty One has done great things for me—holy is his name" (Luke 1:46–47,49).

Reflect on your history with God. Like Mary, rejoice with a song of praise in your heart. ❖

PRAYER

O Lord, as I think of my years with you, I think of . . .

IT'S NO WONDER!

My heart, O God, is steadfast; I will sing and make music with all my soul.

PSALM 108:1

The hooded figures begin to chant, *"Te Deum laudamus: te Dominum confitemur. Te aeternum Patrem omnis terra veneratur ... Sanctus, Sanctus, Sanctus, Dominus Deus Sabaoth. Pleni sunt coeli et terra maiestatis gloriae tuae ..."*

This composition known as the *Te Deum* is ancient, dating before the fifth century. It was heard in monasteries and convents every Sunday at the end of Matins, except during penitential seasons. The Latin hymn can sound depressing — hardly in the same league as the psalm writer's claim to sing God's praises. "Awake, harp and lyre! I will awaken the dawn. I will praise you, LORD, among the nations" (Psalm 108:2–3).

But do not let the Latin fool you. "We praise thee, O God," begins the traditional English translation of *Te Deum laudamus*. "We acknowledge thee to be the Lord. All the earth doth worship thee, the Father everlasting ... Holy, holy, holy, Lord God of Sabaoth; Heaven and earth are full of the majesty of thy glory ..." The words continue: *laudabilis, laudat, laudamus*: praise, praise, praise.

Still today, in convents, monasteries, churches and gatherings in homes and in private meditations, God is praised from the original Latin to a contemporary translation of the *Te Deum*: "You are God: we praise you; You are the Lord: we acclaim you; You are the eternal Father: all creation worships you ... Holy, holy, holy Lord, God of power and might, heaven and earth are full of your glory."

Join the chorus in your own morning worship. "My heart, O God, is steadfast; I will sing and make music with all my soul." ❧

PRAYER

God, I will add my words of praise and say ...

HE TURNS HIS EAR AND LISTENS

I love the LORD, for he heard my voice; he heard my cry for mercy. Because he turned his ear to me, I will call on him as long as I live.   PSALM 116:1–2

"She is growing up, but she is still a little girl," the adults say of the teenager, giving new meaning to the phrase "talking down to children." Will they listen? They can barely hear her soft voice. Besides, she's only a child, they say.

Then God turns his ear and listens.

A young man has been running, stumbling, falling for years. Raised in a tough neighborhood, his so-called friends will not listen, and enemies are deaf to his cries for mercy. Down in the dumps, down on his luck, down for the count.

Then God turns his ear and listens.

She is old now, and she is sick. The medical staff bustles in and out, dispensing pleasantries with her pills. Stopping neither to wait for the answer to their near-rhetorical questions nor to hear the questions she has. Besides, it's not a good idea to get "too close" to the dying.

Then God turns his ear and listens.

Any of the three people above could have written Psalm 116, because God bends down and listens. For the small, the beaten down, the weak, he hears and answers their prayers. Saving from death (see verses 3,8), comforting the afflicted (see verse 10), lifting those who stumble (see verse 8) and comforting the dying (see verse 15). He listens to you, giving you reason to pray as long as you have breath.

Pray now, pray always to the One who turns his ear, listens and answers. In thankfulness to answered prayer, worship him. ❖

PRAYER

O God, I especially appreciate your listening ear because . . .

day149

THE WORD ON THE WORD

I seek you with all my heart; do not let me stray from your commands. I have hidden your word in my heart that I might not sin against you. Praise be to you, LORD; teach me your decrees.   PSALM 119:10–12

The facts that stack up about Psalm 119 are fascinating, the stuff that wins party games—or at least impresses others.

- Longest psalm (176 verses)
- Longest chapter of the Bible
- An acrostic poem of 22 stanzas (one for each letter of the Hebrew alphabet), with the eight verses of each stanza starting with the Hebrew letter of that section
- Near the exact midpoint of many Bibles
- A remarkable array of words that refer to the Scriptures—laws, decrees, commandments, principles, word, statutes, commands

These facts may be fascinating, but following the Word of God is not a trivial pursuit. The psalmist was inspired to write Scripture about the Scriptures. He was making a commitment to God himself and urging others to do the same. Wandering from these commands? You are wandering from God. Hiding his Word in your heart? You are hiding God himself there.

The contemporary Christian singer Sara Groves has written the song "The Word" to express the vital connection we can have with God through the Scriptures. Just as the psalm writer realizes the only way not to sin is to hide the Word in his heart, Groves recognizes that she has tried to help herself while her Bible sits upon the shelf. She delights that the Word was, and the Word is and the Word will be.

We can praise our God by learning his principles. We can live a life that sings God's Word. Commit today to hide and study God's Word. Then celebrate that Word! ✤

PRAYER

Thank you, O Lord, for your Word ...

SHINING IN THE DARKNESS

Your word is a lamp for my feet, a light on my path. PSALM 119:105

Food. Water. Clothing. Shelter. Warmth. These are some of the basic needs for life, the minimum we need to survive. But without another key resource, we are immobilized, too frightened to move. We need light

This writer yearned for the light that is God's Word. Not a cozy fixture in the corner, with God as interior designer. No, he needed—we need—a lamp for our feet, a light for our path. The psalmist had suffered. He had had sorrows—as do we—and his experience told him that only God's illumination would help (see verses 107,153).

The path, God's path, was dangerous. The wicked had set traps (see verse 110), and they were close to him (see verse 150). Even without these foes, darkness could bring stumbling (see verse 165) or cause someone to stubbornly wander off the path (see verse 176).

The strength of the light intensifies through time, as Peter testifies to the early church: "We also have the prophetic message as something completely reliable, and you will do well to pay attention to it, as to a light shining in a dark place, until the day dawns and the morning star rises in your hearts" (2 Peter 1:19).

The psalm writer had the law. The first Christians had the law, the histories, the prophecies and the Psalms. We have all this plus the illumination of the New Testament books. But we also have the greatest light, the Word become human. "The light shines in the darkness, and the darkness has not overcome it" (John 1:5).

Walk the path of prayer and praise, guided by the light of God's Word and his Son. Ask that God would illumine your way throughout the day. Thank him for his guidance. ✤

PRAYER

O God, I need your light today . . .

MY HELP LINE

I lift up my eyes to the mountains — where does my help come from?   PSALM 121:1

Flying into Portland or Seattle can be exhilarating. The views of the Pacific Northwest are tremendous — when it's not raining! Most beautiful are the conical volcanic mountains, with names like Adams, Hood, Rainier and Baker, as they raise their massive, snowcapped peaks to the sky, sentinels of the coastlands.

One other sentinel used to stand in line just as stately. But in May 1980, in a spectacular and deadly display, Mount St. Helens blew its top. Thirteen hundred feet shorter than it used to be, Mount St. Helens today looks like a cone of sand that a child heaped up on the beach. In this world of flux, even our grandest mountains are subject to change.

That's a lesson worth recalling when we're inclined to trust too much in any sort of worldly security. Great fortunes have been lost. Faithful allies have betrayed others. Carefully guarded health has faltered. Knowledge, credentials, position — all have proved inadequate over time. Even the earth itself, we're warned, will one day be swallowed up in fire (see 2 Peter 3:7).

Where, then, can we find real security during our times of need? It's a mark of wisdom to be able to say from the heart, "My help comes from the LORD, the Maker of heaven and earth" (Psalm 121:2).

Worship is righteous if its object is the only One who is worthy. Worshiping God is a mark, too, of knowing what to value, whom to adore. Let us cling in all ways to this caring Father and be safe.

As you go through your day, use the times when you find yourself needing help as a reason to turn to God. ✤

PRAYER

O Lord, today I need your help ...

THE CONTRACTOR AND THE CREW

Unless the LORD builds the house, the builders labor in vain. Unless the LORD watches over the city, the guards stand watch in vain.   PSALM 127:1

Solomon, author of this psalm, knew a little something about building houses. After all, he had built one for the Lord.

No doubt Solomon heard many times from his father, King David, about the time David had desired to build the house of the Lord. The prophet Nathan spoke too soon in assuring David that the Lord was with him in his plan to build a temple. God sent the prophet back to the king with a message that essentially conveyed, "No, you will not build a house (temple) for me, but I will build a house (dynasty) for you" (see 2 Samuel 7:1–16). David had to be content with knowing his son would fulfill his construction dreams.

We can labor all we want at projects that seem desirable or meritorious to us, but if they are not in accordance with God's will, our efforts are in vain. Want to be a leader of the masses? It's no good if God gave you an artist's soul. Dream of a ministry that would be dangerous and all-consuming? Not while you're raising those children God gave you.

We may get huffy sometimes at what seems to be God's stubborn insistence on his own way. But we're better off in every sense if we'll fall in with his will instead of trying to get him to fall in with ours. We'll be more productive and more satisfied if we accept God as the general contractor and take our place—and an honored place it is—as a carpenter on his crew.

What are your plans for today? What about the next year, or even five years? Ask God to be the builder of your plans both for today and the future. Thank him today for making you part of his crew. ♣

PRAYER

Lord, I surrender my plans to you ...

day153

LIVING IN HARMONY

How good and pleasant it is when God's people live together in unity! PSALM 133:1

In this brief psalm, David writes of the joy of harmonious relationships, of how precious and pleasant a commodity is unity. It is wonderful when brothers and sisters live together in harmony, but unfortunately, it is also rare.

Consider the disciples Jesus chose—the very ones you would suppose would live and work together well. Jesus chose men with differing personality types and professions. And as we read through the Gospels, we see that they did not always live together in unity. And they were the nucleus of the church!

It seems that not much has changed. The church we know today is an inspiring, infuriating, faithful, hypocritical, cooperative, divisive, generous, selfish, foolish and wise conglomeration of half-reformed sinners. The bride of Christ—can't live with her, can't live without her. That's us.

Yet Christ loves his bride, and so we must learn to do the same. We must work at getting along, facing squarely our own flaws and bearing with those of others. For unity is worth the effort, however much it may at times not seem so. A cord of three strands is not easily broken. Fellow rejoicers double the joy of the rejoicer; fellow weepers halve the sorrow of the weeper. As the psalmist wrote, how wonderful when brothers and sisters live in unity!

Unity also makes our worship more powerful. Is there someone at work, at church, in your neighborhood or even within your household with whom you are experiencing discord? Look today for ways to live together in unity. ✤

PRAYER

Lord, let unity begin with me ...

FULL EXPOSURE

You have searched me, LORD, and you know me. You know when I sit and when I rise; you perceive my thoughts from afar.   PSALM 139:1–2

Clothing has both functional and symbolic value. But beyond that, we put on clothes because of something deep in the human psyche—something disturbing and unnamed related to the shame of exposure.

This was birthed in us through our first parents. Only when Adam and Eve became guilty of sin did God provide them with clothes. A connection was forged at that time between sin (a matter of the spirit) and shame over bodily nakedness, because human beings are spiritual-physical creatures—soul bodies.

The psalm writer realized this truth. He could not find a place where God was not present. He could not think or say anything that God did not already know.

We may pile on all the clothes we like, but we're still totally exposed before God. This is a disturbing thought when we're feeling guilty. We may even want to run away from God like the prophet Jonah did, but we'll find God is still pursuing us no matter how far away we try to run from him.

When we come to believe—really believe—that God has forgiven us through Christ, however, we can begin to grow comfortable with our exposure before him. We can stop messing around with fig leaves. When God calls, "Where are you?" we can answer immediately, "Here I am, Lord!" ✤

PRAYER

Here I am, Lord ...

day155

CRUEL WORLD, KIND LORD

*Answer me quickly, L*ORD*; my spirit fails. Do not hide your face from me or I will be like those who go down to the pit.* PSALM 143:7

It's clear, even from a quick glance at this psalm, that David was losing hope and was caught in a downward spiral of fear and depression.

David was not alone. Many people suffer from clinical depression. The causes of depression are diverse, and thankfully in some cases medical treatments can blow away the dark clouds of suffering. In addition to medication, however, it is entirely appropriate for those who are struggling to seek the Lord for relief from their painful mental state and its causes, as David did when penned in by his enemies.

We all would like a life that goes from victory to victory, attended by peace, comfort and laughter. But God sees fit to take us through times when we must do what we thought we were incapable of doing, when we lose what we thought we could never live without or when we are forced to give up dreams we thought constituted our reason for being. All of this naturally registers in our emotions.

We must recognize that our suffering is due directly or indirectly to human sin and not to any cruelty on the part of God. Even more important, we must remember that God works with us in our struggles, deepening and maturing our faith. And what of the worship from those who are in the midst of, or have come through, a testing period? It reaches depths of meaning and authenticity that one can achieve in no other way.

When depression hits, do as David did. Turn toward the Lord, not away from him. Reach out to him in prayer and worship, trusting that he will draw near to you. ✤

PRAYER

Lord, help me turn to you through the dark clouds . . .

THE GREAT BURDEN BEARER

The LORD upholds all who fall and lifts up all who are bowed down.   PSALM 145:14

Everyone has burdens—whether they are financial, health related or circumstantial. Sometimes, though, as David expresses in this psalm, our burdens seem more than we can bear. We struggle and stumble under the weight of these worries and concerns, wondering how we can go on.

But sometimes, like David, we remember that the answer to our problem is found in the great burden-bearer, our God.

In his book *Dark Symbols, Obscure Signs*, Riggins R. Earle Jr. recounts the story of a former slave, Charlie, who encounters his old master 30 years after escaping. Here is their conversation:

The former master asked, "Charlie, do you remember me lacerating your back?"

Charlie said, "Yes, mars."

"Have you forgiven me?"

"Yes, I have forgiven you."

The white man next asked, "How can you forgive me, Charlie?"

Charlie replied, "I love you as though you never hit me a lick, for the God I serve is a God of love, and I can't go to his kingdom with hate in my heart."

The old master held out his hand and said, "I am sorry for what I did."

Shaking hands, Charlie answered, "That's all right, mars. I done left the past behind me."

God not only lifted from Charlie the burden of unjust servitude, he more importantly lifted from Charlie a burden of bitterness. That bitterness, while justifiable, would have become debilitating. Consider what load or burden you can leave with the Lord today. ✤

> **PRAYER**

Father God, I offer you this burden . . .

HE GIVES WISDOM

For the LORD *gives wisdom; from his mouth come knowledge and understanding. He holds success in store for the upright, he is a shield to those whose walk is blameless.*

PROVERBS 2:6–7

Decisions. Choices. Alternatives. Judgments. We face them every day. How we long for wisdom to make good decisions when the way ahead is not clear! How we wish to know what is the right action to take in a difficult situation. How we yearn for good judgment when facing choices that appear gray. How badly we need a treasure of good sense to deal with the complexities of life.

"The LORD gives wisdom"—that's a promise we can claim. Nothing we will face is beyond the understanding of the One who created us. God's wisdom is available to us—but we need to ask for it. We need to pour out our lack of understanding, our confusion, our fears and our doubts before him. Then we need to be patient and wait for his sure response.

A short song, which appeared in the *Sarum Primer of 1514*, illustrates beautifully the need to commit daily to seeking and trusting God's wisdom and guidance in all aspects of life. The songwriter penned these words: "God be in my head, and in my understanding; / God be in mine eyes, and in my looking; / God be in my mouth, and in my speaking; / God be in my heart, and in my thinking; / God be at mine end, and at my departing."

Spend a few moments now committing your head, eyes, mouth, heart and life to God as an act of worship. Ask him to guide you throughout the day. ✤

PRAYER

Oh, how much I need your wisdom, Lord …

WHAT ARE YOU WITHHOLDING?

Honor the LORD with your wealth, with the firstfruits of all your crops; then your barns will be filled to overflowing, and your vats will brim over with new wine.

PROVERBS 3:9–10

As the opening chords to the familiar hymn "Take My Life and Let It Be" floated through the sanctuary, the pastor instructed his congregation, "The words are so simple. And here they are set to Mozart's very singable Nottingham tune. Easy to go on musical autopilot. But don't you dare. Don't sing anything you don't mean. Especially verse four."

The first verse started strong. "Take my life and let it be consecrated, Lord, to Thee." *And while you're at it, take my moments and my days.* Verses two and three continued the glad offerings: hands, feet, voice — *Hey, God, I'm singing my heart out for you!* — *and lips. What's so hard about this?* Then came the fourth verse.

"Take my silver and my gold. Not a mite would I withhold." Suddenly the singing was more tentative. *Not a mite? What's a mite, anyway? God doesn't really mean* ... But those singing knew he did mean it, and they must too. They gained strength through verses five and six, urging God, "Take my intellect, my will, my heart, my love."

In 1878, four years after writing the hymn, Frances R. Havergal wrote to a friend, "'Take my silver and my gold' now means shipping off all my ornaments to the Church Missionary House, including a jewel cabinet that is really fit for a countess ... Nearly fifty articles are being packed up. I don't think I ever packed a box with such pleasure."

"Honor the LORD with your wealth," the proverb instructs. Don't withhold a mite. Consider today how you can honor God with your possessions. ✤

PRAYER

God, today I will offer ...

THE FIRST GLEAM OF DAWN

The path of the righteous is like the morning sun, shining ever brighter till the full light of day.   PROVERBS 4:18

A thin line of deep rose appears in the charcoal sky. Slowly the light increases, and the color changes from rose to orange to gold. Stars fade and disappear. The sky lightens slowly to palest blue, then deepens to the azure of a robin's egg. The first rays of sun streak across the landscape, heralding a new day. Darkness has fled.

The writer of Proverbs pictures the way of the righteous as the first gleam of dawn. God's wisdom brings light to our journey and enables us to walk in "straight paths" (Proverbs 4:11). God's understanding illuminates the dark places in our lives, bringing healing and new life, transforming our confusion into his wisdom. God is light and "in him there is no darkness at all" (1 John 1:5). As we listen to his Word and obey his instructions, his light transforms us. His wisdom comes to us like the gleam of dawn.

We can offer up the prayer asking for illumination first spoken in the sixth century, "Hear us, O never-failing light, Lord our God, the fountain of light, the light of your angels, principalities, powers, and of all intelligent beings, who created the light of your saints. May our souls be lamps of yours, kindled and illuminated by you. May they shine and burn with the truth and never go out in darkness and ashes. May the gloom of sins be cleared away and the light of perpetual faith abide within us."

In what areas of your life do you need God's light today? Perhaps it is an attitude that needs changing, a relationship that requires forgiveness or a neglected sin that should be brought to light and confessed. Ask God to shine his truth on you throughout the day. ✤

PRAYER

Lord, illuminate my darkness with your wisdom ...

THE MOST BELOVED FAMILY MEMBER

Say to wisdom, "You are my sister," and to insight, "You are my relative."

PROVERBS 7:4

"What exactly do you think you're doing?"

He tried to shake it off. Tried to bluff his way through. Muttered, "Don't worry. I know what I'm doing." It never worked. Not with her.

"Oh, you know, do you? Like you knew all the times before? Sit down. And listen this time. I am your sister, you know." She then firmly—but with a sister's concern in her voice and the touch of her hand on his—told him that the friendships he was pursuing were getting him further and further into trouble.

Wisdom is just such a relative. Often personified as a woman in the Bible, wisdom deserves love as does a caring sister. Wisdom is the one to lead your head and your heart back to God.

If a believer's life is to be a holy act of worship every day, wisdom must have her say. And she must be heeded. The stakes are too high, the consequences too deep, the ramifications too wide. Solomon knew well from his own experience the importance of heeding wise warnings.

How do you welcome God's insight? Is it like a sister's or brother's care for you, or a nagging voice that you tune out? God longs for his people—if they are truly to be called his people—to have minds and hearts shaped by and conformed to his ways.

Today, let wisdom lead you back to the altar, with a holy heart and a mind to praise him. ✤

PRAYER

Father God, I thank you for the messengers of wisdom you have sent to me …

BUILDING A WORSHIP FOUNDATION

The fear of the LORD is the beginning of wisdom, and knowledge of the Holy One is understanding. PROVERBS 9:10

At the height of her popularity, it was reported, newspaper columnist Ann Landers received an average of ten thousand letters each month. And nearly all of them were from people burdened with problems. When asked if there was any one predominate issue in the letters she received, her answer was "fear."

None of us likes to be afraid. Fear generates a fight or flight response deep within us. We avoid it whenever we can, and we fight against it when we can't escape it. So what, then, does it mean to fear the Lord? For those who do not know God, dread and terror of punishment are appropriate responses. But for those who truly seek knowledge of the Holy One, fear is transformed by love into reverence and awe.

Fear of the Lord is necessary to worship. It inspires within us reverence for God's majesty and power and illuminates the great gulf between our humanness and God's divinity. Fear induces us to obedience and service; it emboldens us to avoid sin and live a holy life.

The wonderful paradox of fear of the Lord is that this fear ultimately frees you from all other fears. Fear of God gives you wisdom to know he is in charge, not you. It brings knowledge of his holiness — and nothing can challenge that power. Fear of God brings understanding to all other fears and gladdens your heart. ✤

PRAYER

Lord, I fear you because . . .

NO STRAIN, NO GAIN

Truly the righteous attain life, but whoever pursues evil finds death.   PROVERBS 11:19

"Let us strain toward righteousness." So wrote Lactantius, one of Constantine's advisers, a teacher of rhetoric and, later, a defender of the Christian faith.

Some heed the cloister call to pursue righteousness. A few live a hermit's life. Perhaps for them, the pursuit of righteousness and godliness is easier in a setting of solitude. Then again, perhaps not. But for most of us living busy lives, consistent, godly living is a "challenge," to say the least. A strain.

Lactantius knew the challenge, the effort needed, the straining that leads to life. He also saw what evil leads to. In the early fourth century, at the request of the emperor Diocletian, he moved from his native Africa to the city of Nicomedia, in what today is Turkey, to be a professor of rhetoric.

He became a Christian in Nicomedia; ironically, the edicts and persecutions of this same Diocletian made it impossible for him to continue as a public teacher. He had some private students, but he was often in poverty. He wrote and wrote—an impassioned Christian apologist.

Do you hear the call of righteousness? Today, let it lead you to God's presence and the privilege of worshiping him. Strain toward righteousness, toward godly living. Prayerfully consider what that might look like in your life as you heed the call. ❖

PRAYER

O Lord, help me strain toward righteousness . . .

day163

THE PLEASURE OF DISCIPLINE

Whoever loves discipline loves knowledge, but whoever hates correction is stupid.

PROVERBS 12:1

Discipline is one of those poor, unfortunate words, largely misunderstood and usually said with a frown and a sigh. It is continually cast in a negative light—doing hard, unpleasant things, or worse, having some measure of pain inflicted on you by another.

But what is it, really? Discipline is training that frees you to be the best you can be. Good parents discipline their children not to hurt but to help, to protect them from ultimate harm, to point them to a better way.

Champion athletes discipline themselves to achieve success. They spend hours perfecting subtle techniques—twisting this body part or that, dipping or spinning just so. Why do they put themselves through such a rigorous and exacting regimen? Are they masochists? No. They subject themselves to all this because they know discipline brings freedom and reward. To be prepared, to know you are ready for whatever comes, is a wonderful thing. That is why the proverb writer exhorts us to love discipline.

Worshiping God is no different. It takes discipline to get our selfish souls to acknowledge God, and it takes further discipline to learn to honor him rightly. It means reading, studying, observing. It means diligence, discomfort and reordering priorities. It means loving the process, accepting correction.

What place does discipline have in your life? ♣

PRAYER

Lord, I want to honor you rightly . . .

SECURITY THROUGH FEAR

Whoever fears the LORD has a secure fortress, and for their children it will be a refuge.
PROVERBS 14:26

People fear so many things in this troubled world. Even when we're not wrestling with big worries like financial ruin or terrorism, we're haunted by lesser but still potent demons—fear of aging, being alone or fitting in.

The result of all these anxious thoughts is a pervading sense of insecurity. And so what do we typically do? We scramble about trying to guard against this contingency or ward off that possibility. And just about the time we think we've taken care of one worry, another problem appears on the horizon, setting off a whole new round of uncertainty. Is this any way to live?

Solomon's wise observation, "Whoever fears the LORD has a secure fortress," reminds us of a great truth: Real security is found in the Lord. He is the ultimate safe place, a cosmic version of those castles and round towers of Ireland with tiny doorways leading to small staircases that twist upward to fortified "safe rooms" high within. In times of trouble, women and children found refuge and security in these hideaways that were inaccessible to the biggest, most fierce invaders. No wonder the psalms refer to God as our rock and fortress (see Psalm 31:2–3), our shield and stronghold (see Psalm 18:2).

As you encounter stressful situations today, as anxious thoughts creep into your mind or as fears begin to mount, use those moments to turn to God and worship him. ✤

PRAYER

O my rock and my fortress, teach me to fear you . . .

day165

THE HEART OF THE MATTER

The LORD detests the sacrifice of the wicked, but the prayer of the upright pleases him.

PROVERBS 15:8

William Temple, Archbishop of Canterbury (1942–44), wrote, "Worship is the submission of all our nature to God. It is the quickening of conscience by His holiness, nourishment of mind with His truth, purifying of imagination by His beauty, opening of the heart to His love, and submission of will to His purpose."

Contrast this breathtaking understanding of true worship with views that worship is the attempt to please God by engaging in certain prescribed religious rituals.

The problem with this kind of thinking is that it turns God into some kind of religious hall monitor who roams up and down the aisles of the church to see who is participating. He becomes the worship cop who wants to make sure we toe the line. At issue is our compliance—our bodies in the right places going through the right motions, our lips saying all the right things.

But in truth, God wants our hearts. All the religious songs, prayers and litanies in the world don't mean a thing if our hearts aren't right.

If you want to delight God, start with your heart. Allow your worship to flow from a heart that is centered on who God is and who you are in him. ❖

PRAYER

Lord, purify my heart …

day166

WHOSE AGENDA IS IT ANYWAY?

Commit to the LORD whatever you do, and he will establish your plans.

PROVERBS 16:3

William Barclay said that work done for love always has a glory. But how many people work for love ... or as Paul urged, for the glory of God (see 1 Corinthians 10:31)? Listen to the conversations around you. You'll hear phrases like "my job," "my goals" and "my happiness." The fact is, most people view their lives as their own. Even more astonishing, human nature subconsciously thinks, "What matters most in the world is me, and how things affect me."

Then Christ enters the picture, messing up everything. To hear the Bible tell it, life revolves around him, not us. He did not come, as the bumper sticker says, to be our copilot. Nor is his job description to give us divine assistance in accomplishing all our self-centered plans and dreams. No, he came to invite us to have a meaningful part in fulfilling *his* agenda.

That's the idea behind today's often misunderstood verse. Read it again. Think of it against the backdrop of Proverbs 3:5–6: "Trust in the LORD with all your heart and lean not on your own understanding; in all your ways submit to him, and he will make your paths straight."

Do you see? Real life is found in trusting God, not ordering him around as if he were a divine waiter. Satisfaction comes when we seek his will rather than devising our own plans. When we make him central, when we give him our hearts and sign off on his plans, then—at last!—we find direction, success and the significance our souls hunger for. ✤

PRAYER

Lord, show me the truth about my heart ...

THE GREAT COVER-UP

Whoever would foster love covers over an offense, but whoever repeats the matter separates close friends.   PROVERBS 17:9

Close your eyes for a moment and remember the first secret you shared that someone didn't keep. Was it a whisper in third grade of a love unrequited? An embarrassing revelation made to a parent that was then broadcast to the family? Perhaps as an adult you bared your soul to your best friend, only to have your kindred spirit involve others in your most intimate struggle.

Chances are you remember a moment of betrayal from your past; and even now, there's a tender spot in your heart that's strangely sore from the memory. Knowing this, it's even harder to admit that we ourselves have inflicted such pain on others.

That is why Solomon took time to remind us that "cover[ing] over an offense" is a way to show love. We should be willing to overlook the faults of another because, after all, isn't that what our God does for us? "He will not always accuse, nor will he harbor his anger forever ... for he knows how we are formed, he remembers that we are dust" (Psalm 103:9,14). How thankful we are that this all-powerful Savior, full of tenderness and compassion, doesn't do to us what we deserve!

Because we are made in his image, we are called to offer the ultimate form of worship: To be and act like him. "Dear friends, since God so loved us, we also ought to love one another" (1 John 4:11). As an act of worship today, look for opportunities where you can disregard another person's offense and preserve love. ✤

PRAYER

Lord, help me to revel in your mercy and love ...

WAIT BEFORE IT'S TOO LATE

Desire without knowledge is not good—how much more will hasty feet miss the way!

PROVERBS 19:2

Kings, nobles and peasants. History shows people from all walks of life have made errors in judgment that cost them something. In the Shakespearean tragedy *Romeo and Juliet*, the love-smitten Romeo plots his own suicide upon the announcement that his Juliet is dead. In his haste, he ingests poison before he receives the message that she is not gone, but merely drugged. We cringe at the couple's misfortune and scoff at Romeo's hastiness.

It's true, as the proverb writer points out, that acting without the right information will often lead us down a wrong path. Consider another example of fear and misjudgment when in the Old Testament King Saul refused in the heat of battle to wait for the priest Samuel. Instead, Saul hastily offered up a burnt offering to the Lord. Samuel arrived, rebuked him and named the price for Saul's lack of patience. "If you had [obeyed], he would have established your kingdom over Israel for all time. But now your kingdom will not endure; the LORD has sought out a man after his own heart" (1 Samuel 13:13–14).

The stories of impetuous mistakes seem endless. And if we mentally review our past, we find our own errors in judgment—unwritten, perhaps, yet not unseen by an all-knowing God. We excuse ourselves by saying that action must be better than inaction—at least we were doing something. How strange that the very action we avoid is the one God requests of us: wait.

Wait. Seek God today before each decision you need to make. Ask him for guidance and wisdom, and then wait. ✤

PRAYER

Father, give me a heart of wisdom and show me how to wait on you . . .

PURSUING THE RIGHT STUFF

Whoever pursues righteousness and love finds life, prosperity and honor.

PROVERBS 21:21

The old adage says that "cleanliness is next to godliness." No one would argue that maintaining good hygiene is a positive pursuit, but next to godliness? What exactly does that mean? According to the proverb writer, the pursuit of righteousness should be every believer's goal. But what does it take to be a godly man or woman?

The life of the apostle Paul is one illustration. A Pharisee with high credentials and a persecutor of Christians, his conversion was nothing short of a miracle. Paul's desire for godliness consumed him, as he counted all of his education, background and position as nothing. "May I never boast except in the cross of our Lord Jesus Christ" (Galatians 6:14). Paul died a martyr for his faith, but he is honored as the foremost writer of the New Testament, an apostle to the Gentiles and a godly example to every believer.

In today's world, our first priority is often making our life more comfortable. But God asks us to put first things first. His priorities are that we love him with all our being, walk in ways that glorify him and share his love with others in everything we do and say. That's what it means to "pursue" godliness.

For a moment, forget about what others think of you or today's to-do list. Ask yourself if your worship includes pursuing God's priorities. When you put first things first, God promises that "life, prosperity and honor" will follow. ❧

> **PRAYER**

Lord, help me live out a life that overflows with righteousness...

LOOKING UP, NOT SIDEWAYS

Do not let your heart envy sinners, but always be zealous for the fear of the LORD.

PROVERBS 23:17

Few of us like to admit to feelings of envy, yet few of us are immune to them. Your neighbor pulls into his driveway behind the wheel of a new car, and you feel a twinge of discontent with your older vehicle. A co-worker is given the job promotion you hoped for, or perhaps a former classmate achieves the sort of success you've dreamed of. Envy can cause us to look sideways at what others have and down upon our own circumstances, rather than up to God.

Neighbors, co-workers and classmates may not be the type of "sinners" the proverb writer is referring to, but the command not to envy others applies to us all. Envy inhibits our ability to worship. When we focus on what others have, we take our attention away from all that God has done for us. It's been said that a discontented person has the attitude that everything he does for God is too much, and everything God does for him is too little.

The antidote to discontentment is found in today's key verse. Rather than envying others, we are encouraged to develop a healthy reverence for the Lord. God alone has the power to satisfy us, and he has promised to supply everything we truly need.

Worship draws us closer to God so that we can begin to see our lives from his perspective. Whatever your present circumstances, today look for ways to draw every ounce of good from them. Remember that God has promised you both a future and a hope. Keep looking up! ✤

PRAYER

Lord, please root out any envy within me . . .

PAY BACK WITH LOVE

Do not gloat when your enemy falls; when they stumble, do not let your heart rejoice.

PROVERBS 24:17

A story is told about Abraham Lincoln in the closing days of the Civil War. A prominent senator took the floor of the Senate to demand that, as the enemy to the Union, the South should be destroyed. Lincoln listened quietly. When the politician finally ceased his diatribe, Lincoln was said to have calmly replied, "I destroy my enemies when I make them my friends."

We live in a world where vengeance is common. Conventional wisdom demands that if you are struck, you strike back. If someone hurts you, you hurt him. Payback time. Tit for tat. But Proverbs speaks of the unconventional wisdom that is peace-loving and full of mercy. This is the type of wisdom that restrains us from gloating over the misfortunes of our enemies but lets us share their sorrows instead.

Paul's first letter to the Corinthians speaks of a love that "does not delight in evil but rejoices with the truth" (13:6). It is only natural to feel a sense of satisfaction when those who have hurt us receive their "comeuppance." Yet today's key verse cautions us against such a response. Where do we learn to love in such an unnatural fashion?

When we attempt to avenge the wrongs committed against us, we assume the rightful role of God, who alone will judge the earth. Scripture does not state that we will always be treated fairly on this side of heaven, but we are promised that one day God himself will avenge all wrongs.

When you are tempted to shout "unfair" today, remember the One you worship. ✣

PRAYER

Lord, I need your unconventional love for my adversaries ...

day172

HANDLING THE HEAT

Like apples of gold in settings of silver is a ruling rightly given. Like an earring of gold or an ornament of fine gold is the rebuke of a wise judge to a listening ear.

PROVERBS 25:11–12

"Let me offer you a small piece of advice ..."

"You could have done a much better job on that project if only ..."

What is it about words like these that can cause us to bristle? Both unsolicited advice and unexpected criticism can create an almost instantaneous negative reaction if we're not careful. We might feel we are being personally attacked or that our work has been judged to be inadequate.

When we become defensive, however, we are creating barriers to communication that can greatly inhibit our growth. Granted, not every recommendation or critique we receive is well-intended. The key passage for today describes certain types of advice and criticism in lyrical terms—comparing them to choice fruit and precious metal. But the instruction is clear: We are to highly value timely advice and valid criticism.

Responding in a godly fashion to others' suggestions, opinions or critiques can be one of the most challenging disciplines to which we are called as followers of Christ. Thankfully, we have examples in Scripture—leaders such as Moses and David—whose responses to complaints or godly rebukes are models for us yet today.

We can't worship God if our own self-estimation is too high, and God in his wisdom sometimes sends critics not to hurt but to humble us. Today, as you may feel burned by the heat of criticism, remember to take your pain to your heavenly Father for comfort and counsel. ✤

PRAYER

Lord God, please show me a right response to this criticism I received ...

FORGETTING FINANCIAL FANTASIES

Be sure you know the condition of your flocks, give careful attention to your herds; for riches do not endure forever, and a crown is not secure for all generations.

PROVERBS 27:23–24

The legendary multimillionaire John D. Rockefeller, far and away the richest man of his generation, was once asked how much money it would take to satisfy him. His reported reply? "Just a little bit more."

At worst, his response reveals the innate greed of the human heart. At best, it highlights humankind's universal feelings or restlessness—or perhaps insecurity—about not having enough.

Clearly the great majority of us will never know firsthand what it's like to be as rich as Rockefeller. But we can grasp the crucial truth that, contrary to our frequent daydreams about money, riches and social standing, they do not provide true security. Fortunes can and do disappear. Power and influence are quick to evaporate.

In today's key verses, readers are encouraged to forget financial fantasies and to focus instead on the down-to-earth realities of discipline and hard work. The common shepherds in Bible times who lived off the land found a simple but good life. In an agrarian society, they had no choice but to depend on God for his provision. And he proved faithful again and again.

The lessons for us? Be diligent. Do your work well. Exercise simple faith. No matter what your job or financial condition, being a true worshiper demands that as you work, you look to God and rely on him. The issue isn't the amount of money in your bank account, but the amount of trust and gratitude in your heart. ❖

PRAYER

Lord, my security lies in . . .

AN UNSOLVED MYSTERY

Who has gone up to heaven and come down? Whose hands have gathered up the wind? Who has wrapped up the waters in a cloak? Who has established all the ends of the earth? What is his name, and what is the name of his son? Surely you know! Every word of God is flawless; he is a shield to those who take refuge in him.   PROVERBS 30:4–5

Author A. W. Tozer insisted that the single most important thing about any individual is what he or she believes about God.

Spiritually sensitive people know this is true. This probably explains why, via sermons, theology books, weekend seminars and worship music we strive so hard to understand God for ourselves and struggle so much to explain him to others. But do we do all this in the humble effort to love and serve him better? Or is our deeper motive to figure out God and make him less mysterious?

One thing is for sure: If we could answer every nagging question about God's character and accurately predict his every action, then in a real sense there would be no need for trust. We'd have God in a box.

Trying to remove all mystery about the Almighty is futile. You may as well try to catch a hurricane in a Mason jar. The great God of the Bible is inexplicable and unpredictable. The whole universe can't contain him. In fact, the only reason we know anything about him at all is because he has graciously revealed himself in creation; in Jesus, the living Word; and in the written Word.

It's not wrong to want to learn about God—in fact, that's what worship is all about. Christians should spend time reading and studying and trying to know him better. But keep in mind that finite creatures can never fully grasp an infinite Creator. It is this sense of mystery that keeps our hearts filled with wonder. ♣

PRAYER

O great triune God, I praise you because your greatness is . . .

THE WORK OF WORSHIP

Speak up for those who cannot speak for themselves, for the rights of all who are destitute. Speak up and judge fairly; defend the rights of the poor and needy.   PROVERBS 31:8–9

Have you ever heard someone say that his or her favorite verse in the Bible is "God helps those who help themselves"?

The only problem is that this so-called verse is not in the Bible! Its source? Ben Franklin's *Poor Richard's Almanac, 1757*. In fact, the Bible says almost the opposite—instructing God's people to help those who can't help themselves.

Take the passage above, for example. In the most literal sense, the first nine verses of Proverbs 31 are advice from a queen mother to her son, the king. She's urging him to rule his people with mercy and compassion, reminding him to use his exalted position and immense power to help the helpless. But the principles in these verses apply to all followers of Christ (see Psalm 82:3–4; 2 Corinthians 9:8–9). We're called to be imitators of God (see Ephesians 5:1) and, let's face it, who cares for the poor more than he does (see Proverbs 14:31)?

When's the last time you got your hands dirty helping out in a low-income neighborhood? Visited inmates in a nearby jail? Paid a visit to an orphanage or nursing home? Helped a mentally challenged person? Challenged unfair treatment of immigrants?

Worship is not just about singing or praying at a certain time and in a certain place. It is a mindset. It is a way of life. It is a heart that beats for God and looks constantly for ways to spread his righteous reputation in the world. When we live as worshipers, every place is holy, every moment is significant and every action is eternal. Find opportunities to do the work of worship today. ✤

PRAYER

Father, stir up a holy compassion in my heart today . . .

FINDING MEANING IN LIFE

A person can do nothing better than to eat and drink and find satisfaction in their own toil. This too, I see, is from the hand of God, for without him, who can eat or find enjoyment?   ECCLESIASTES 2:24–25

Perhaps no one in history has illustrated this longing for meaning in life more than Solomon. The second son of David and Bathsheba, the boy grew up to become Israel's third king. Blessed with unearthly wisdom (see 1 Kings 4:29–34), Solomon enjoyed a reign of remarkable prosperity and unprecedented peace. He oversaw the building of Jerusalem's greatest and most glorious temple. He dabbled in engineering and botany, and became famous worldwide. But over time, proving that even wise people can do stupid things, he accumulated a household of 700 wives and 300 mistresses—many of them foreigners and worshipers of other gods.

Not surprisingly, Solomon's heart for the one true God cooled. His restlessness multiplied. Eventually he found himself in the ultimate mid-life crisis—a time of frantic searching, boredom and despair.

His diary from this period, the ancient book of Ecclesiastes, reads like the bitter ramblings of a depressed old skeptic. "Utterly meaningless! Everything is meaningless" (Ecclesiastes 1:2). Yet at the end of this book, after experimenting with every pleasure and pursuit this world has to offer, he concluded, "Here is the conclusion of the matter: Fear God and keep his commandments, for this is the duty of all mankind" (Ecclesiastes 12:13).

What was Solomon's great discovery? That a life divorced from God is no life at all. That meaning and joy in life can only be found by relating rightly to the source of life. To fear God is to worship him. To worship him is to make him the top priority in your thoughts and actions. ❖

> **PRAYER**

Lord, my life has meaning because ...

ETERNAL LONGINGS

He has made everything beautiful in its time. He has also set eternity in the human heart; yet no one can fathom what God has done from beginning to end. ECCLESIASTES 3:11

The French author Simone Weil once remarked that beauty and affliction are the only two things that can pierce the human heart. King Solomon observed the same truth some ten centuries earlier in the book of Ecclesiastes.

Their point was that this world—and that includes your life—is full of mystery and transcendence. Haven't you experienced fleeting moments of such wonder and sweetness that you felt like laughing and weeping all at once? Haven't you faced head-scratching, heart-hurting hard times that crashed like a hurricane through your soul? Of course you have. This is the universal human experience.

Tragically, most people plod through their days unaware of the deep drama unfolding all around them. They miss the world's haunting beauty—or quickly dismiss it—even as they try frantically to remove every shred of discomfort and pain from their lives. Their hearts are then numb to everything in creation meant to point us to a better world still to come. Roses, sunsets, tax audits, even cancer—if we look with deeper eyes—can each direct our attention to the One who is writing, directing and playing the lead role in the divine drama we call life.

Don't ignore, deny or—worst of all—try to deaden the eternal longings deep in your heart. Savor the rich beauty all around you throughout the day. Search in and behind the affliction in your life. God is speaking. He is wooing you. The whole world is his sanctuary. Your entire life is meant to be a response to him. Let those who have ears to hear, hear. ✤

PRAYER

Father, open my eyes today . . .

GOD'S WARNING SIGNALS

Do not be quickly provoked in your spirit, for anger resides in the lap of fools.
ECCLESIASTES 7:9

Strong emotions—if we handle them wisely—can function like warning lights on the dashboards of our lives.

Do you find yourself extremely discouraged, even depressed? Feeling insignificant, even worthless? How about anxious or even panicky? If so, these "trouble lights"—continuing with our automotive analogy—would indicate you need to "pull over" and "look under the hood." Or better yet, pull into "God's garage" for a quick checkup or tune-up.

Strong emotions are a flashing signal that something isn't quite right. In such times, if we ignore them and continue barreling on down the highway of life— pedal to the metal—we risk causing real damage to ourselves and others. What these powerful feelings are indicating is that it is time to stop driving. Find a rest area. Put your life on blocks, even if only for a few minutes. With God's help, examine your heart.

Nowhere is this more important than in dealing with the common emotion of anger. By developing a holy habit of regular heart monitoring and maintenance, we avoid the common tendency for minor irritations to escalate into full-scale rage. As we learn the important discipline of self-control, we also learn to avoid saying or doing things in anger that we later regret.

This kind of reflective living makes us proactive instead of reactive people. It turns potentially negative emotional moments into occasions for prayer and insight. When you feel yourself starting to boil over today, stop. Talk to God, and ask him to redirect your emotions. ✤

PRAYER

Father, I am angry about . . .

DILIGENT GENEROSITY

Ship your grain across the sea; after many days you may receive a return.

ECCLESIASTES 11:1

Robert Gilmour LeTourneau, owner of more than 200 patents, made a fortune designing and selling massive earth-moving equipment. But he was perhaps most famous for his lavish charity. Later in life, he made it his goal to give away not 10 percent of his income—the standard Christian tithe—but 90 percent! His reasoning? "God has a bigger shovel than I have."

Such generosity is hard for us to fathom because we live in an uncertain world. But then we come to a verse like the above, which basically says, "Throw caution to the wind. Take financial risks. More specifically, be ready and willing to help others in trouble."

Why? Why would anyone live like that? First, because of the way relationships tend to work. Generous people typically find help when they are in trouble because the people they have helped are often the ones to return the favor. On other occasions the help comes from unexpected sources.

But even if we never "get it back" in this life, there is a second reason to be generous. Living by giving is a prime way we can worship God. Every time we write a check to help someone or an organization, or take a meal to someone in need, we have a prime opportunity to act out this prayer: "God, you have blessed me, so that I might bless others. You have been faithful to me in the past, and I know you will be in the future. I trust you to continue to provide. May this small gesture bring great honor to your name."

When you lend a helping hand to people, turn a trusting heart heavenward. Acknowledge God as the provider of every good thing in your life. ✤

PRAYER

Father, help me to give . . .

day180

A REFLECTION OF GOD'S ROMANTIC HEART

You are a garden locked up, my sister, my bride; you are a spring enclosed, a sealed fountain.
SONG OF SONGS 4:12

In his autobiography, *Just As I Am*, Billy Graham writes of his initial impressions of the woman he would one day marry. "If I had not been smitten with love at the first sight of Ruth Bell, I would certainly have been the exception. Many men at Wheaton thought she was stunning. Petite, vivacious, smart, talented, witty, stylish, amiable and unattached. What more could a fellow ask for?"

Billy forgot one adjective in describing his future wife: *determined*. She sensed God calling her to be a missionary in Tibet while Graham sensed the call to preach the gospel. Many months, discussions and what might be termed arguments later over the future of their relationship, Billy finally put this question to Ruth: "Do you believe that God brought us together?" When she answered yes, he replied, "In that case, God will lead me, and you'll do the following."

Perhaps not the classic proposal, but when the answer "yes" came several months later, their relationship became a lifelong union and commitment.

After more than half a century of marriage and successfully raising five children, this starry-eyed husband and wife still celebrated the Creator's gift of intimacy. They looked into the portrait of romantic love that King Solomon painted in Song of Songs as if it were a mirror. Not only did they see their love for each other in these verses, they also saw a reflection of God's love.

Can you see it too? Can you feel the arms of God embracing you with the gift of a new day? Listen as he calls you his beloved. Respond with a heart filled with love for the faithfulness and grace that he has lavished on you this day. ✤

PRAYER

Lord, knowing that you consider me beloved, I feel . . .

GOD'S ETERNAL FLAME

Place me like a seal over your heart, like a seal on your arm; for love is as strong as death, its jealousy unyielding as the grave. It burns like blazing fire, like a mighty flame. Many waters cannot quench love; rivers cannot sweep it away. If one were to give all the wealth of one's house for love, it would be utterly scorned. Song of Songs 8:6–7

Every year 4.5 million people visit Arlington National Cemetery. Most of them pay their respects at the grave of President John F. Kennedy, which is marked by an eternal flame that was incorporated into the grave marker at the request of JFK's widow. Even though the flame apparatus had been tested to withstand rain and wind, a month after the assassinated president was buried, a group of students from a Catholic school accidentally doused the flame by sprinkling holy water on it. An alert uniformed guard relit it with a portable lighter.

When the Kennedy grave was expanded in the late sixties, a more elaborate fuel line was constructed underground. As part of the plan, a constantly flashing electric spark near the tip of the nozzle relights the gas should the flame be extinguished accidentally. All the same, for purposes of maintenance around the gravesite, the flame is occasionally turned off manually. It's not eternal after all.

In contrast, the picture of love found in these verses from Song of Songs presents a real eternal flame. The love pictured here can't be quenched. Although the description is of human love, it also points to the giver of love. The intense flame of his affection can never be doused or turned off.

Human love can be strong. But the love of our heavenly Father is stronger. It can be seen in two nail-pierced hands. ✤

> **PRAYER**

Jesus, as I ponder your love, I am moved to say . . .

FROM THE PRAYER CLOSET TO THE STREET

*Learn to do right; seek justice. Defend the oppressed. Take up the cause of the fatherless;
plead the case of the widow.* ISAIAH 1:17

She was born August 26, 1910, in Skopje, Macedonia. Her wealthy parents named
her Agnes Gonxha Bojaxhiu. They had no idea their daughter would one day
change her name or change the course of history. In 1928, she joined a religious
order and took the name Teresa. In 1950, this diminutive lady in her now familiar
white habit founded a religious order in Calcutta.

Under her servant leadership, the Missionaries of Charity operated hospitals,
orphanages and shelters for lepers and the dying poor. Amazingly, the ministry
Mother Teresa started has grown to include branches in 50 cities in India and 30
other countries. She dedicated every day of her adult life to caring for the dying,
the disabled, the mentally ill, the unwanted and the unloved. As far as she was
concerned, she was loving, cleaning and feeding as "Jesus in disguise."

In her 87 years of life, this giant of the faith proved that worship is more than
having personal devotions. It is personally serving the needy around us. That's
what Isaiah is driving at in this passage. Genuine praise extends beyond the prayer
closet to the people we encounter throughout the day.

Even though lingering in the Lord's sweet presence is definitely easier than
helping a homeless person to a shelter, it is incomplete. Worshiping with our hands
and feet is harder than with our lips. Today, instead of folding your hands in your
favorite chair, walk downtown and give someone a hand. ✤

PRAYER

Help me, Father, to see the needs around me that break your heart . . .

A TRUE VISION OF HOLINESS

"Woe to me!" I cried. "I am ruined! For I am a man of unclean lips, and I live among a people of unclean lips, and my eyes have seen the King, the LORD Almighty." Isaiah 6:5

In writing about Isaiah's encounter with God in his classic *The Holiness of God*, R. C. Sproul observes, "In that single moment, all of [Isaiah's] self-esteem was shattered. In a brief second he was exposed, made naked beneath the gaze of the absolute standard of holiness ... The instant he measured himself by the ultimate standard, he was destroyed—morally and spiritually annihilated."

No wonder Isaiah said, "Woe to me! I am ruined! For I am a man of unclean lips, and I live among a people of unclean lips."

The Bible is filled with stories of the way people respond to the holiness of God. Shortly after creation, Adam and Eve distanced themselves in the garden from a holy God. Camouflaging themselves among the foliage, they played the first recorded game of hide-and-seek (see Genesis 3:8). When David recognized the gravity of his sin with Bathsheba, he cast himself on God's mercy, all the while feeling estranged from the One he had ultimately violated (see Psalm 51).

A common thread of dread runs through these encounters with God. The brilliance of God's pure presence reveals the imperfection of our sinful lives. We either want to run away and hide or we want him to leave us alone. The disparity is normal. This awareness of his holiness and our sin is redemptive knowledge. It motivates us to act on the feelings of guilt and shame now uncovered. It brings us to a point of confession, seeking forgiveness and finding God's love anew. It reminds us that the One we worship is truly worthy of our praise and adoration even though we aren't. ♣

PRAYER

Lord, I confess ...

WHAT'S IN A NAME?

For to us a child is born, to us a son is given, and the government will be on his shoulders. And he will be called Wonderful Counselor, Mighty God, Everlasting Father, Prince of Peace. ISAIAH 9:6

"For to us a child is born ..." So begins the familiar passage read every year at Christmas—the assurance of a child, a Son, who would enter our world to save it. Our thoughts immediately turn to the babe born in a lowly stable. But let's consider the other names given to this child and the promise contained within each one.

- Wonderful Counselor—The One we worship holds the counsel of God from eternity; he defends God's people with unprecedented integrity and grace.
- Mighty God—He is nothing less than the Almighty Creator in human flesh, the One who is capable of achieving the necessary and seemingly impossible.
- Everlasting Father—As the image of the invisible God, the eternal One we worship is like a father. He is involved in our lives.
- Prince of Peace—He is the One who reconciles us to God; he is the giver of peace in our hearts and ultimately, when his kingdom is established, of peace among the nations.

These names stir within us a desire to praise Jesus in gratitude for the many ways he transcends time and space and touches our lives.

Whisper these timeless names under your breath. Better yet, why not write all four titles on an empty sheet of paper and hang it on the refrigerator or near your place of work? During the day, as you glance at those names, imagine the Lord invisibly serving you in those ways. ❧

PRAYER

Lord Jesus, when I consider this list of names for you, I think ...

GREETING DEATH WITH A SONG

Surely God is my salvation; I will trust and not be afraid. The LORD, the LORD himself, is my strength and my defense; he has become my salvation.　　　ISAIAH 12:2

Art Bernier was a devout Christian. His optimism was contagious. Those who encountered him at Seattle Pacific University where he worked as a custodian knew Art as a spark plug; he made sure others' days were filled with joy and life. His last days of life, however, were spent in a hospital filled with pain due to inoperable cancer.

As one nurse nervously attempted to find a vein to administer morphine, she hit a nerve. The discomfort was so intense that Art swore at his white uniformed helper. In addition to the intolerable pain, Art felt remorse. He pressed the call button summoning the nurse back to his room and begged her forgiveness. But that was only one of the indicators that Art Bernier was a believer.

As death drew nearer, this 70-year-old man didn't recoil in fear. The words of Isaiah could easily have originated with him. He found the ability in his heart to trust God and not be overwhelmed with anxiety. Although his strength was ebbing away on a daily basis, this man who had sung in church most of his adult life still attempted to sing from his hospital bed. He sang about Jesus and the strength his Savior gave. Whatever fear he might have had about journeying through the valley of death's shadows was met with songs of praise.

Don't minimize the place and power of praise in your life. When personal worship becomes a pattern of life, it serves us well when death comes knocking. In the meantime, think about songs that celebrate the Savior's love. Do it now wherever you are. ♣

PRAYER

Holy Father, move me by the power of your Spirit to freely praise you . . .

day186

OF KERNELS AND CROSSES

My people who are crushed on the threshing floor, I tell you what I have heard from the
LORD Almighty, from the God of Israel.   ISAIAH 21:10

In Biblical times, farmers would use their oxen to drag a heavy sledge back and
forth across a pile of harvested grain to separate the kernels from the chaff. Afterward, they would toss the whole mess into the air with a pitchfork and let the wind
blow the chaff away from the kernels. Then they would gather up the grain and
set fire to the chaff.

It's easy to see why threshing and winnowing became prominent Biblical symbols, isn't it? For instance, trials in life can crush us, forcing us to give up our
cherished sins—the chaff—and leaving only what is God-pleasing—the kernels. That's what happened in Isaiah's time to the Israelites, who suffered repeated
invasions and finally were exiled before they gave up idolatry. It can happen to us
too. We can be "threshed and winnowed."

God is not the author of evil, but he permits evil to enter our lives when it suits
his larger purposes for the world or his smaller purposes for our lives individually.
As we are living for Christ, these trials become woven into the pattern of our dis-
cipleship. They are not just random troubles but "crosses" we have to bear.

Learning to accept God's threshing and winnowing work in our lives is gradu-
ate-level Christianity. We're justified in trembling before the prospect. But if we're
committed to a path of devotion that will take us into the heart of God, we will
choose to worship God even when the sledge is dragging behind us.

Today, thank God for the threshing and winnowing you are experiencing. Be
specific. ♣

PRAYER

In times of threshing and winnowing, Lord, I feel...

day187

THE COST—AND GAIN—OF DISCIPLESHIP

Trust in the LORD forever, for the LORD, the LORD himself, is the Rock eternal.

ISAIAH 26:4

"In Peru, Christians don't expect to get something for serving Jesus," said Pastor Zapata. "They expect to give something." To illustrate, Pastor Zapata showed his foreign guests a row of white crosses, each representing a local Christian killed by Communist insurgents. As if that wasn't proof enough, inside Pastor Zapata's village home was the body of another pastor who had been killed by guerrillas the night before. Expressing their grief, members of the dead man's family surrounded his body where it lay covered with a blanket.

Outside, though, the scene was joyous. Despite a steady rain, the congregation of the murdered pastor sang praise choruses. Guerrillas had killed their pastor, destroyed their church building and burned many of their homes, yet they sang praise to God.

These believers, and countless others whose stories are shared through the Voice of the Martyrs organization, had learned the lesson Isaiah taught: Trusting in God is never the wrong choice. He is the eternal Rock to whom we can cling in life and in death—we trust in him *always*.

For many believers, suffering won't reach levels anywhere near the pain known by the martyred church. For others, it may. But regardless of our circumstances, we need God's strength—a strength that endures.

If we hold on to our eternal Rock, and do not let go, we will one day find ourselves in that place where a praise-inspiring vision of God fills our whole sight.

Allow the testimony of Pastor Zapata to stir you today to pray for the persecuted church—that they will continue to trust in the Lord, the eternal Rock. ✤

PRAYER

I will cling to you, eternal Rock ...

THE POTTER AND HIS WORKS

You turn things upside down, as if the potter were thought to be like the clay! Shall what is formed say to the one who formed it, "You did not make me"? Can the pot say to the potter, "You know nothing"?   ISAIAH 29:16

Have biomolecules built up over eons on Earth's surface, as naturalistic dogma predicts? According to Hugh Ross and Fazale Rana in their book *Origins of Life*, the Earth has been bombarded by massively destructive meteorites many times, narrowing the window of life's sustainability to a period far too short for evolution.

Did life originate on early Earth in the form of extremophiles—tiny creatures that are able to withstand very high or very low temperatures? Apparently not, since biologists now admit that even the simplest extremophiles are too complex to have arisen on their own.

Did microscopic life arrive on Earth aboard a meteorite from some other place in the universe, perhaps Jupiter's watery moon Europa? No. Europa's ice layer has now been proved much too thick (miles deep) to permit life to exist farther down. Meanwhile, numerous lines of evidence are making it look more and more as if Earth is the only place in the universe capable of hosting life.

These are just a few of the theories that origin-of-life scientists have considered—and dropped. While the theory of evolution has worn an air of invincibility since the Scopes trial, the proof isn't really there.

Meanwhile, we who believe in creation have no room for smugness. How many of us proclaim that God had a purpose for creating life in general, while at the same time we question whether God has a purpose in creating us individually? The Potter (to use Isaiah's imagery) knew exactly what he was doing when he made each of us pots. Thank him for creating you as you are and for each "pot and jar" you encounter throughout the day. ✤

> **PRAYER**

Lord, you are the Potter, I am the clay ...

day189

SHATTERING YOUR COMPLACENCY

You women who are so complacent, rise up and listen to me; you daughters who feel secure, hear what I have to say! In little more than a year you who feel secure will tremble; the grape harvest will fail, and the harvest of fruit will not come. ISAIAH 32:9–10

When is it easier or harder to live for God?

When life is going well, health is good, the career is going well and all aspects of life have seemingly fallen into place, it's sometimes easier to let other aspects of life slip. Devotional time doesn't seem as pressing a matter. Cutting corners in the workplace is deemed appropriate. Maintaining relationships doesn't have that high a priority.

But when life is tough, when job security is threatened, the test results come back negative or the marriage relationship is rocky, finding time to spend with God is not as difficult. Friendships and relationships become crucial. Living for—and with—God is paramount.

At the time Isaiah delivered this prophecy, the people of Israel's countryside were taking it easy after harvesting their crops. That would not have been bad, except that they apparently were feeling self-sufficient and had little concern about God and his desires for them. Little did they know—until Isaiah warned them—that they were mere months away from seeing their pleasant fields and vineyards utterly devastated (perhaps by an invasion of the Assyrians). Their complacency was about to be shattered.

Where has complacency crept into your attitudes, habits or relationships? Use this time as your personal wake-up call and confess those areas to God. ❖

PRAYER

Lord, as I examine my life, I find …

THE SILENCE OF LISTENING PRAYER

Hezekiah received the letter from the messengers and read it. Then he went up to the temple of the LORD and spread it out before the LORD. And Hezekiah prayed to the LORD.
ISAIAH 37:14–15

Being silent before God may seem a strain for those of us who are not used to it; it can make us restless and often uncomfortable. But prayer can never truly be two-way communication until we learn to listen as well as speak. In fact, if prayer ever feels like an unreal exercise to us, it may be because we are doing all the talking!

It is not that we should necessarily expect to hear God give us specific instruction on a matter (how nice when he does, as in the case of Hezekiah) or even expect to feel the "nudge" that some Christians talk about. It's more about stretching open a space in our spirits for God to begin to fill with himself. Listening prayer, in that way, changes us over time.

Through listening prayer, we learn more about the One to whom we are praying. We cannot "know that [he is] God" until we are willing to "be still" (Psalm 46:10). And so listening prayer has the power to bring our wills more nearly into line with God's will.

Facing a crisis or decision? As an act of worship today, spread it out before the Lord as Hezekiah did his threatening letter. Speak. Wait. And listen. ✤

PRAYER

Speak now, Lord, for your servant is listening...

A NEW SONG FOR ALL NATIONS

Sing to the LORD *a new song, his praise from the ends of the earth, you who go down to the sea, and all that is in it, you islands, and all who live in them.*   ISAIAH 42:10

"Missions is not the ultimate goal of the church. Worship is," declared John Piper in his book *Let the Nations Be Glad!* "Missions exists because worship doesn't."

Indeed, you could say that the goal of missions is to make the worship of God part of a culture in the widest possible way. Only when "new songs" are sung to God in the Yaminahuas language (Amazon), the Buhi language (Philippines), the Occitan language (Provence) — as well as in every other language and via every culture on earth — will the praise of God swell to its fullest extent, with every harmonic layer adding to the richness of the chords. God deserves and desires no less. Someday these nations will gather together and worship God in heaven.

After peeking into heaven, the apostle John reported, "After this I looked, and there before me was a great multitude that no one could count, from every nation, tribe, people and language, standing before the throne and before the Lamb. They were wearing white robes and were holding palm branches in their hands. And they cried out in a loud voice: 'Salvation belongs to our God, who sits on the throne, and to the Lamb'" (Revelation 7:9 – 10).

In John's vision the angels added their amen to the praise coming from the diverse crowd of human beings (see Revelation 7:11 – 12). Let us do the same.

Today, look for ways to incorporate other cultures into your routines. Celebrate the diversity God has given to us. ✤

PRAYER

Lord, I offer my voice to those of other nations in singing your praise . . .

A LONG OBEDIENCE IN THE SAME DIRECTION

Even to your old age and gray hairs I am he, I am he who will sustain you. I have made you and I will carry you; I will sustain you and I will rescue you.   ISAIAH 46:4

There's something charming about a young believer who is full of enthusiasm for the Lord. But there's something truly inspiring about a man or woman who has walked with God through all the stages of life.

Time magazine profiled Billy Graham in an article titled "A Christian in Winter." The evangelist fulfilled his calling and upheld moral standards over decades, and has become an example of consistent obedience to Christ.

What sort of Christians will we be in the winter of life? There's no question that God will remain faithful to us, as Isaiah 46:4 assures us, but will we be faithful to him?

If we remain faithful, we will receive the blessings of old age, as was so beautifully expressed by the late Dean of Westminster Abbey and Master of Balliol, Benjamin Jowett, in a letter to a friend:

> *Though I am growing old, I maintain that the best part is yet to come — the time when one may see things more dispassionately and know oneself and others more truly, and perhaps be able to do more, and in religion rest centered in a very few simple truths.*
>
> *I do not want to ignore the other side, that one will not be able to see so well, or walk so far, or read so much. But there may be more peace within, more communion with God, more real light instead of distraction about many things, better relations with others, fewer mistakes."*

Our bodies may fail us, but God never will. The habit of daily worship can help bind us to Christ with bonds time can never weaken. ❧

PRAYER

Lord, build a foundation of faithfulness within me . . .

day193

HIS LOVE IS HAND WRITTEN

See, I have engraved you on the palms of my hands; your walls are ever before me.

ISAIAH 49:16

"No doubt about it," they lamented. "God has deserted us. Probably even forgotten us."

The poster children for short-term memory disorder, the people of Israel thought—for the umpteenth time—that even though they were the chosen people, they had become the rejected people. Or perhaps they had their own foretelling of Tevye's prayer in the musical *Fiddler on the Roof*: "It is said we are the chosen people. Could you please choose somebody else?"

Isaiah encourages them, "For the LORD comforts his people and will have compassion on his afflicted ones" (Isaiah 49:13). God *has* comforted and *will* comfort. A small word in the next verse, however, reveals much: *but*. Despite the history, despite the promises, "But Zion said, 'The LORD has forsaken me; the Lord has forgotten me'" (verse 14).

Does the *but* describe your response to God's promises to comfort? How strongly do you complain that he has forgotten you? His response to the charge of forgetting is the same as it always has been: "Never!" The proof, added to all the centuries of evidence? A remarkable image: "I have engraved you on the palms of my hands."

What do we know of his hand? It is a hand of power, of fighting and smiting, but also of amazing comfort and protection. Along with the people of Israel and Isaiah we can say, "In the shadow of his hand he hid me" (Isaiah 49:2).

God does not simply know us "like the back of his hand." He turns over his hands and shows us the palms. These same palms that later bore the nail prints of crucifixion, the ultimate proof that he has not forgotten us. May we lift up our hands today in gratitude and praise. ✤

PRAYER

O God, I thank you for your hands . . .

MY WAY IS THE HIGH WAY

"For my thoughts are not your thoughts, neither are your ways my ways," declares the LORD. *"As the heavens are higher than the earth, so are my ways higher than your ways and my thoughts than your thoughts."*   ISAIAH 55:8–9

The Great Wall of China. Heart transplants. Airplanes. The isolation of radium. Armistices. Computers. A Mozart concerto. How amazing is each one? Who could think up such things? What sort of mind can create this kind of beauty?

Apart from the fact that it was God who inspired and directed these "manmade" accomplishments, he can still resoundingly say his ways are greater, his thoughts are higher. Why? Through this prophecy he beckons his people to realize how he has worked, is working and will work through history to bring all of his creation back to himself.

Through the prophet Isaiah, God proclaims, "As the rain and the snow come down from heaven, and do not return to it without watering the earth and making it bud and flourish, so that it yields seed for the sower and bread for the eater, so is my word that goes out from my mouth: It will not return to me empty, but will accomplish what I desire and achieve the purpose for which I sent it" (Isaiah 55:10–11).

Rain and snow. Seeds growing. Plants flourishing. These are the actions of a God totally in control. Give thanks today for the high ways and thoughts of God that are expressed in the beauty of creation around you. ✤

PRAYER

Your ways, O God, are so much higher than mine...

day195

THAT OLD SIN PROBLEM

But your iniquities have separated you from your God; your sins have hidden his face from you, so that he will not hear.   ISAIAH 59:2

The father seems to have finally lost patience with his wayward children. About time, some say. He is ready to cut them out of the will. They say they want to visit, but he will likely turn them away.

Such was the relationship between God the Father and a young man of high intelligence but low morals who was born in AD 354 in what is now known as Algeria. The young man struggled with God intellectually as a student and teacher of rhetoric and philosophy. He struggled with God spiritually as the son of a devout Christian and protégé of Saint Ambrose, the great bishop of Milan.

The young man's name was Augustine. His writings and his leadership of the early church following his baptism by Ambrose, ordination as a priest and eventual consecration as the bishop of Hippo in the region of his birth are legendary.

Augustine understood as have few others the enormity of the "problem" Isaiah described in the key verse for today — "your sins have hidden his face from you." He knew that God had turned away; indeed, his most famous book is the autobiographical *Confessions.*

What reason is there for hope that God will save us? The words immediately before today's dire verse remain eternally true. "Surely the arm of the LORD is not too short to save, nor his ear too dull to hear" (Isaiah 59:1).

Call to him now. He will turn back to you. He will listen. ✤

PRAYER

Father God, have mercy on me . . .

A NAME OF FAME

"As the new heavens and the new earth that I make will endure before me," declares the LORD, *"so will your name and descendants endure. From one New Moon to another and from one Sabbath to another, all mankind will come and bow down before me," says the* LORD. ISAIAH 66:22–23

After a battle in which his namesake had fled from a skirmish, Alexander the Great approached the young soldier and rebuked him, "Either change your name or live up to it."

Names, particularly family names, carry great importance. Passing on the family name—through a business or simply through an enduring lineage—has been important since history began. For some, it is even an obsession. "It's the end of an era. If he doesn't produce a son, he's the last of the line. The family name dies with him."

Names are important to God too. Consider the emphasis given in Scripture to *the* name. "The name that is above every name, that at the name of Jesus every knee should bow" (Philippians 2:9–10). To conclude the prophecy given through Isaiah, however, God chose to emphasize not his own name but that of his people. They will have an enduring name. Here God is assuring them that, through the Messiah he will provide, they will always be his family. The family name will never die out, never disappear.

Always a part of God's people. Always one of his children. How will you honor God's name today? ❖

PRAYER

Father God, thank you for calling me by name . . .

day197

FROM THE START

Before I formed you in the womb I knew you, before you were born I set you apart; I appointed you as a prophet to the nations. JEREMIAH 1:5

Former chaplain of the United States Senate Dr. Lloyd John Ogilvie once preached a sermon called "When God First Thought of You." In this memorable message, Dr. Ogilvie contended that each of us existed in the mind of our Creator before we were conceived in our mother's womb. His point was this: When God first decided that we would be given life on earth, there was a specific purpose in his plan for each one of us. It wasn't random. It was by design.

That's the same principle presented by Jeremiah in the opening chapter of his book. God has a personal knowledge of those he has created. His love is specific and personal. He knows intimately those he loves. And that knowledge is complete. From the very point of conception, a loving God is aware of what makes each person special.

In light of that keen awareness, God weaves together a meaningful plan that is based on the needs and gifts of each person. Jeremiah's assignment was to speak prophetically to the unresponsive nation of Israel. For you, his call to love your neighbor might seem equally challenging. But it is just as meaningful because God knows what you can uniquely accomplish for his sake.

Understanding God's intimate knowledge of each person may call for personal confession. Nothing about your thoughts, attitudes and actions escapes his all-seeing eyes. But that knowledge might just as easily prompt you to praise him. Imagine—the Creator of the universe understands you like none other—and still loves you. Amazing! So whether you need to confess or praise him, do it now. Personal worship times include both. ✤

PRAYER

Lord, you know me like none other ...

day198

BE HONEST TO GOD!

Do not trust in deceptive words and say, "This is the temple of the LORD, the temple of the LORD, the temple of the LORD!" If you really change your ways and your actions and deal with each other justly ... then I will let you live in this place, in the land I gave your ancestors for ever and ever. JEREMIAH 7:4–5,7

A pastor in a liturgical church attempted to welcome his congregation from the pulpit with the ritualistic greeting "The Lord be with you!" But the microphone wasn't working properly. After several failed attempts at being heard, he cleared his throat and loudly said, "Something appears to be wrong with the sound system." Without thinking, the congregation replied with the expected response, "And also with you!"

Although this story may coax a smile, it hints at a timeless tendency. It is possible to codify our worship so that it becomes routine and without thought. Symbols and responses can replace a sincere encounter with the living God. In Jeremiah's day, the temple in Jerusalem was such a symbol. As long as God's people could look up and see the sun glistening off the gold-gilded roof of Solomon's temple, they felt they were safe from God's judgment. Their walk with the Lord had been reduced to false reliance on external relics and repeated practices.

Perhaps you recognize that tendency in yourself at times. You catch yourself saying "Praise God!" out of habit. The prayer you say before digging in at dinner is repetitious and offered without thinking. Still, reprogramming your pattern of praise may not be as easy as you think. If you're willing, however, it can be done.

As you think about the kind of vital relationship you desire with the Lord, speak your mind. Wouldn't you like to be entirely honest? Well, you can. Avoid God-talk. Don't resort to religious clichés. Speak to God in prayer as you would to your best friend in the world. ✤

PRAYER

Lord, this is the real me, coming before you ...

GETTING TO KNOW HIM

"Let the one who boasts boast about this: that they have the understanding to know me, that I am the LORD, *who exercises kindness, justice and righteousness on earth, for in these I delight," declares the* LORD.   JEREMIAH 9:24

Obtaining knowledge is a core value of the human experience. But not every person embraces that value with equal affection. An Arab proverb says, "He who knows and knows that he knows is wise. Follow him. He who knows and knows not that he knows is asleep. Wake him. He who knows not and knows not that he knows not is uneducated. Teach him. He who knows not and knows that he knows not is a fool. Shun him."

As far as God is concerned, our knowledge of him is the most important possession we have. That comes through loud and clear in this passage from Jeremiah. For Hugh Steven, veteran missionary with Wycliffe Bible Translators, that was the credo of his life. When asked what our purpose in this life is all about, he would answer, "To develop a capacity for knowing God so we will have the means by which to worship and enjoy him in the world to come."

Our ability to truly know God is rooted in our willingness to listen and observe. But that sure is difficult when spouses, children and work deadlines deserve and demand attention. Yet God says our knowledge of him is unequalled by any task on earth (no matter how noble). That should trigger within us the desire to sit in his presence and learn.

What is it you want—or need—to know about God today? Write down one question; then find time to pursue the answer. Make it a habit to "truly know and understand" God. ✤

PRAYER

Lord, I want to know you by persistently seeking your face . . .

A NEAR IMPOSSIBILITY

Can an Ethiopian change his skin or a leopard its spots? Neither can you do good who are accustomed to doing evil.   JEREMIAH 13:23

In the fall of 1959, author John Howard Griffin set out on a personal odyssey. He exchanged the privileged life he'd known as a Southern white man for the disenfranchised world of a jobless black man by undergoing a medical procedure to change his skin color. His best-selling book *Black Like Me* chronicles his eye-opening lessons but ends with his returning to his life as a Caucasian.

Tired of hypocrisy and sin, we too often try to remake ourselves. But apart from God, we're unsuccessful. The attitudes and values with which we were raised are more powerful than most realize. When coupled with a human nature that seeks pleasure over morality and self-interest over justice, choosing to do what is right is more easily agreed to than accomplished.

These words Jeremiah recorded leave little wiggle room, and they make us uncomfortable. In fact, these words invade the very center of our will. We may want desperately to change an attitude, behavior or thought pattern, but we simply aren't strong enough. We can't stop displeasing the Lord and being hurtful to others on our own. That is a fact of human nature.

Only God can bring about the means for you to take on a new identity. Only his Holy Spirit can change the leopard spots—or spots of sin.

What "spots" do you want taken away today? Ask God for his help and trust him to remove them. ❖

PRAYER

Wash me, Lord...

day201

IN SEARCH OF GREENER PASTURES

Blessed is the one who trusts in the LORD, whose confidence is in him. They will be like a tree planted by the water that sends out its roots by the stream. It does not fear when heat comes; its leaves are always green. It has no worries in a year of drought and never fails to bear fruit.

JEREMIAH 17:7–8

The state of Washington is a state of contrasts when it comes to its landscape. On the west side of the Cascade Mountains, it is lush and green. Eastern Washington, however, is flat and arid, actually resembling the wheat fields of Kansas. The portion of the state that is dotted with inlets and lakes and benefits from the runoff of melting snow from Mount Rainier boasts a year-round vibrancy.

All the precipitation you ordinarily associate with the Pacific Northwest allows the residential lawns and grassy parks of Seattle to remain green all 12 months of the year. Where there is moisture and proximity to bodies of water, there is life and color. Where there is the absence of those natural resources, there is brown wilderness.

In this passage Jeremiah isn't giving us an agricultural lesson on growing healthy plants and fruit-bearing trees. He's calling us to observe what's true in nature so we might learn a spiritual lesson. People who trust in the Lord and make him their hope and confidence will be like the trees the prophet describes—lush and fruitful.

Have you found that the water of God's Word stimulates spiritual growth? When you find dry times during your day, when you feel under stress or far from God, allow this image of lush greenery to stir your thoughts toward God, the One who can refresh you. ✤

PRAYER

Lord, refresh my arid heart today . . .

IN THE NAME OF GOD

But you must not mention "a message from the LORD" again, because each one's word becomes their own message. So you distort the words of the living God, the LORD Almighty, our God. JEREMIAH 23:36

Jim Jones was a popular pastor in Northern California. This effective communicator had a charismatic personality and was successful in bridging the chasm that often divides whites and blacks. His interracial church was known as The People's Temple. But something in Pastor Jones snapped; he became consumed with his own ideas.

To get support from the congregation, he would attribute his inspiration to divine revelation. One of those "revelations" resulted in the majority of his congregation relocating to the small country of Guyana in South America. The communal cult was known as Jonestown. Relatives of church members who followed Pastor Jones south of the equator were troubled. They had reason to believe that Jim Jones was a manipulative cult leader, but they had no idea what the tragic consequences of his leadership would bring. On November 18, 1978, 914 members of The People's Temple committed mass suicide because a man who equated himself with God told them to drink Kool-Aid laced with poison.

That kind of cult phenomenon is not without precedent. Israel's history is stained with evidence of such scandal. Jeremiah had harsh words for those who claimed their prophetic words were from God. Even today it's tempting at times to attribute our gut instincts to God's leading when in actuality they are selfish desires wanting to be fulfilled.

Be honest when you evaluate why you want to change churches, why you're tempted at times to leave your mate, why you reinterpret Scripture to be politically correct. Remember that God alone is our authority. ✤

PRAYER

Lord, I bow to your authority . . .

day203

AN ANTIDOTE TO MOTION SICKNESS

"For I know the plans I have for you," declares the LORD, "plans to prosper you and not to harm you, plans to give you hope and a future. JEREMIAH 29:11

Perspective is everything. When you have a view of what's up ahead, your current circumstances aren't as troubling as they might otherwise be. For example, have you ever noticed that the person driving the car never gets carsick? That's because the driver sees the upcoming curves and makes the necessary mental adjustment in advance of what his body (and the car) are about to experience.

Curiously, a person's emotional equilibrium can also be impacted by knowing what is ahead. Perhaps it has to do with the fact that the person feels as though he or she is in control of the situation.

In these familiar words recorded in Jeremiah, God reminds us that he is in complete control. Even though we can't see around the bend, he can. Even though our lives may feel out of control, our paths are following an itinerary of his choosing. And despite the fact that we sometimes get upset or lose our balance on the journey, God reminds us that his route is a good one. Our destination is a future filled with hope, and our safe arrival is guaranteed.

Based on recent disappointments or disasters you've had to endure, isn't it good to know that God is in control? He *does* have a plan! ❖

PRAYER

Father God, help me trust you instead of worrying . . .

PUT ON YOUR DANCING SHOES

Then young women will dance and be glad, young men and old as well. I will turn their mourning into gladness; I will give them comfort and joy instead of sorrow.

JEREMIAH 31:13

When residents of Palestine, West Virginia, think back on the war with Iraq, one soldier's name and face comes to mind more than any other—19-year-old PFC Jessica Lynch. This homegrown hero was among the soldiers of the 507th Ordnance Maintenance Company who were ambushed, captured and presumed dead. But the worst fears of her family were not realized. More than a week after her capture, U.S. Special Operations Forces raided the hospital near Baghdad where the wounded POW was being held as a hostage. The mourning of a small town tucked in the Appalachian Mountains gave way to incredible joy.

Remarkably, that scene is similar to the one Jeremiah describes. Anticipating the return of the exiled Jews to Jerusalem, he pictures God's people dancing before the Lord in worshipful joy. No ballroom dancing here. This dancing is a spiritual celebration, a tangible act of praise by which God's faithfulness against the backdrop of peril and injustice is celebrated.

Based on what the prophet says, we have every reason to believe that turning mourning into dancing and sadness into joy is standard with God. That's his plan. Because we know him, our ultimate destiny is heaven, and we have the solid assurance that one day all sickness, death and sorrow will be banished—we will be perfect and complete. All of this earth, including our pain and sorrow, is temporary. Only our joy and dancing will last forever!

Whatever your sorrow is today, keep your eyes on Christ and gain God's eternal perspective. Then join in the celebration and get ready to dance! ✣

PRAYER

Lord, you turn my sorrow into joy now . . .

THE WRITE STUFF

So Jeremiah took another scroll and gave it to the scribe Baruch son of Neriah, and as Jeremiah dictated, Baruch wrote on it all the words of the scroll that Jehoiakim king of Judah had burned in the fire. And many similar words were added to them.

JEREMIAH 36:32

Theologically trained Kenneth N. Taylor was concerned that his ten children didn't understand the family's devotional reading of the King James Version of the Bible. After all, it was written in seventeenth-century English. So beginning in 1954, he started paraphrasing the New Testament into modern English.

After seven years of writing and rewriting, he submitted the manuscript to several publishing houses. Much to his chagrin, he was rejected by all of them. Still, Taylor was convinced there was value in the work for more than just his own children. He refused to give up. At last, he and his wife, Margaret, decided to use their limited savings to self-publish his work. The result was a best-selling paraphrase called *The Living Bible* and the beginnings of a successful publishing company known as Tyndale House.

That same determination characterized Jeremiah. When King Jehoiakim destroyed the prophet's only copy of his prophecy, he could have despaired. Instead, Jeremiah picked up his devastated ego off the ground and started all over again. This time, according to Scripture, "many similar words were added to them."

It's nearly impossible to sing praise to God as we brew our morning coffee when a reputation we have spent a lifetime building has been stained by false rumors. It's asking too much to put a smile on our faces when the enemy isn't a two-faced friend but a doctor's diagnosis.

Jeremiah went beyond what any of his peers would have expected. God planted in his heart the ability to persevere. He will do the same for you. ✤

> **PRAYER**

Lord, give me the strength to keep going . . .

TOPPLING YOUR TOWER OF STRENGTH

Should you then seek great things for yourself? Do not seek them. For I will bring disaster on all people, declares the LORD, but wherever you go I will let you escape with your life.

JEREMIAH 45:5

As American troops moved from the Persian Gulf into the major cities of Iraq, they encountered towering statues bearing the likeness of Saddam Hussein. Within days of Iraq's liberation, these idol-like images were toppled and destroyed. The destruction of these statues was a symbol of the regime's demise.

The larger-than-life likenesses that dominated towns and cities throughout this dictator's land illustrated that the tendency to seek great things for one's self permeates history.

The desire to exercise godlike control over others and to seek glory for ourselves is not bound by culture or time, and it is not limited to despots. It is an ongoing temptation in a fallen world.

As God's people, however, we have a choice whether to cave in to those impulses or resist them. For most people the temptation is not to become a Saddam-like dictator. Rather, it is to make a name for ourselves or try to take control of a situation that overwhelms. Ever since a couple in a garden opted to hedge their bets and ended up hiding buck naked in a hedge of another kind, we are naturally oriented to seeking great things for ourselves.

When you feel this urge to glorify yourself, pause and turn to God. Ask him to reveal your hidden motives. Confess your tendencies to him. Then seek his help. ✤

PRAYER

Lord, I will glorify you instead of myself . . .

A CITY FOR THE BIRDS

"The terror you inspire and the pride of your heart have deceived you, you who live in the clefts of the rocks, who occupy the heights of the hill. Though you build your nest as high as the eagle's, from there I will bring you down," declares the LORD.   JEREMIAH 49:16

The city of Petra flourished in sixth century BC. It was located in the area south of Amman in modern-day Jordan. Taking advantage of the soft stone, the residents of this ancient town carved cliff dwellings and caves in which to live. The ornate architecture has survived amazingly well in the arid climate of the Middle East, the most famous of which is the Treasury building.

Surrounded by towering hills of rust-colored sandstone, Petra enjoyed natural protection against invaders. A narrow canyon leading into the valley of Petra no more than ten feet across (and less than four feet at some points) also provided increased security. The Lord's warning against pride and a false sense of security as recorded by Jeremiah apply very well to this forgotten empire. Although the ancient Edomites who lived there claimed the safe vantage point of eagles and the enviable fortress-like surroundings, they were still destroyed. When they failed to honor and worship Israel's God, their glory was reduced to a ghost town.

If you have climbed the hills of Petra, you can easily see how futile it is to build a life on anything but the firm foundation of a growing faith in God. But it doesn't take a trip to the Middle East to grasp that truth. Reread these verses from Jeremiah. Feel the passion with which the Lord speaks. Hear the cry of the eagle in flight. See the weeping refugees of a civilization being led away into captivity.

Ask the Lord what false securities exist in your life. Ask him to chip away at the veneer that prevents you from daily acknowledging your need of him. ❖

PRAYER

Lord, I truly need you today . . .

IN PRAISE OF GODLY SHEPHERDS

My people have been lost sheep; their shepherds have led them astray and caused them to roam on the mountains. They wandered over mountain and hill and forgot their own resting place. JEREMIAH 50:6

Dr. Robert G. Tuttle Jr. is a respected theologian and author. Although he had gleaned much about Biblical culture from his graduate work, he made a firsthand discovery about shepherds while escorting a tour group in Israel. One morning, the group climbed aboard a bus for a ride through the Judean countryside. The Israeli tour guide explained to Dr. Tuttle and his companions that shepherds in the Middle East never drive their flocks from behind. Instead, he said, they always lead them by going ahead of them.

Within a few minutes Tuttle called to the front of the bus, asking the guide to look out to the hillside. "I thought you said that shepherds in this part of the world never drive their sheep," he said. "Look over there!" As the guide looked through the bus windows, he saw a man charging after a flock of sheep attempting to get away. "Oh, sir," the tour guide said with a chuckle in his voice. "That's not a shepherd. That's a butcher."

Although Tuttle had not seen a wayward shepherd after all, he would have had he lived in Jeremiah's day. The spiritual shepherds of God's flock did not live up to what was expected of them. Their lives lacked integrity and their concern for the people of God left much to be desired.

Hopefully, you attend a church where your shepherd considers the call to care for your soul a privilege. If so, thank the Lord for him as you quietly intercede for significant others in your life. Ask God to fill him with insight and inspiration as he feeds you each week in worship. ✤

PRAYER

Lord, please hear my prayer for my pastor . . .

OUR ONLY REAL HELP

Arise, cry out in the night, as the watches of the night begin; pour out your heart like water in the presence of the Lord. Lift up your hands to him for the lives of your children, who faint from hunger at every street corner.　　　　　　　　　　LAMENTATIONS 2:19

The era was not good for prophets. The nation was a spiritual and moral mess. The people had turned their backs on the one true God. Worse, they had begun worshiping pagan gods and participating in the vile rituals of their neighbors. Despite countless warnings from numerous prophets, the populace refused to turn from their self-willed ways.

At last God sent judgment on his beloved people in the form of the invading Babylonians. Lamentations describes this tragic event, a disaster that easily could have been avoided—the divine judgment of Jerusalem in 586 BC.

Lamentations is a grim and gritty book. What does it have to do with worship? On one level it is a stark warning against worshiping whatever is not God. On another level, it is a reminder that even when we have been unfaithful to God and are wallowing in the consequences of our rebellion, he is still the One we need. And he stands ready to forgive and restore us.

Feeling far away from God? Realizing you made some wrong choices? Wanting to come back to God? Then do as the prophet urges: Pour out your heart to God. Reach up to him in prayer. ✣

PRAYER

Lord, I pour out my soul to you ...

LOST IN WONDERING LOVE

Because of the LORD's great love we are not consumed, for his compassions never fail. They are new every morning; great is your faithfulness. LAMENTATIONS 3:22–23

The rebellious southern kingdom of Israel (Judah) had resisted God's repeated appeals to turn away from their sinful ways. They had not been swayed by the fall of the northern kingdom of Israel. They had ignored every warning of impending judgment. Yet when, on divine cue, the brutal Babylonians arrived to destroy Jerusalem, Jeremiah was not shocked and amazed by God's power and justice, but lost in wonder at God's faithful compassion. In the midst of all the violence and suffering, Jeremiah saw fresh, daily reminders of God's tender mercy.

What an amazing promise! No wonder so many Christians memorize this passage or display it in a frame on the living room wall. God's love is unfailing and endless. Judgment cannot obliterate his great mercy. It comes to us daily, like a gorgeous sunrise. And—don't miss this!—he is faithful. He will do what he says. We can lean fully on him.

Perhaps the most stunning aspect about Jeremiah's great testimony of trust is the fact that he utters it in the bleakest of times.

God's faithful mercy surrounds you today. Wonder at it; then respond with praise. ✤

PRAYER

Give me eyes to see, Lord, your unfailing love ...

day211

IN HIS PRESENCE

Like the appearance of a rainbow in the clouds on a rainy day, so was the radiance around him. This was the appearance of the likeness of the glory of the LORD. When I saw it, I fell facedown, and I heard the voice of one speaking. EZEKIEL 1:28

John of the Cross, a sixteenth-century monk and mystic, is remembered for his passionate devotion to Christ. "I no longer want just to hear about you, beloved Lord, through messengers," he once wrote. "I no longer want to hear doctrines about you, nor to have my emotions stirred by people speaking of you. I yearn for your presence."

This should be the hunger of every redeemed heart—to be with God. To see him face to face. To bask in his presence. To revel in his grace and love.

Scripture says we were made by God and for God (see Colossians 1:16). He is our true home. No wonder we never quite fit anywhere else. As Augustine put it, "You have made us for yourself, O God. And our hearts are restless until they find their rest in you."

Of course, those who encounter God as Ezekiel did as described in this passage are bowled over and forever changed. Moses glowed. Jacob built altars. Job shut his mouth and, as far as we know, never questioned God again. David wrote songs and danced with all his might. Isaiah came unglued. Zechariah was struck dumb. Mary sang in adoring wonder.

One truth is that we are ever in the presence of God. We can go no place where he is not (see Psalm 139). Every moment of every day offers opportunities for worship.

Today, take advantage of each moment—mundane or miraculous—to respond to God's precious presence. ❖

PRAYER

Lord, I long to see you, to be with you . . .

OUR NEW AND IMPROVED HEARTS

I will give them an undivided heart and put a new spirit in them; I will remove from them their heart of stone and give them a heart of flesh. Then they will follow my decrees and be careful to keep my laws. They will be my people, and I will be their God.

EZEKIEL 11:19–20

"Change my heart, O God," the praise chorus goes. "Make it ever true. Change my heart, O God. Let me be like you."

It's a beloved song and a wonderful sentiment. But if you want to be theologically correct, it's an unnecessary request for Christians to make—sort of like praying for God to be with us.

The fact is, every believer in Jesus already has a changed heart. It's a done deal. That's the promise and the essence of the gospel, the new covenant. When you put your trust in Christ, an invisible but very real spiritual heart transplant occurs—your old, hard, sin-prone heart gets replaced with a new heart. That's what this passage in Ezekiel is alluding to—a new heart that responds to God and connects with him.

This explains why the apostle Paul speaks about believers having a brand-new nature (see 2 Corinthians 5:17). We are brand-new people with new desires and new capacities to honor God.

So, according to the Bible, the Christian life is a matter of learning to say no to the impulses of our unredeemed human nature and letting our new, true nature surface in our daily lives. The God who lives in us wants to direct us, fill us, use us and satisfy us. Becoming a fully devoted worshiper starts in the heart.

Today, consider singing that chorus this way, "Change my mind, O God. Let me see what's true. Change my mind, O God. You have made me new!" ✤

PRAYER

Change my mind, O God ...

FOR BETTER, FOR WORSE

Later I passed by, and when I looked at you and saw that you were old enough for love, I spread the corner of my garment over you and covered your naked body. I gave you my solemn oath and entered into a covenant with you, declares the Sovereign LORD, and you became mine. EZEKIEL 16:8

Ezekiel 16 is a tragic chapter that recites God's long-term love and faithfulness for Judah and the people's callous tendency to play with God's affections. Anyone who has ever felt the bitter sting of unrequited love—or worse, the piercing pain of betrayal—will identify with God's wounded heart.

The sobering truth is that the ancient Jews weren't the only ones who treated God in this manner. We all have a tendency toward spiritual adultery. We are forever tempted to chase after other gods.

The amazing thing is that, in spite of our hurtful habits, God doesn't cut his losses and move on. He keeps pursuing and wooing and loving.

How can you wrestle with these facts and not be moved? How can you not be changed? God wants you desperately, despite all your fickleness and failure. He wants you for his glory and for your deep, eternal happiness. Do you dare believe it?

Find a ring that you typically don't wear and put it on your right ring finger as a reminder of God's never-failing marriage vows to you. ❖

PRAYER

Father God, I pray that I might comprehend your love in a new way . . .

day**214**

MAKING A SPIRITUAL U-TURN

Rid yourselves of all the offenses you have committed, and get a new heart and a new spirit. Why will you die, people of Israel? For I take no pleasure in the death of anyone, declares the Sovereign LORD. Repent and live! EZEKIEL 18:31–32

What is repentance, and why is it important? Simply defined, the word means to "change one's mind," and it implies a turning away from sin to God.

Repentance is God's deepest wish for his creatures. He yearns for people to have life—spiritual life, eternal life. The clear message of Jesus is that our Creator longs for us to enjoy the richest existence imaginable (see John 10:10). He desperately wants us to experience his vast mercy and grace and to be spared his perfect yet severe justice. We cannot experience God's amazing favor, however, until, like the prodigal son of the New Testament, we acknowledge our foolish actions and make a U-turn for home.

Even after we've become the children of God through faith in Christ (see John 1:12), we need a kind of ongoing repentance. Daily we wander off course. Daily we need to stop, turn and come back to God. And every time we do this—every single time—we find God to be like the father in the prodigal son story. Arms open wide, eyes filled with joy and relief, ready to throw a party in our honor.

As the old country preachers used to say, "If that doesn't ring your bell, your clapper's broke."

As you go about your chores and routine today, allow each U-turn sign you see prompt you to thank God for his grace and mercy that awaits you as you turn back to him. ♣

PRAYER

God, thank you for calling me home . . .

EXHIBIT A FOR GOD'S TRUTH

Son of man, with one blow I am about to take away from you the delight of your eyes. Yet do not lament or weep or shed any tears.   EZEKIEL 24:16

The life of Gladys Aylward, a missionary to China during and after World War II, reveals a stirring story of faithful obedience to God despite incredible suffering.

Upon delivering the orphans she led to safety, Gladys was gravely ill and almost delirious. She had suffered beatings from the Japanese; she was ill from relapsing fever, typhus, pneumonia, malnutrition, shock and fatigue. Yet through her ordeal Gladys had learned to choose Christ over anything else life had to offer — so much so that she turned down a marriage proposal from the man she loved. Gladys knew she could not continue God's work with the orphaned children if she were married.

It is a lesson many obedient servants of God have had to learn. Take, for example, Ezekiel. There he was, the faithful prophet, tending to God's business, doing right, when, as an object lesson to the nation, God took his beloved wife. She had been the light of Ezekiel's life. What a terrible loss! Then came the odd — unique to this situation — command: Ezekiel was forbidden to mourn.

Ezekiel's experience is a powerful reminder that we are part of a story that is much bigger than our own private lives. We have important roles to play, and huge, cosmic realities are at stake — like God's reputation and his glory, as well as the need for a lost and rebellious world to be pierced by the power and trustworthiness of God.

When we suffer in this life but continue trusting God, we become exhibit A — walking advertisements for the truth and the power of the gospel. ✤

PRAYER

Father, when I hurt, give me the grace to refuse self-pity . . .

day216

THE GOD OF EARTH AND TIME

I will bring them back from captivity and return them to Upper Egypt, the land of their ancestry. There they will be a lowly kingdom ... "On that day I will make a horn grow for the Israelites, and I will open your mouth among them. Then they will know that I am the LORD."
EZEKIEL 29:14,21

Scholars note that at least one-fourth of the Bible was prophecy at the time it was written. In other words, one out of every four verses announced in advance what God was planning to do on earth! And many of these prophecies, like the one above about Egypt, have already been fulfilled.

So what difference does this make to one who wants to be a worshiper of God? Fulfilled prophecies show us God's faithfulness and trustworthiness. What he says he will do! We can count on him.

Prophecy also demonstrates the sovereignty of God. The world—despite appearances to the contrary—is not spinning wildly out of control, but moving toward its appointed end. God truly does have the whole world—and all of human history—in his good, big hands.

Finally, the inclusion of so much prophecy in the Bible accentuates God's love and concern for his people. He wants us to understand what lies ahead. He wants us to be prepared for all that is to come.

Today, as you look at the news headlines—probably including at least one story about tension in the Middle East—pause and worship the God of Egypt, Israel and the entire world. He is worthy to be praised! ✦

PRAYER

Father in heaven, my times are in your hands ...

MAKING REAL CHANGE

I will give you a new heart and put a new spirit in you; I will remove from you your heart of stone and give you a heart of flesh.   EZEKIEL 36:26

Two high school seniors concocted a plan to rid themselves of using foul language. Each time one heard the other curse, he would deliver a swift, hard punch to the offender's arm. At the end of this weeklong endeavor, both boys sported bruised, aching biceps. And their speech was just as crude as ever.

Willpower alone does not suffice. This is the message God proclaimed to the world through the prophet Ezekiel. Call it "new covenant theology." Under the old covenant, God gave his people laws on tablets of stone. Under the new arrangement, God gives his children totally new hearts. The old system pressured people from the outside; the new system empowers Christians from within.

Formerly, people were motivated by a sense of duty and obligation — "I ought to obey God." Now, because of the indwelling Christ, Christians are motivated by joy and holy passion — "I get to live for Christ!" We live differently because we are different. In the words of the apostle Paul, "Put on the new self, created to be like God in true righteousness and holiness" (Ephesians 4:24).

Stop trying to change yourself with your own power. It doesn't work. Instead, let Jesus bring the deep, fundamental changes of the new birth to the surface of your life. Lean on him and yield your will to his. This is the essence of a life of true worship.

Today, offer to Jesus as a sacrifice of worship an attitude or habit you want him to change. ✣

PRAYER

Lord, I offer you my heart to change . . .

day218

ZEALOUS FOR HIS REPUTATION

Therefore this is what the Sovereign LORD says: I will now restore the fortunes of Jacob and will have compassion on all the people of Israel, and I will be zealous for my holy name. EZEKIEL 39:25

God announced through Ezekiel that he was "zealous" for his name. Understand that God is not needy or insecure. He is not like the corrupt dictators of our time who demand allegiance using fear and intimidation and who plaster their pictures and monuments all over the countryside in a pathetic attempt to hang on to power. On the contrary, God says in a sense, "Worship me, make me the focus of your life because, quite simply, I deserve nothing less. I am the great treasure of the universe. To give your life to anything or anyone else would be illogical—and wrong."

All that God did in the time of Ezekiel, and all that he does now, is designed to show the world his greatness. And—here's the mind-boggling part—he calls us to embrace that same job description. *We* are to be zealous for God's glory. *We* are to pray continually that his name might be honored (see Matthew 6:9). *We* are to conduct our lives in such a way that everything we do—every single thing—enhances God's holy reputation (see 1 Corinthians 10:31).

In other words, live today so that people shake their heads in wonder, lift their eyes to heaven and say, "Wow. What an amazing God!" ✤

PRAYER

Lord, be the great passion of my life. Make me zealous for your glory. And cause my life to spread your righteous reputation ...

day219

HEAVINESS AND LIGHT

Then the Spirit lifted me up and brought me into the inner court, and the glory of the *LORD filled the temple.* Ezekiel 43:5

The great hymn "Immortal, Invisible" concludes with this verse: "Great Father of glory, pure Father of light, / Thine angels adore Thee, all veiling their sight; / All praise we would render; O help us to see / 'Tis only the splendor of light hideth Thee!"

Purity. Light. Brightness. Splendor—all to an infinite degree. This was Ezekiel's experience as, in a wild vision, he watched the glory of God fill the temple.

The Hebrew word translated *glory* refers literally to the heaviness or worth of something. The idea is brilliance and greatness, beauty and perfection. In the days of Moses, the glory of God took the form of an immense cloud or a bright pillar of fire. In John's visions in Revelation, the glory of God is accompanied by smoke, and it causes a sparkling effect. It is brighter than the sun itself. Because it is always such an awesome thing, people hide their eyes in fear when confronted with the unveiled glory of God. And they typically hug the ground, flattened by the breathtaking weight of his majesty.

Every day you are surrounded by the glory of God. And even harder to comprehend, you are indwelled by this same God of glory. Yes, you are his modern-day temple! The only question is whether or not you have eyes to see. Will you make yourself a fit habitation for him? And will you respond in reverence and worship?

Let each church building you pass today serve as a reminder of God's glory indwelling you. ✣

PRAYER

Fill me, O God, with your glory . . .

day220

LARGE AND IN CHARGE

He changes times and seasons; he deposes kings and raises up others. He gives wisdom to the wise and knowledge to the discerning.　Daniel 2:21

Years ago, an American missionary couple serving on the African continent was given a telegram containing the terrible news that their son had been killed in an automobile accident back in the United States. They wired back a two-word answer: *No accident.*

No accident? How could they respond this way in the face of such tragic news? Only because they knew that God is sovereign and that he oversees the affairs of men, women, cultures and entire nations. He determines the course of world events; he removes kings and sets others on the throne. He "gives wisdom to the wise and knowledge to the discerning," said Daniel.

When tough times come for you and your family—death, illness, divorce, financial reversal—how do you respond? With hand-wringing, sleepless nights, desperation and fear? Such reactions are certainly typical, even understandable. Yet the men and women who place their trust in our Sovereign God can know that this is not a random, senseless universe. It is under the control of its Creator. *There are no accidents.*

That's good to know in a world where words like *terrorism*, *bankruptcy* and *unemployment* strike fear in our hearts. We have no guarantees of safety, security, health, wealth and unending blessedness, but we do have the assurance that the God who determines the course of world events, removes kings and sets others on the throne and gives wisdom to the wise and knowledge to the discerning is pleased to allow us to call him "Father." ✤

PRAYER

Father, here are my fears . . .

day221

NONNEGOTIABLE

Now when Daniel learned that the decree had been published, he went home to his upstairs room where the windows opened toward Jerusalem. Three times a day he got down on his knees and prayed, giving thanks to his God, just as he had done before.

DANIEL 6:10

Daniel certainly built his relationship with God on a foundation of love and trust. Prayer was as natural to Daniel as breathing and eating. It was the expression of his heart. It was conversation with his God. Throughout his life, from the time he was brought as a young captive into the king's court through each succeeding administration in which he served, Daniel practiced daily prayer. It was his lifelong habit.

So when the edict was handed down that anyone praying to any god would be put to death, Daniel didn't flinch. He refused to let anything keep him from spending time with God. It was, for him, a nonnegotiable. Nothing mattered more than his communion with God—not food, drink, the opinion of others or even a death threat.

Contrast our often tepid prayer lives with that of Daniel, who refused to let a death threat keep him from going before the Lord openly and regularly. If we're honest, most of us struggle with simply communicating with God on a regular basis. We're pressed for time, concerned about how others see us, not as consistent in our prayer life as we know we should be. For many Christians, prayer is the first thing to go when life gets hectic and out of control.

Fortunately, God meets us where we are, not where we ought to be. Confess your lack of prayer and even your lack of desire to pray, and ask God to fan the flame. ✤

PRAYER

Father, fan the flame of prayer in my life ...

day222

THIS MEANS WAR

Then he continued, "Do not be afraid, Daniel. Since the first day that you set your mind to gain understanding and to humble yourself before your God, your words were heard, and I have come in response to them. But the prince of the Persian kingdom resisted me twenty-one days. Then Michael, one of the chief princes, came to help me, because I was detained there with the king of Persia." DANIEL 10:12–13

Have you noticed how many distractions, obstacles and detours you encounter on your way to your weekly worship service or even your own daily devotions? Weird, out-of-the-ordinary kinds of things that keep you from spending time with God and other Christians?

Daniel 10:12–13 makes it clear that there is conflict in the spiritual realm when God's people pray (see also Ephesians 6:10–18). Prayer is one of our mightiest weapons in this battle—the supernatural equivalent of air support in a military campaign—and our enemies will try to neutralize this advantage and keep us from praying if they can.

We must recognize the reality of Satan, demons and spiritual warfare in our walk with the Lord. (Jesus certainly did! See his confrontation with Satan in Matthew 4:1–11.) If not, we're sitting ducks. This battle is difficult enough when fighting our own sin and spiritual inertia. Don't make it harder by underestimating or completely discounting the truth about our opposition and the intensity of the conflict. That's a sure-fire way to become a casualty in the spiritual war.

Make an assessment today of the defenses you already have in place to conduct spiritual warfare. Based on your evaluation, devise a strategy so that you will be battle-ready when Satan and his cohorts attempt to derail you and undermine your faith. ✤

PRAYER

Lord, open my eyes to the reality of the battle in the spiritual realm ...

day223

KEEPING WORSHIP REAL

Though you, Israel, commit adultery, do not let Judah become guilty. Do not go to Gilgal; do not go up to Beth Aven. And do not swear, "As surely as the LORD lives!"

HOSEA 4:15

Home for the summer after her freshman year in college, Beth was eager to share what God had been doing in her life. Her pastor invited her to share her story during a service. She hesitated, confident in her spirit but not in her speech. "Would you like me to ask Mr. Kelly to give you some tips?" the pastor asked. Although known primarily as the director of their incredible choir, Mr. Kelly was quite a public speaker.

His instruction helped immensely. As her last lesson ended, Beth handed Mr. Kelly a small gift. He read the note she had written about how God had blessed her and how grateful she was that Mr. Kelly had helped her praise God through her speaking.

"There's something you should know about me," he said. "I'm not a Christian. I'm an agnostic."

Beth was shocked. "But the choir? Your solos? The hymns? The amazing anthems glorifying God?"

"I simply love good music and pulling off a good performance," he replied.

Look up the word *hypocrisy* in an illustrated dictionary, and a picture of Mr. Kelly might well be in the margin, alongside the people of Gilgal and Beth Aven. Now look at the word's origin in the Greek, *hupokrisis*, "playing of a part on a stage." God beseeches his people, as he did through the prophet Hosea, to worship him without pretense. Pause right now to consider your own worship habits. What, if any, part of your worship is merely playing a part? ✚

PRAYER

O God, please show me any way in which I am only playing a part…

THE SEEDS OF RIGHTEOUSNESS

Sow righteousness for yourselves, reap the fruit of unfailing love, and break up your un-plowed ground; for it is time to seek the LORD, until he comes and showers his righteousness on you.   HOSEA 10:12

An impossible task. How could this ground ever yield a harvest?

"Let us trust Mother Nature," some say. "Her drops of sun and rain, the nutrients in her soil—these are the true means of growth."

"What?" others counter. "Stop your poetic ramblings. They don't begin to disguise your laziness. We have days of work ahead of us to have any hope of producing crops. Especially with this drought."

Faith or good works? The answer in farming is both. And when the farmer is the Great Farmer and the soil is our own hearts, the answer is the same. God will shine his light on us, shower us with righteousness and feed us from his Word. But we must get our hearts ready, we must break up any hard ground, we must clear out the rocks and stones, we must allow seeds of only high quality to be planted.

What hard ground do you need to break up today so God will find the soil of your heart ready for planting and receptive to the best seed? Confess those areas to God and ask that he will warm, water and feed a righteous heart, willing and able to praise him. ✛

PRAYER

God, please feed my heart . . .

OFFER YOUR SACRIFICE OF PRAISE

Take words with you and return to the LORD. *Say to him: "Forgive all our sins and receive us graciously, that we may offer the fruit of our lips."*   HOSEA 14:2

Giving thanks before serving holy communion, the celebrant says, "We celebrate the memorial of our redemption, O Father, in this sacrifice of praise and thanksgiving. Recalling his death, resurrection, and ascension, we offer you these gifts."

These words are from the *Book of Common Prayer*, the worship "manual" of the Episcopal Church, the expression of faith a group of believers have "in common." But the call to a sacrifice of praise and thanksgiving is for individuals as well. And it has gone out for millennia.

Put it all before the Lord, said the prophets and priests. Offer your petitions. Offer yourself. Why a sacrifice of praise? Sacrifice of praise refers to thank offerings to God—real, heartfelt repentance, not just a "going through the motions" nod to him. It is a continual reminder that we are to offer something, something of value.

Sometimes the offering is costly. "It's a real sacrifice of time," complains the person who really would rather not part with those precious minutes. "I'd be sacrificing my career advancement," says the employee who debates cutting back on hours to care for a family member. "I'd be sacrificing feeling hurt and deprived," thinks the one not used to giving thanks during the hard times.

The author of the letter to the Hebrews echoed Hosea 14:2. "Through Jesus, therefore, let us continually offer to God a sacrifice of praise—the fruit of lips that openly profess his name" (Hebrews 13:15).

Offer your petitions today. Offer yourself. Offer the sacrifice of praise. ✤

PRAYER

Lord God, please accept my offering of praise . . .

A CHANGE OF HEART

"Even now," declares the LORD, *"return to me with all your heart, with fasting and weeping and mourning."*   JOEL 2:12

"But God, they are *still* heading in the wrong direction! I wonder if they are even able to change. And when are you going to say 'Enough is enough' to them?"

Repent, turn, change. This is what the prophet Joel had been telling the people of Judah. As a faithful communicator of God's message to his people, did he wonder if God's offer was for a limited time? Was there small print that said, "Must be redeemed by ____"?

"Yes, Joel, my people can change," God seems to say. "And I continue to be gracious and merciful and slow to anger. Tell the people again, 'Return to the Lord your God.' My offer still stands."

We too can marvel at God's patience and God's offer. The same invitation, the same call to repentance hits our ears. "Turn to me now. Give me your hearts." How are you going to respond?

Bryan Duncan expressed his gratitude that our gracious God could accept and redeem him in the song "A Heart Like Mine." That God could want him—want you—and seek him—seek you. How could his heart be worthy, asks Duncan. But he knows it is God's redemption that makes it so.

Our response? With abandon, every heartbeat can be given to God. Every heartbeat of a redeemed heart can beat to a new purpose.

Repent, turn, change. Come to God today with "fasting and weeping and mourning" for those areas in your life that need a change of heart. ✣

PRAYER

My Lord, who is gracious and merciful, my heart beats for you . . .

DISCIPLINED IN LOVE

Hear this word, people of Israel, the word the LORD has spoken against you—against the whole family I brought up out of Egypt: "You only have I chosen of all the families of the earth; therefore I will punish you for all your sins."   AMOS 3:1–2

"You don't love me anymore. That's why you're doing this."

A father is about to punish his child. This accusation is not completely unexpected—after all, didn't he throw the same allegation at his own father? Nevertheless, it catches him up short.

"Don't love you anymore? Are you *kidding*? It's because I love you that I'm doing this. This is going to hurt me more than it hurts you."

The children of God had been riding along on a caravan of prosperity. "Times are great. And with a king like Jeroboam, we can't lose. Who needs God when you're sittin' pretty like us?" Israel is about to be called up short. They are sitting ... but it's not pretty.

"Hear this word, people of Israel, the word the LORD has spoken against you," warned the prophet Amos. "You only have I chosen of all the families of the earth; therefore I will punish you for all your sins."

God rescued them from Egypt and cared for them in the wilderness. Wanderers, yet still watched over. "Know then in your heart that as a man disciplines his son, so the LORD your God disciplines you" (Deuteronomy 8:5).

This is the way of God with his people, his beloved children. How has God brought his loving discipline into your life? Today, thank him for correcting your course because he loves you. ♣

PRAYER

Father God, when I sense that you are disciplining me, I will ...

WATERED-DOWN WORSHIP?

Away with the noise of your songs! I will not listen to the music of your harps. But let justice roll on like a river, righteousness like a never-failing stream!   AMOS 5:23–24

> There are those who are asking the devotees of civil rights, "When will you be satisfied?" ... We can never be satisfied as long as our bodies, heavy with the fatigue of travel, cannot gain lodging in the motels of the highways and the hotels of the cities. We cannot be satisfied as long as the Negro's basic mobility is from a smaller ghetto to a larger one ... No, no, we are not satisfied, and we will not be satisfied until justice rolls down like waters and righteousness like a mighty stream."

The speaker was Dr. Martin Luther King Jr., the speech given on the steps of the Lincoln Memorial on August 28, 1963. It is what has come to be known as his "I Have a Dream" speech. His dream was for justice; his words were from the book of Amos. He had used the same words in December 1955 to encourage the African-Americans of Montgomery, Alabama, at the start of the successful 381-day bus boycott—a boycott that had begun with the quiet bravery of Rosa Parks.

Had the boy Martin heard the prophet's call for justice from his father's pulpit in Atlanta's Ebenezer Baptist Church? In the days before the boycott, had he preached from this passage as a young pastor there in Montgomery?

The call for justice is linked forever with the call to worship. The heart of God is grieved when our worship is hollow; our adoration becomes an abomination when we ignore injustice and the oppression of others. ✜

PRAYER

O God, let justice roll on like a river in ...

day**229**

THE LORD WILL BE KING!

Deliverers will go up on Mount Zion to govern the mountains of Esau. And the kingdom will be the LORD's.   OBADIAH 21

"Are we there yet?" the voice implores from the backseat. The driver sighs. It's going to be a long trip. Like the child on a car trip barely begun, we implore from the backseat, "Father God, are we there yet? When will this agony be over?"

"How long ... how long ... how long, O Lord?" God's people have implored from the backseat since the trip out of Egypt. But the Father's hands are firmly on the wheel—the destination will be reached, the goal will be achieved, his kingdom will come. As the prophet Obadiah preached, "The kingdom will be the LORD's."

Benedictine nun Julian of Norwich was born in 1342. She became deathly ill in her early thirties, but God miraculously gave her not only her health but a unique, long-term perspective. In *Revelations of Divine Love* she wrote:

> *I saw full surely that he changeth never his purpose in no manner of thing, nor never shall, without end. For there was no thing unknown to him in his rightful ordinance from without beginning. And therefore all thing was [sic] set in order ere anything was made, as it should stand without end; and no manner of thing shall fail of that point ...*

At times, life seems amiss. The job search stalls. Health concerns arise. A spouse walks out the door. In the midst of these moments, it is easy to think that victory has been delayed, the final destination is far off. Yet, we need to remember that God is in control.

Worship the King. He is already there, awaiting you. ✣

> **PRAYER**

Father God, your kingdom come; your will be done ...

WHEN ALL HOPE IS LOST

When my life was ebbing away, I remembered you, LORD, and my prayer rose to you, to your holy temple. JONAH 2:7

Helen Keller was a famous example of a "hopeless case" who proved to be not so hopeless after all. But lesser known is the fact that Anne Sullivan, the woman who drew Helen Keller out of her dark and silent world, was once considered a hopeless case too.

Anne was born in Massachusetts in April 1866 to poor Irish immigrants. Her father worked little and drank much, and her mother suffered from tuberculosis. Anne herself contracted trachoma, which went untreated and resulted in near-blindness. When her mother died, Anne and her brother, Jimmy, wound up in the state poorhouse in Tewksbury, where they boarded with prostitutes, mental patients and other troubled people. Before long, Jimmy died and Anne was left with no caring relative, little eyesight and no prospects for a future.

The turning point came when a team from the Board of Charities arrived at the poorhouse. Anne literally threw herself at the head of the team and begged to be given an education at a school for the blind. Her plea was heard, and at age 14 she was enrolled in the Perkins Institute for the Blind, where in six years she went from elementary school classes to graduation as valedictorian. During that time, a brilliant operation restored her sight, and Anne thereafter devoted herself to the care of the blind.

When we're out of hope, that's the time to turn our thoughts to God and hope again. Remember Jonah's prayer today when you feel overwhelmed or without hope. Turn your thoughts once again to God. ✢

PRAYER

Lord, I need hope today...

day231

AMEN TO MERCY

He prayed to the LORD, "Isn't this what I said, LORD, when I was still at home? That is what I tried to forestall by fleeing to Tarshish. I knew that you are a gracious and compassionate God, slow to anger and abounding in love, a God who relents from sending calamity."

JONAH 4:2

A man was all in favor when his church decided to start running evangelistic small groups in members' homes. He even volunteered to host one of the groups. Imagine his surprise, though, when he opened his door on the first night and saw standing there the neighbor about whom he had called the police several times for playing music too loudly and letting his dogs bark. He slammed the door shut.

It's a reaction as old as Jonah.

The recital of God's graciousness and compassion, his slowness to anger and unfailing love, constitutes a virtual refrain in the Old Testament (see Exodus 34:6; Psalm 86:15; 103:8; Joel 2:13), and everywhere but here they are recited to the praise of God. In the mouth of Jonah, God's great qualities of kindness became recast, sneeringly, as liabilities. The reluctant prophet wanted to see the Assyrians, his nation's archenemies, served out with punishment, not mercy.

If giving this kind of response to God's grace wasn't going to be a temptation for us as well, it's not likely the Lord would have told the story about a young man who went sullen over the merciful treatment shown his prodigal brother (see Luke 15:11–32). Nor would the Bible include Jesus' teaching about workers hired early in the day who complained about the equal payment to people hired later that same day (see Matthew 20:1–16).

God has grace in store even for people we do not like and for those we think do not deserve it. Commit to praying for someone you find hard to accept. ✤

PRAYER

Lord, help me to show your grace ...

WHEN YOU FACE PERSECUTION

But now many nations are gathered against you. They say, "Let her be defiled, let our eyes gloat over Zion!" But they do not know the thoughts of the LORD; they do not understand his plan, that he has gathered them like sheaves to the threshing floor.   MICAH 4:11–12

In part, Micah may have been looking ahead to the near future when God would give the Israelites victory over their foes. But Micah may have also been looking toward the end times, when God will decisively destroy the enemies gathered against his people. With either perspective, the principle is the same: God protects his own.

That's good to remember in a world where claiming the name of Christ can put your life at risk. Did you know that more Christians were martyred in the twentieth century—about 26 million—than in all the preceding centuries of the Christian era combined—(an estimated 17 million before the year 1900)? Did you know that today around 200 million Christians in 60 nations face persecution in some form?

We might reasonably ask where God is for these people. But he is suffering with them, and preparing a glory for them weightier by far than what they have endured (see Romans 8:18).

We might also ask why all this matters for us, we in America who face little persecution. Some believe that as our society embraces generalized spirituality and relative morality, people who defend the exclusive claims of Christ will become an embattled minority, resembling the early church.

Pray for the persecuted church today. Also, if anyone is persecuting you, ask Christ to reveal himself to them, as he did to the persecutor Saul of Tarsus, so they may escape the judgment awaiting those who set themselves against God's people. ❖

PRAYER

Protect me, Lord, I pray . . .

SIMPLE GOODNESS

He has shown you, O mortal, what is good. And what does the LORD require of you? To act justly and to love mercy and to walk humbly with your God.   MICAH 6:8

If you read the verses preceding Micah 6:8, you will find some rhetorical questions the prophet posed on behalf of his fellow Israelites. God had indicted the nation for plunging into all manner of immorality and idolatry. So Micah asked, "Will the Lord be pleased with thousands of rams, with ten thousand rivers of olive oil? Shall I offer my firstborn for my transgression, the fruit of my body for the sin of my soul?" (Micah 6:7). Answer: *no!* The people needed no new act of contrition but rather to start living out the simple commands of justice and righteousness that God had already given them.

How could the Israelites have been so foolish as to think they could buy off God? But wait! Do we ever think we can make up for our sins by going to more church services? Volunteering for more ministry projects? Adding a zero to the check we drop in the offering plate? Praying until our knees bear a permanent impression of the carpet? Fasting till we look like famine victims? Sometimes we may. In this we're no wiser than the guilty Israelites.

In fact, we who know about grace coming through faith in Christ have even less justification for trying to buy off God with worship than did our Old Testament predecessors. We can make no "sacrifice" that will strike a single one of our sins off God's ledger, nor should we try. We have only to believe in God's Son and then do what we know is right.

Do what is right. Love mercy. Walk humbly with your God. Spend time in silence before him right now. Ask him to reveal to you where you need to be more obedient, more merciful and more humble. ✤

> **PRAYER**

Help me, Lord, to do what I know is right...

THE WAR BIBLE

The LORD is good, a refuge in times of trouble. He cares for those who trust in him.

NAHUM 1:7

Herbert, an aging World War II veteran, set his granddaughter Alyssa on his knee one day and told her that he had a special gift for her. He brought out a small leather-covered Bible. "I carried this Bible with me all through the war," he explained. "As I tramped across Europe, fighting battles or just wondering what was going to happen next, this book was my comfort. It helped me trust that God would take care of me and my wife and baby back home."

Next, Herbert opened the Bible to a well-thumbed page and read Nahum 1:7 aloud. "This verse was my special promise," he told Alyssa. "In the war I clung to the truth that God was with me, even in times of trouble. Somehow, knowing that God was aware of my fear helped me enter the refuge of his peace. And after all these years, what I know is that the Lord is good."

Reading Nahum on the march in Europe, Herbert may or may not have realized that this little prophetic book was written in a context of war similar to what he was experiencing. The "Nazis" of Nahum's day were the Assyrians, who had already conquered the northern kingdom of Israel. Would they conquer Judah too? No, the Lord would be a refuge to protect the remnant of his followers in the land.

The Lord is still good. He knows each of us by name and knows what we face in the "battles" of our lives. We can trust that when trouble comes he will be our strong refuge. ♣

> **PRAYER**

Be my safe place, O God, my God . . .

MADE RIGHT BY FAITH ALONE

See, the enemy is puffed up; his desires are not upright—but the righteous person will live by his faithfulness.
         HABAKKUK 2:4

That's one small step for a man, one giant leap for mankind.

Ask not what your country can do for you, but what you can do for your country.

Give me liberty, or give me death.

Most Americans—hopefully!—can identify those quotes as being spoken by Neil Armstrong, John F. Kennedy and Patrick Henry, respectively. They were words that, when they were spoken, galvanized a nation and changed the course of history.

Less well-known to modern people, but no less pivotal, are these words from the prophet Habakkuk in approximately 600 BC: "The righteous person will live by his faithfulness." This message—just three words in the original Hebrew text—echoed by the apostle Paul in Romans 1:17, set forth the uniquely Biblical message that we are made right with God not by any works of righteousness of our own, but strictly by faith. This doctrine of justification by faith sets Christianity apart. It also makes it difficult for many people to come to terms with God's wonderful salvation. We don't do anything to earn it; we don't add anything to it; we just receive it by his grace, through faith—period.

The truth that we are made right with God by faith, not works, changed the lives of great men and women down through the centuries and helped launch the Protestant Reformation. Salvation is the gift of God from first to last. Let the beauty and the wonder of that reality cause you to bow before our gracious God in adoration, gratitude and praise. ❧

PRAYER

Lord, thank you that I am made right with you by faith . . .

A FATHER'S JOYFUL SONG

The LORD your God is with you, the Mighty Warrior who saves. He will take great delight in you; in his love he will no longer rebuke you, but will rejoice over you with singing.   ZEPHANIAH 3:17

Ask any parent if there is any more difficult or time-consuming job than raising a child. You lose sleep, patience, money, time, hair and, occasionally, your sanity. You make unbelievable sacrifices for a person who has no marketable skills, adds nothing to the family finances, makes incredible demands on you at all hours of the day and night and doesn't even say "Thank you." And yet ...

When it's time for bed or even a nap, there is nothing more satisfying than holding that child close to your heart. For many parents, these are their most cherished moments.

It seems unbelievable, but that is how God feels about you. Zephaniah 3:17 says, "He will take great delight in you; in his love he will no longer rebuke you, but will rejoice over you with singing." Does that not sound like a picture of a proud parent, holding a child close, totally content just to be together?

As amazing as it seems, God thoroughly enjoys spending time with you. Remember that, especially on those days when it would be easier just to roll over and reset the alarm or turn a deaf ear to his call. ✤

PRAYER

Father, to know that you want to spend time with me makes me feel ...

day237

FOR THE GLORY THAT WILL BE

"But now be strong, Zerubbabel," declares the LORD. *"Be strong, Joshua son of Jozadak, the high priest. Be strong, all you people of the land," declares the* LORD, *"and work. For I am with you," declares the* LORD *Almighty.* HAGGAI 2:4

At age 16 in 1895, Edward bought his first camera and took 50 pictures. When he developed the film, however, he was distressed to see that only one had turned out—a picture of his sister by the piano. Edward's father criticized the effort, causing Edward to contemplate giving up photography. But then his mother praised the one successful photo. With this encouragement, Edward Steichen went on to become one of the world's greatest photographers.

Timely encouragement can make the difference between premature surrender and glorious victory. In the fall of 520 BC, the Jewish exiles who had returned to Jerusalem started rebuilding the temple. Yet as the days passed, instead of being proud that their work represented a turning point in the nation's religious life, they became disappointed in the structure they saw taking shape in front of them. Stone by stone, they were putting up the best worship house they could manage, but they knew it fell far short of the original temple's grandeur. They just did not have the resources Solomon had.

That's when God stepped in to encourage the builders. For the present, he assured them of his presence. For the future, he painted a picture of the glory that would in time come to the temple. His encouragement gave them the extra incentive they needed to finish construction.

When we are attempting something for the glory of God, he has the same encouragement for us. What is on your desk or on your to-do list that is overwhelming you? Remember God's words of encouragement and renew your commitment to keep on going. ❖

PRAYER

Let me know your nearness, God . . .

CHRIST, OUR PRECIOUS JEWEL

"See, the stone I have set in front of Joshua! There are seven eyes on that one stone, and I will engrave an inscription on it," says the LORD Almighty, "and I will remove the sin of this land in a single day."　　　　　　　　　　　　　ZECHARIAH 3:9

It was February 10, 1908, and Amsterdam diamond cutter Joseph Asscher was feeling extremely nervous. This was the day set for Asscher to cut the largest diamond ever found—the Cullinan diamond, weighing 3,106 carats (1.37 pounds). In attendance were representatives of the stone's owner, Britain's King Edward VII, as well as notary publics, a doctor and two nurses.

Asscher had spent two months studying the rough diamond and making special tools for cutting and polishing this gem of unheard-of size. A slight miscalculation in his attack and the stone would shatter into a thousand pieces. Slowly and carefully, Asscher lifted his mallet. Then, with finesse, he struck the blade. Nothing happened. Screwing up his courage again, Asscher struck a second time. This time the stone split perfectly. Asscher promptly fainted, then spent the next two weeks in a hospital recovering from nervous exhaustion.

The jewel that Zechariah saw in his vision may not have looked much like the Cullinan diamond, but it was much more valuable. In the possession of Jeshua (first high priest after the Jewish exile), the stone in the vision had seven "eyes," or facets, indicating total awareness. Theologians concur: This jewel represents the Messiah, our Lord Jesus. His is the name engraved on the stone. He is the one who wipes out sins.

It is remarkable to consider that we, in a sense, "possess" this matchless jewel. If Asscher trembled before a hunk of compressed carbon, we should be in awe that the Spirit of Christ dwells within us. In the words of 2 Corinthians 4:7, we have "treasure" inside us! ✣

PRAYER

Lord Jesus, I cherish the gift of your Spirit . . .

NO POSERS ALLOWED

Ask all the people of the land and the priests, "When you fasted and mourned in the fifth and seventh months for the past seventy years, was it really for me that you fasted? And when you were eating and drinking, were you not just feasting for yourselves?"

ZECHARIAH 7:5–6

According to polling data, in a typical week in the United States

- 43 percent of adults attend a religious service
- 25 percent of all adults attend Sunday school
- 42 percent of adults read the Bible
- Nearly 80 percent of adults pray

In view of all this religious activity, the question that begs to be asked is, So why isn't our nation more righteous? The answer is simple: It's perilously easy to act religious without really caring much about God.

Of course, hypocrisy is nothing new. In the period after the Jewish exiles returned to Judah from Babylon, they asked God whether or not they should continue to fast in the fifth and seventh months as they had done during the exile to mourn the destruction of Jerusalem. God essentially replied, "You weren't really fasting for me while you were in exile, and to this day you're still thinking of yourselves when it comes to worship." Harsh words. It makes one wonder what God would say about *our* worship.

How many of the 43 percent of adults who attend a religious service do so for selfish purposes instead of honoring God? What portion of the 80 percent who pray do it to give themselves a sense of calm rather than to bring themselves into line with God's will?

We may not be among those who have self-serving motives for our worship activity, but given God's attitude toward hypocrisy, it behooves us to check from time to time to make sure. ✣

PRAYER

Judge my motives, Lord . . .

THE FACE IN THE CRUCIBLE

This third I will put into the fire; I will refine them like silver and test them like gold. They will call on my name and I will answer them; I will say, "They are my people," and they will say, "The LORD is our God." ZECHARIAH 13:9

Kay Arthur begins her book *As Silver Refined* by describing the patient labor of a craftsman as he builds a fire, crushes silver ore, fills his crucible with the mineral, watches the metal melt and impurities rise to the top and repeatedly reheats the silver and skims off the dross. Then Arthur writes, "Once more he bends over the crucible, and this time he catches his breath. There it is! In the silver he sees what he has waited for so patiently: A clear image of himself, distinct and sharp."

It's easy to see why Biblical writers turned to the practice of metal refinement for symbols of spiritual realities (see Psalm 12:6; 66:10; Proverbs 17:3; 27:21). In Zechariah's case, a remnant of people in the land were to be purified by their circumstances so they would renew their covenant with God. But the message is of more than one of historical interest; we too may be refined like silver. God uses the flames of tribulation to burn away sinful impurities from our spirit so that his image in us is distinct and sharp.

But let's not be overly pious about our suffering, particularly that which is due to our own actions. If you sense that your current hardship may be God's way of purifying you and bringing out his image in your life, dedicate yourself to cooperate with him.

Thank God today for the refining process you are undergoing right now. ❖

PRAYER

Purify my heart, Lord . . .

ONLY OUR BEST WILL DO

"When you offer blind animals for sacrifice, is that not wrong? When you sacrifice lame or diseased animals, is that not wrong? Try offering them to your governor! Would he be pleased with you? Would he accept you?" says the LORD Almighty.   MALACHI 1:8

In the movie trilogy of the *Lord of the Rings* directed by Peter Jackson, there were battle scenes with scores of soldiers wearing chain mail. The designers decided that interconnected plastic rings would look most realistic on screen. So a pair of young men spent three and a half years linking 12.5 million plastic rings by hand for all the soldier costumes. In an interview, one of the young men raved about the experience.

Many people found the *Lord of the Rings* movies to be good entertainment, but would you want to spend three and a half years of your life attaching one plastic ring to another? Every day people pour their souls into endeavors—like beating their time on the running track by a fraction of a second or putting together a marketing plan that will knock the socks off a client. The point is not that anything is wrong with these pursuits, but rather, do we give to God our very best, as others give to their vocations and avocations?

God criticized the priests of Israel for offering flawed animals on the altar even though the law clearly stated that God was to get only unblemished beasts. You can almost hear the hurt in God's voice because the flawed offerings showed how little the people cared about him. He must be hurt the same way when we approach our ministries in a slipshod, good-enough-for-church-work way. How thrilled he is when we offer our lives as living sacrifices each day (see Romans 12:1)!

Review your agenda for today. Commit to giving your best in each and every endeavor as an act of worship. ✤

PRAYER

Lord, I offer you . . .

I-DOLATRY

"Surely the day is coming; it will burn like a furnace. All the arrogant and every evildoer will be stubble, and the day that is coming will set them on fire," says the LORD Almighty. "Not a root or a branch will be left to them."　　　　MALACHI 4:1

Oscar-winning actress Meryl Streep once commented in an interview on the rampant pride in Hollywood. "It's sort of exhausting, this self-congratulatory atmosphere in which the movie community lives. It's unbearable. We're not that important in the world, but we certainly think we are."

While pride is one of the classic seven deadly sins, it has also long been recognized as being the most fundamental sin. Pride is what caused Lucifer to be cast out of heaven; he preferred to be devil-in-chief rather than an angel commander saluting God. Pride in who we are or what we own or what we have accomplished likewise causes us to put ourselves in the place only God should occupy.

The Jews in Malachi's time had seen arrogant people temporarily getting away with doing what they wanted instead of obeying God. And so the people had concluded, "It is futile to serve God" (Malachi 3:14). But God assured everyone that the arrogant would in time certainly go through the fire of destruction—and a most thorough destruction at that (see Malachi 4:1).

Catherine of Siena reported that God said to her, "You are she who is not, and I am Who Is." Of course, each of us has value that has been given to us by God, and there is such a thing as acceptable pride in oneself. But in comparison to who God is, we are nothing. Let us put no other god—certainly not ourselves—before him.

Let your pride in your work—whether at home, school, or the office—take a backseat to God today. ♣

PRAYER

Forgive me for my pride, Lord. May I put you first, always ...

day243

THE POWER OF ONE NAME

She will give birth to a son, and you are to give him the name Jesus, because he will save his people from their sins. MATTHEW 1:21

As the new millennium was about to begin, Bryan Brand and his wife were hosting a Bible study on the book of Acts in their home. They noticed how people in the Scriptures always responded very strongly to the name of Jesus. From those observations, Bryan got the idea to create billboards around St. Louis on which simply the name of Jesus would appear.

The very first sign was put up in November 1999. Like those that appeared subsequently, it featured white letters on green background to mimic interstate signs. The signs carried no additional words. Since the Jesus Name Project (as it was called) began, testimonies have been shared about marriages saved, forgiveness extended and God's working in other ways—all through the power of one name.

For two millennia prior to Bryan Brand's brainstorm, the power of Jesus' name has resulted in freeing people from their sinful, self-destructive lifestyles. Since an angel instructed an uneducated carpenter to name his wife's child Jesus, the world has witnessed unimagined wonders that are rooted in Jesus' name.

No doubt, you can attest to how simply whispering that name has calmed your fears. No day is complete for the believer without saying or singing his name. Whether with an ancient hymn like "At the Name of Jesus," the favorite Gaither tune "There's Just Something About That Name" or a new worship chorus that celebrates the Savior, sing it out today as a reminder that he takes delight in saving us from desperate situations. ❧

PRAYER

Lord Jesus, I need you today . . .

TURN, TURN, TURN

From that time on Jesus began to preach, "Repent, for the kingdom of heaven has come near." MATTHEW 4:17

In the '60s, The Byrds recorded and released a song entitled "Turn, Turn, Turn." Although they were a secular rock group, this particular single on the Top 40 charts was straight out of Scripture. With clarity and a singable tune, they taught a generation of flower children the words Solomon recorded in Ecclesiastes 3. The essence of the lyrics is quite straightforward. Every season of life with its distinct—and varied—occasions demands a unique response. Wise is the person who faces the music—whether a jig or a dirge.

But the kind of turning Jesus invites us to is not seasonal. It is a turning that we must make throughout our lives. Because the broad stroke of sin paints us into a corner when we feel like rejoicing as well as when we feel like crying, we will do well to seek the Lord on a daily basis. It is always appropriate to turn from our self-centered ways and turn toward him.

When we fail to go to the Lord regularly, it takes its toll. Seasons of joy and contentment become fewer and farther between. Worship becomes difficult and less meaningful.

As long as we are on this earth, we need to practice repentance. Daily. Hourly. By the minute, if necessary.

Today is your chance to turn, confess your sins and accept the Lord's forgiveness. ✣

PRAYER

I'm sorry, Father, for . . .

THIS LITTLE LIGHT OF YOURS

In the same way, let your light shine before others, that they may see your good deeds and glorify your Father in heaven.   MATTHEW 5:16

Before both the summer and winter Olympic Games, the ritual is the same. A torch is lit from an eternal flame atop Mount Olympus in Greece before it is transported to the country where the Games will be hosted. Months prior to the opening ceremonies, as excitement for the Olympics builds, ordinary citizens are given the privilege of carrying the torch, each for several hundred yards. Little by little, mile by mile, the Olympic flame makes its way toward the stadium in the city where the Olympics will be held. Local newspapers may herald the identity of individuals who run in the torch relay, but the significance is in the flame, calling attention to the event it symbolizes.

Similarly, Christlike behavior and acts "shine before others." They are not intended to draw attention to individual people, but to point to the goodness of God. Just as the Olympic torch reminds those who see it of the events soon to follow, so our good works remind others of the source of all goodness. But it's awfully easy for our passion for service to be doused. Worries over finances, stressing out over teenage kids, spending too much time with our personal hobbies—all can dim our flame. Fortunately, hearing the words of Jesus kindles a renewed desire to let our lights shine.

Do something today that will allow your good deeds to shine for your heavenly Father. Make an anonymous donation to a local charity. Sweep a neighbor's sidewalk without telling him or her. If anyone asks, say you are doing it for Jesus! ❖

PRAYER

Lord, show me ways to shine for you . . .

TRY A CANDID CONVERSATION

*And when you pray, do not keep on babbling like pagans, for they think they will be
because of their many words.* MATTHEW /

The hit Broadway musical *Fiddler on the Roof* offers its audience not only some first-class entertainment but also a wonderful refresher course on intimate, candid prayer with God. The main character in the play is Tevye, a poor milkman who models candor when talking to God. He brings up both small things—such as his poor son-in-law's need for a sewing machine—and big things—like world peace.

Can't you hear Tevye as he gestures with animated passion and looks up to the sky as he speaks? Although many prayers punctuate the musical, one in particular illustrates Tevye's approach. He says, "Motel and Tzeitel have been married for some time now. They work very hard and they are as poor as squirrels in winter. But they are so happy they don't know how miserable they are. Motel keeps talking about a sewing machine. I know. You are very busy now. Wars. Revolutions. Floods and plagues. All these little things that bring people back to you. But couldn't you take a second and get him a sewing machine?" Then, before Tevye is finished, he lets the Lord know that he really needs a new horse.

We can't help but think as we hear this conversational approach to prayer that this is what Jesus had in mind. In this passage he makes a case for communication with the Father that is honest and spontaneous, not rote and ritualistic.

How would Jesus evaluate your prayers? Do they tend to follow a formula? Today, tell God about the small matters that are weighing on your heart along with the big issues. Talk to God just as if he were sitting right there with you. ✤

PRAYER

Dear God, to be totally honest with you, I admit that …

day247

IT'S A BEAUTIFUL LIFE

If you, then, though you are evil, know how to give good gifts to your children, how much more will your Father in heaven give good gifts to those who ask him! MATTHEW 7:11

While lecturing at Colorado College in 1893, Katherine Lee Bates hiked Pikes Peak in the Rocky Mountains, where she was overwhelmed by the beauty of God's creation. From her viewpoint at the 14,110-foot summit, the 34 year-old Wellesley professor gazed at the breathtaking panorama. Picking up her pen, she scratched out the lyrics to a hymn that celebrates the beauty of our country's natural resources.

"America the Beautiful" continues to be treasured as a portrait of God's blessings to those who claim the United States as their homeland. Although not specifically referring to this passage in Matthew, Katherine Bates' lyrics affirm it. As the song goes, God sheds his grace—his good gifts—on us, wherever we may call home. The wonder of creation displayed on every continent is unmistakable. So too are the gifts we often take for granted—health, food, shelter, clothing, employment, family, friends.

The gifts the heavenly Father wraps up and delivers to us are chosen with us in mind. They represent a personal knowledge of those who receive them. It is the kind of gift-giving characterized by mothers and fathers who know exactly what it is their children need—and desire. It is the kind of gift-giving that celebrates the uniqueness of the recipient.

Such beautiful gifts from a good God call for a response. Find a pen and sheet of paper and begin to list what you're grateful for. Identify the gifts God has given to you, which celebrate the uniqueness of who you are. ❖

PRAYER

Wonderful Father, thank you for how you have lavished me with good gifts . . .

A BIRD'S-EYE VIEW

And even the very hairs of your head are all numbered. So don't be afraid; you are worth more than many sparrows.   MATTHEW 10:30–31

Photos of Earth taken from the space shuttles are incredible. The clarity of these images photographed from hundreds of miles away is absolutely amazing. Even more remarkable is how these same images can be magnified and yet hold their crisp quality. We can distinctly see the rooftop of a high-rise in a city's financial district with this high-technology imaging. Zoom in more and you can even see the sidewalk in front of any given building.

In a sense, this technology helps us understand how it is possible for God to have the omniscience Jesus attributes to him. If a camera mounted to an orbiting capsule can magnify activity on our planet with computer-governed precision, surely the Creator of the universe can focus on the minutest details of his creation. Nothing escapes his glance.

As a result, we have no reason to question our circumstances. He sees all and knows all.

As you struggle with issues at work or in your marriage that no one has a clue about, isn't it good to know that your Father in heaven is fully aware? Our lives are never out of view. We can take comfort in his care. It is also a reality that motivates our praise. It frees us to praise God no matter where we are. Today, as you are stuck in commuter traffic or out mowing the lawn, praise the One who is always watching! ✤

PRAYER

Heavenly Father, may your constant glance also motivate my obedience . . .

LIBERTY'S ORIGINAL INVITATION

Come to me, all you who are weary and burdened, and I will give you rest. Take my yoke upon you and learn from me, for I am gentle and humble in heart, and you will find rest for your souls. For my yoke is easy and my burden is light.   MATTHEW 11:28–30

The Statue of Liberty is more than one of the most photographed landmarks in America. It symbolizes the legacy the United States has earned as a nation. Historically, we have welcomed the oppressed and homeless of many lands who have sought sanctuary within our borders. The colossal woman who guards New York Harbor beckons the needy. The inscription on her base leaves no room for doubt: "Give me your tired, your poor, / Your huddled masses yearning to breathe free." This inscription is from "The New Colossus," a sonnet written in 1883 by Emma Lazarus.

Nineteen centuries before Frédéric Auguste Bartholdi, the French artisan, sculpted Lady Liberty, the Son of God did far more than offer would-be citizens a new form of government and the wide-open spaces of limitless opportunity. He invited them to immigrate to a spiritual realm, free from the unending exhaustion of carrying guilt.

Sound inviting? Jesus is gentle, humble and not overly demanding in what he expects. Can't you picture his smiling countenance? It's a loving glance that calls you to quit striving to please others or prove yourself worthy.

"Come to me," Jesus encourages, and "I will give you rest." Rest from the tyranny of your schedule. Rest from the anxieties and worries that burden you right now. Rest that comes from deep within the soul. Pause right now, and in silent worship, meditate on these words. Say them again to yourself. Give to Jesus whatever burdens you are bearing today. ✣

PRAYER

Lord Jesus, I release these burdens to you . . .

MORE THAN YOU BARGAINED FOR

Again, the kingdom of heaven is like a merchant looking for fine pearls. When he found one of great value, he went away and sold everything he had and bought it.

MATTHEW 13:45–46

Originally it was called Seward's Icebox and Seward's Folly. Secretary of State William Seward convinced President Andrew Johnson to buy the Alaska Territory from the Russian government for $7.2 million. That reduces down to two cents per acre. Seward was aware that, in addition to the political presence the territory on the Bering Sea would represent, the wealth hidden within the vast wilderness of "the great land" was well worth the price the czar demanded. Still, Seward didn't live long enough to fully realize the fortune in gold and oil—let alone the beauty of its natural resources—his purchase would bring to the United States. If he had, he would have been willing to offer the Russians whatever it took to secure a land of unprecedented abundance.

In Jesus' parable, he compares the assurance of salvation to a priceless pearl. The merchant was so convinced of the pearl's value, he liquidated all of his other holdings to secure a one-of-a-kind find he would never encounter again. Giving up things "for the sake of Christ" is a plus, not a minus. And as with the hidden resources of Alaska, personal salvation offers an abundance that can only be discovered after the fact.

No doubt you have experienced that for yourself. Nonetheless, at times you may forget just how valuable this life is—a life of forgiveness and fulfillment made possible for you by Jesus' death.

What activities, pursuits or priorities are you holding on to right now that prevent you from fully realizing the abundance of life in Christ? Like the merchant, do whatever you need to do in order to gain that which is priceless. ✣

PRAYER

Jesus, help me explore the great expanse of my life that has yet to be developed by you ...

WORSHIP THAT IS GENUINE

You hypocrites! Isaiah was right when he prophesied about you: "These people honor me with their lips, but their hearts are far from me. They worship me in vain; their teachings are merely human rules."　　　　　　　　　　　　　　　　　　MATTHEW 15:7–9

The questions came fast. Intense. Double-edged. Fraught with traps. A press conference? More like an inquisition with an audience. The Pharisees and religious teachers shot their arrows of interrogation at Jesus. He shot his responses right back at them.

He who had so recently walked on water now walked around their questions. "Jesus, what are your motives? Where are your priorities?"

Jesus pointed back through the centuries to the messengers of old whose message was still current today. As Ezekiel wrote, "My people come to you, as they usually do, and sit before you to hear your words, but they do not put them into practice. Their mouths speak of love, but their hearts are greedy for unjust gain" (Ezekiel 33:31).

Jesus may also have been pointing ahead to the apostle Paul's warnings against the worship of traditions instead of worshiping the one true God. "These rules, which have to do with things that are all destined to perish with use, are based on merely human commands and teachings" (Colossians 2:22).

Do your lips honor God with prayers, with songs? That's good. But how far away is your heart? This is the test Jesus put before those he talked with that day in Jerusalem (see Matthew 15:1–9). At issue is the genuineness of your worship.

In your worship—both personal and corporate—what rules have you observed that have more to do with following human tradition than following God? Identify the one to which you are most prone and ask God's help in conquering it. ❖

> **PRAYER**

God in heaven, I want to honor you with my lips and my heart . . .

A PEACE OF HIS MIND

Then the master called the servant in. "You wicked servant," he said, "I canceled all that debt of yours because you begged me to. Shouldn't you have had mercy on your fellow servant just as I had on you?"   MATTHEW 18:32–33

The parable of the unforgiving debtor is blunt. Unforgiving equals wicked? Yes, replies Jesus. He concludes the parable with, "This is how my heavenly Father will treat each of you unless you forgive your brother or sister from your heart" (Matthew 18:35). Receiving forgiveness from God, reaching up in thankfulness to God, releasing forgiveness out to others, rewarded back with the peace of God.

In God's great economy, the beneficiaries must soon be the benefactors. The debtor in the parable owed millions of dollars, yet all of it was forgiven by the king. Our sin is the spiritual equivalent of such a debt, yet all of it is forgiven by the King of kings. The newly forgiven debtor in the parable was owed a comparatively small sum by another servant, perhaps a few thousand dollars. Yet he did not extend any mercy.

Do we reach up in thankfulness, and then reach out in forgiveness to others as an expression of that gratitude? Or do we make no connection at all between the two debts?

Who is it that you need to extend forgiveness to today? As an act of worship, reach up in thankfulness to God. Reach out with forgiveness to that person. Be rewarded with peace. ♣

> **PRAYER**

King of kings, help me to freely forgive ...

"BUT WITH GOD ..."

Jesus looked at them and said, "With man this is impossible, but with God all things are possible."

MATTHEW 19:26

Too bad he had already walked away. The rich young man never heard the words of possibility.

"Teacher, what good thing must I do to get eternal life?" he had asked eagerly (Matthew 19:16). He smiled at the reply; he had indeed obeyed all the commandments. Could it really be this easy?

"What do I still lack?" he inquired further (Matthew 19:20). But he soon stopped smiling, wondering if he could possibly have heard Jesus correctly. Sell all he had? Give the money to the poor? The Gospel account tells us, "When the young man heard this, he went away sad, because he had great wealth" (Matthew 19:22).

Jesus watched him walk away, and then warned that it would indeed be hard for the rich to enter the kingdom of heaven. Even his disciples seemed to despair. Then Jesus uttered the words "But with God ..."

God's grace and power apply to far more than the salvation of a rich young man. Everything is possible.

The contemporary singer Nicole C. Mullen expresses this conviction in her song "Call on Jesus." We can think we are beyond saving, we can be hiding, we can be in despair. But when we call on Jesus, "all things are possible" — mounting on wings like eagles', watching mountains fall, being assured that he will move heaven and earth to rescue us when we call.

Rejoice that all *is* possible with God. Drink in the hope that is poured out with the words "But with God ..." ✤

PRAYER

God of the possible, I thank you for ...

A FAIL-SAFE PRAYER

If you believe, you will receive whatever you ask for in prayer.   MATTHEW 21:22

Prayer in fervent belief—the kind of prayer Jesus called for from his disciples—does get answered. But to come with such a guarantee of 100-percent effectiveness? Surely such a prayer must be long and deeply theological, probing the ontological nature of the godhead.

Actually, effective prayer contains only four short words: "Your will be done" (Matthew 6:10).

Is part of you disappointed? Were you thinking that prayer professionals had discovered a new, more logical, empirically tested approach? A new posture? Perhaps a particular language that "gets through" to God better and faster?

Go to God in prayer—confident prayer, slapped with a label that says it will never fail. "Your will be done ..." Whatever comes after comes under the never-fail umbrella—a seemingly hopeless relationship, unemployment, a child on what seems, from every earthly angle, to be the wrong path, illness, a difficult decision ...

"Your will be done," when said in utter surrender and genuine faith, is the perfect test of the saying, "Prayer changes things or it changes us." Open your hands and offer up the something or the someone into God's care. Keep your hands open to receive the answer—*his* answer. ♣

> PRAYER

Heavenly Father, your will be done ...

ALL, ALL, ALL

Jesus replied: "'Love the Lord your God with all your heart and with all your soul and with all your mind.' This is the first and greatest commandment." MATTHEW 22:37–38

The answer came so quickly. "How had he had time to sort through all 600 laws?" wondered the experts in religious law. "And that commandment? Why, even children know this ..."

"Oh."

Are we sometimes like the Pharisees who questioned Jesus that day—asking him what we ought to know? These "experts in religious law" more than likely had memorized these verses from Deuteronomy as young children: "Hear, O Israel: The LORD our God, the LORD is one. Love the LORD your God with all your heart and with all your soul and with all your strength. These commandments that I give you today are to be on your hearts" (Deuteronomy 6:4–6). With his answer, Jesus reminded them that nothing had changed—God's requirements were the same before and then.

"With all your heart." Is your affection for the Lord genuine, wholehearted?

"With all your soul." Is your soul sold out to God? Is it him you trust for your spirit's eternal life?

"With all your mind." Are your thoughts subject to the omniscient One? Is your thirst for truth and for him, who is the source of knowledge?

You know what God expects. You know what he deserves. You must love the Lord your God with all ... with all ... with all. Give to God your all in love. Ask him to govern your mind. Tell him you love him wholeheartedly. Trust him with your very soul. ♣

PRAYER

Lord God, I want to love you with all my heart, soul and mind ...

"WHEN DID WE EVER . . . ?"

He will reply, "Truly I tell you, whatever you did not do for one of the least of these, you did not do for me."   MATTHEW 25:45

"Lord, when did we see you hungry or thirsty or a stranger or needing clothes or sick or in prison, and did not help you?" (Matthew 25:44).

Ah, but they had. And so have we.

Certainly Saint Francis of Assisi never neglected "the least" of Jesus' brothers and sisters, did he? Not the humble, kind, bless-the-beasts-and-the-children monk we see in paintings and in our imagination. Not the "Mother Teresa" of the thirteenth century. In fact, a rule of the Franciscan order said, "They should be glad to live among social outcasts, among the poor and helpless, the sick and the lepers, and those who beg by the wayside."

Saint Francis had not always been so. Raised in luxury and privilege, he did his best to avoid dealings with the disgusting outcasts of his day. When he got near them, he would pinch his nose against the smell.

But he encountered God and was transformed into a remarkable servant who taught us how to serve Christ with all people. In *The Lessons of St. Francis*, John Michael Talbot describes one incident in Assisi's life: "One day when Francis was riding down a road near Assisi he saw a leper approaching from a distance. He felt all the familiar feelings—the discomfort, the fear, the nausea, the desire to flee—as the lonely leper came closer and closer. But Francis, ennobled and enabled by God's grace, got down off his mule, walked up to the leper, and kissed him."

The verses in today's larger passage in Matthew link our compassion, or its lack, to the final judgment (see Matthew 25:31–46).

Watch for "the least" today. Give them your best. And by so doing, worship and serve the Most High. ✤

PRAYER

Lord, show me how to serve your people . . .

EAT, DRINK AND BE ... THANKFUL

While they were eating, Jesus took bread, and when he had given thanks, he broke it and gave it to his disciples, saying, "Take and eat; this is my body." Then he took a cup, and when he had given thanks, he gave it to them, saying, "Drink from it, all of you. This is my blood of the covenant, which is poured out for many for the forgiveness of sins."

MATTHEW 26:26–28

Passover meal. The Last Supper. The Lord's Supper. Agape feast. The Blessed Sacrament. Eucharist. Holy Communion.

Known by many names, this meal began as the last, sad Seder among friends one evening in Jerusalem. Today, we eat this bread and drink this wine in remembrance of what happened over the next few days.

Jesus broke the bread for them; his body was broken for you. He poured the wine for them; his blood was poured out for you. In the words of the apostle Paul, "For whenever you eat this bread and drink this cup, you proclaim the Lord's death until he comes" (1 Corinthians 11:26).

One of the most traditional names for this remembrance is the Eucharist. The word gets to the heart of why we celebrate, why we remember, for it is derived from the Greek word *eukharistia*, meaning "gratitude."

Henri J. M. Nouwen writes in *With Burning Hearts: A Meditation on the Eucharistic Life*: "Jesus is God giving himself completely, pouring himself out for us without reserve."

When you eat bread or drink juice or wine, allow these simple elements to remind you of Christ's body broken for you, of his blood given for you. Then eat, drink and be thankful. ✤

> PRAYER

Lord Jesus, when I think of how your body was broken for me, I ...

HIS COMMANDING PRESENCE

Go and make disciples of all nations ... [teach] them to obey everything I have commanded you. And surely I am with you always, to the very end of the age.   MATTHEW 28:19–20

That day up there on the mountain, Jesus assured them of his remarkable power when he said, "All authority in heaven and on earth has been given to me" (Matthew 28:18). Then he commissioned them with the greatest of commissions: "Go and make disciples of all nations" (verse 19).

Assured, commissioned and now reassured. "I am with you always, to the very end of the age." The God of complete authority. The God of complete assurance.

Jesus gives you, today's disciple, the same Great Commission. Destinations and details will vary, but the commission is the same for all of us: "Go and make disciples." Mundane or magnificent, the assignment from God—the living of a life that is an act of worship to him—can overwhelm us. But the promise of his presence is steadfast.

Fernando Ortega's music often takes the lyrics and imagery of yesterday—including Scripture and traditional hymns—and gives them a fresh setting and instrumentation. In "Hear Me Calling, Great Redeemer," you can see yourself coming down from the mountain, afraid yet assured that God will go before you through the valley.

Hold on to his hand, hold on to the truth that the commission he has given you comes with the same reassurance he gave the disciples. God will be with you. Always. ✣

PRAYER

God, be with me ...

day259

CHANCE OF A LIFETIME

"Come, follow me," Jesus said, "and I will send you out to fish for people." MARK 1:17

There's Abram, a businessman in Ur, who heard a voice and uprooted his family to a place only God knew. And because Abram was just crazy enough to follow this weird, wild call, he not only found eternal treasure, he also changed the course of human history.

There's Moses, on the back side of nowhere, trying to keep up with a flock of smelly sheep, just killing time, when, out of the corner of his eye, he saw a flaming bush. He paused to check it out. And his life — and the world — would never again be the same.

History recounts the stories of men and women who heard God summon them. People who dared to give up their small ambitions to pursue eternal realities, countless saints who were willing to hitch their wagons — and lives — to God's direction and who attempted outlandish, impossible things.

Such was the case with the disciples. Jesus gave the simple summons, "Come, follow me." Come and leave their families, their livelihoods, their lives? Follow a Nazarene carpenter-turned-preacher? But what about ... what if ... what would ...?

Here's the deal: Christ is still looking for disciples. More amazing, he continues to invite average — dare we say "flawed" — folks to join him in his cosmic cause. When we pursue Jesus, life takes on a new urgency. Our gifts and abilities are suddenly focused on kingdom needs and opportunities.

Since Jesus Christ is the focal point of the universe, the supreme value, the only truly worthy One, doesn't it make sense to follow him, to learn from him and to encourage others to do the same? ✤

PRAYER

Lord Jesus, give me a heart full of reckless abandon for you ...

AWESOME AND AWE-FULL

They were terrified and asked each other, "Who is this? Even the wind and the waves obey him!"
MARK 4:41

When was the last time you were truly awed?

Maybe it was with a sense of wonder at the vast beauty of a mountain range or an ocean view. Perhaps it was with speechless amazement at the birth of a child. Or with raw fear when caught in the path of a tornado, hurricane or the raging flow from a flooding river.

The disciples of Jesus certainly had plenty of awe-filled moments. In the passage cited above, they were caught with Jesus in a sudden storm on the Sea of Galilee. It must have been a severe squall—at least four of these men were experienced fishermen, and they were absolutely panicked.

Awakened from a peaceful sleep, Jesus calmly rebuked the tempest. And immediately the sea became as smooth as glass.

But the storm wasn't over. Not by a long shot. Banished from the sea, the storm kicked up in the racing hearts and spinning minds of the Twelve. Dripping wet, the men were left to ponder what they had just experienced. Maybe they bailed a bit of water. Maybe they just looked at each other. They may have watched Jesus as he resumed his nap, stared off in the distance or did whatever it was he did next. Is there any category for something like this?

One thing is true. When God in his glory is manifest in our midst, we experience awe.

Allow God to invade your day. Look for his glory, his manifestation in the tasks you have before you today. Worship him in those moments. ✤

> **PRAYER**

My Lord and my God, I am awed by . . .

TIME TO RETREAT AND RECHARGE

The apostles gathered around Jesus and reported to him all they had done and taught. Then, because so many people were coming and going that they did not even have a chance to eat, he said to them, "Come with me by yourselves to a quiet place and get some rest."

MARK 6:30–31

In *The Unquenchable Worshipper: Coming Back to the Heart of Worship*, Matt Redman observes, "So often when my worship has dried up, it's because I haven't been fueling the fire. I haven't set aside any time to soak myself under the showers of God's revelation."

The fact is, we were designed by God to need a regular amount of downtime. Jesus knew this. After sending his disciples out on a ministry tour, what does Jesus do? He tells them it's time to get away and get some rest. And actually, there is a work-rest rhythm built into the fabric of the universe. How else do we explain the seasons, hibernating animals and dormant fruit trees? Sometimes the most fitting and God-honoring act is to simply *be* with God rather than to *do* for him.

Ah, but we are a hyper-efficient, get-it-done, type-A generation with places to go, people to see and things to do. Armed with our smartphones, GPSs and assorted to-do lists, we launch into our days with a vengeance. Is it any wonder that our souls are weary and burned-out? "Expend extra energy focusing on God? Give my time and my attention and affection to him? You've got to be kidding. I'm lucky to make it to church once a week!"

When our hearts are exhausted and drained, chances are we're thinking about anything but God. Today, look at your schedule and ask God if you need a break from activity to focus on intimacy with him. ❖

PRAYER

Lord, teach me the invaluable discipline of rest . . .

WHO IS HE, REALLY?

"But what about you?" he asked. "Who do you say I am?" Peter answered, "You are the Messiah."   MARK 8:29

No matter how much it tries, the world can't get over Jesus. Every couple of years or so, at least one of the major news magazines does a cover story on some aspect of the Nazarene's life. Or one of the networks will air a special about him. We are haunted by Jesus—and rightly so.

"Who do you say I am?" "Who do *you* say I am?" "Who do you say *I* am?" No matter how it is posed, this is the question above all questions. It is the question Jesus continues to ask each person and every generation. And whether or not we answer it with our lips, we answer it with our lives every day.

Peter got it right. He recognized that Jesus was much more than an intriguing political revolutionary, more than a good teacher, even more than a great prophet. He saw him as the long-promised Messiah—the son of God, sent to rescue people from sin, sent to reign over the world.

Later, writing to other worshipers of Jesus, Peter noted, "Though you have not seen him, you love him; and even though you do not see him now, you believe in him and are filled with an inexpressible and glorious joy, for you are receiving the end result of your faith, the salvation of your souls" (1 Peter 1:8–9).

Today, ask yourself the question, "What does my life say to the world about who Jesus is?" Let the joy of knowing Jesus be evidenced by what you do and say throughout the day. ❧

PRAYER

Jesus, I say that you are . . .

day263

FOR WHAT PURPOSE?

For even the Son of Man did not come to be served, but to serve, and to give his life as a ransom for many.
MARK 10:45

Why did Christ come into the world? To teach? Do miracles? Start a new religion?

In John 6:38, Jesus states his purpose this way: "I have come down from heaven not to do my will but to do the will of him who sent me." And what exactly was the will of God for Jesus? Well, according to today's verse, it was to serve and to die. Or we might even say it was to serve by dying.

Could it be that our purpose is similar to Christ's? Not to do what we want, but to die to our own agendas and live boldly for God's? To do the Father's will? To serve God by serving others?

And what if we take the risk? What if we give ourselves away—our whole lives as one giant sacrifice of worship to God? This is what Jesus did. It is how he lived. No wonder he was able to say, "I always do what pleases [the Father]" (John 8:29). And no wonder the Father in heaven echoed this assessment, stating of Christ, "This is my Son, whom I love; with him I am well pleased" (Matthew 17:5).

What would it mean for you to offer your life as a giant sacrifice of worship to God? Spend some time reflecting on what you need to change—attitudes, habits or daily commitments—so that your life focuses on serving others. ✤

PRAYER

Father in heaven, I give my life to you ...

GOD-WORTHY LOVE

To love him with all your heart, with all your understanding and with all your strength, and to love your neighbor as yourself is more important than all burnt offerings and sacrifices. MARK 12:33

"Talk is cheap," the old saying teaches, and nowhere is that more true than in the spiritual realm. It is one thing to know the right answers, to be able to quote chapter and verse, to discuss the finer points of theology. It is another matter altogether to put words into practice, to be doers of God's Word.

The discussion surrounding today's verse—between Jesus and a devoutly religious young man—gets to the heart of worship, the essence of life. What's the bottom line? Why have we been created in the first place? How should we spend our lives? Of all the good things we can focus our attention on, what is the best, the most important?

The young man knew the truth in his head: Loving God. Loving him with all that we are and have. Thinking of him. Pursuing him. Ordering our lives around him. Serving him. Seeking to honor him. And out of that consuming love, loving others compassionately. The man understood all this and could articulate it. He just wasn't able to take the steps necessary to live out the truth.

If you are struggling today to love God as he so richly deserves, call on him to fill you with heavenly passion. Ask him for a God-worthy love, and direct that love back toward heaven. ✢

PRAYER

Lord, fill me with your love ...

WORSHIP AND YOUR WEALTH

Calling his disciples to him, Jesus said, "Truly I tell you, this poor widow has put more into the treasury than all the others. They all gave out of their wealth; but she, out of her poverty, put in everything—all she had to live on."   MARK 12:43–44

You don't need a PhD in economics to know that it takes a chunk of money to live these days. We have basic needs: food, clothing, shelter. And paying taxes isn't an option. What about transportation, insurance, education costs and saving for retirement? Pay for all the necessities—and maybe a small luxury every now and then—and you might watch your checking account balance drop dangerously close to red numbers.

So here's the million-dollar question: Why would anyone in his or her right mind put money in a church offering plate or write a check for world missions? But how we handle money is perhaps the single best indicator of what we really believe. As the German theologian Helmut Thielicke once wisely observed, "Our pocketbooks have more to do with heaven and also with hell than our hymnbooks."

Jesus watched worshiper after worshiper come into the temple and give God a few financial leftovers. It didn't cost these people much of anything. Then he noticed a destitute widow giving her last two coins. There's no indication she gave to get. Rather, it was a quiet act of love, a bold step of faith. If this life is all there is, she was crazy. If it really is possible to store up treasure in heaven (see Matthew 6:19–21), she was a spiritual and financial genius.

What does how you handle material means say about your spiritual health? Does it reflect a thankful heart absorbed with God and the business of God?

Worship God today with your money—make a donation (perhaps anonymously) to your church or local charity. ❖

PRAYER

Lord, show me new ways I can worship you by being generous . . .

day266

OUR HEROIC VICTIM

"Abba, Father," he said, "everything is possible for you. Take this cup from me. Yet not what I will, but what you will."   MARK 14:36

We look upon this agonizing scene in Gethsemane like we might gawk at a train wreck. It is stomach-turning and riveting, all at the same time. On the one hand, disasters—whatever form they take—always devastate lives. On the other hand, they almost always produce heroes. In this life-and-death moment, Christ is both.

Jesus is about to become the ultimate "innocent victim." He was beaten senseless by a band of bored, brutal soldiers, and then executed in cold blood. And why? For what crime? For speaking words of grace and truth.

But this kneeling figure, covered in blood, sweat and tears, is also a hero of epic—no, make that eternal—proportions. "God made him who had no sin to be sin for us, so that in him we might become the righteousness of God" (2 Corinthians 5:21).

Jesus willingly volunteered for this grimmest of duties. But who can fault him for the dread and horror that descended on his soul?

In his book *Moments with the Savior*, author Ken Gire describes the moment well: "His hands are no longer clutching the grass in despair. They are no longer clasping each other in prayer. They are raised toward heaven ... reaching for the cup from his Father's hand."

Today, worship Christ in two ways: first, by thanking him for his sacrifice, and second, by living sacrificially yourself. ✤

PRAYER

Jesus, I want my whole life to be a worshipful response to you ...

THE TORN CURTAIN

With a loud cry, Jesus breathed his last. The curtain of the temple was torn in two from top to bottom.
　　　　　　　　　　　　　　　　　　　　　　　　　　MARK 15:37–38

Call it what it was. Obscene. Sickening. An ancient R-rated scene. A brutalized man, skewered to wood, bleeding, suffocating, crying out. Mockers laughed while mourners wept.

God creates the human race, knowing we will rebel, knowing we will put him (literally) through hell, knowing we will cost him the priceless life of his innocent Son.

But he implements the plan of salvation anyway. And the result? At the worst of moments, a mysterious phenomenon occurs. Scripture records that the veil inside the Jewish temple is torn from top to bottom. The thick tapestry that keeps humans out of the "most holy place" is inexplicably ripped down the middle. This curtain is, for all practical purposes, the "wall" that signifies man's separation from God. Suddenly it is no more.

Herein is love. And here is the reason we worship. The torn curtain is why, today, you can throw back your head and laugh and weep. It is why we dance with joy. It is why we lie face down before our Creator. He takes the ugliest incident in the universe and turns it into humankind's most hopeful hour. What an amazing God!

Thank God that because of the cross, because of the torn curtain, you are in his presence right now. Spend a few moments there in grateful praise. ✤

PRAYER

Father in heaven, thank you for opening a way of access to you . . .

ORDINARY PEOPLE, EXTRAORDINARY GOD

My spirit rejoices in God my Savior, for he has been mindful of the humble state of his servant. From now on all generations will call me blessed.   LUKE 1:47–48

Mary was right. Two thousand years after she lived, we still remember this humble village girl chosen by God to become the mother of his Son.

God has always used ordinary people in extraordinary ways to further his plans. Paul described one early congregation: "Not many of you were wise by human standards; not many were influential; not many were of noble birth" (1 Corinthians 1:26): And ever since, the church has advanced largely through the work of average people.

In the fifth century, the son of a minor church official in Britain was captured by pirates and sold as a slave in Ireland. He escaped from his captors several years later, but eventually returned to Ireland to preach the gospel. By the time of this ex-slave's death, nearly the entire island had chosen Christianity. Today he is called St. Patrick.

In the seventeenth century, a former soldier and office clerk named Nicholas Herman joined a religious order in France and spent decades working in the order's kitchen. His status was low, but that didn't stop him from writing his influential *The Practice of the Presence of God* under his adopted name of Brother Lawrence.

While we may consider ourselves less wealthy, less intelligent or less influential than others, such limitations in no way prevent God from choosing us to partner with him in doing wonderful works. It's a blessed opportunity, indeed. ✣

PRAYER

Give birth to great things through me, God . . .

day269

HOMESICK FOR A PLACE WHERE WE HAVE NEVER BEEN

And she gave birth to her firstborn, a son. She wrapped him in cloths and placed him in a manger, because there was no guest room available for them.　　　　LUKE 2:7

Many of us can attest to a longing for heaven. We have moments—and they may occur at the oddest times, even when things are going the best for us—when somehow, down deep, we think, *I don't belong here. This world is not my home.*

We can take comfort in knowing that it was the same way for Jesus. He was in the world, and the world was made by him, but the world knew him not (see John 1:10). His displacement started when he was born, when his mother had to give birth to him in a stable because there was no room for them at the inn. Later he would say that he had no place to lay his head (see Luke 9:58). Finally, in a parallel to his displaced birth, he would be crucified outside the walls of Jerusalem. Our Lord was an unwelcome stranger on this earth.

Now Jesus is at home in his Father's mansion, and he is preparing a place for us there. Sojourners through this life, we are justified in every bit of longing we feel for heaven. Of course, God has a purpose for us on earth, just as he had for Jesus, and we must carry out that purpose. And along the way, as it is possible and appropriate, we may enjoy the limited good this world has to offer. But the time will come—soon—when the door will open and we will hear the Father say, "Welcome home, my dear, dear child."

Allow the words of this familiar account of the Lord's birth to cause you to worship the One who does not belong to this world. Let them remind you that this also is not your true home. ✤

PRAYER

Lord, where you are is where I belong . . .

ALL CREATURES HERE BELOW

When all the people were being baptized, Jesus was baptized too. And as he was praying, heaven was opened and the Holy Spirit descended on him in bodily form like a dove. And a voice came from heaven: "You are my Son, whom I love; with you I am well pleased."

LUKE 3:21–22

In *Enjoying Intimacy with God*, J. Oswald Sanders wrote, "We are now, and we will be in the future, only as intimate with God as we really choose to be."

Do you feel close to God right now? Do you desire to be closer to him? One way to grow closer to God is to know more about who he is. He reveals himself primarily through Jesus.

One of the most striking characteristics of Jesus when he lived on earth was that he was humble. Jesus was not proud or conceited as the Son of the King, and he displayed his humility from the start of his earthly ministry by submitting to baptism at the hands of John the Baptist. Did he need to repent like other people, as baptism signified? No, the One who was fully God and fully man was completely sinless. He was baptized because he wanted to identify with those he came to save.

Because of his humility and obedience, Jesus was accepted by the Father. As Jesus prayed, heaven was opened "and the Holy Spirit descended on him in bodily form like a dove." In company with this supernatural act, God announced in the hearing of those present, "You are my Son, whom I love; with you I am well pleased."

Though humble, Jesus is fully worthy of our worship. John, the man who baptized him, declared of Jesus, "He must become greater; I must become less" (John 3:30). In the same spirit, we should raise up Jesus and lower ourselves. This is the way to intimacy with God. ✤

PRAYER

Jesus, I worship you because . . .

THE SERVANT-WORSHIPER

The Spirit of the Lord is on me, because he has anointed me to proclaim good news to the poor. He has sent me to proclaim freedom for the prisoners and recovery of sight for the blind, to set the oppressed free. LUKE 4:18

John Teter, an evangelist with InterVarsity Christian Fellowship, tells about meeting a 6-foot-tall, 280-pound wrestler who was a student at Compton College. The young man called himself Colossus.

Teter invited Colossus to attend a Bible study for spiritual seekers, and Colossus agreed. At the end of the first Bible study session, Teter asked Colossus to pray. The wrestler began, "O great Odin! This is your servant-warrior Colossus."

Startled, Teter interrupted and asked Colossus who he was praying to. "Odin," explained Colossus. "He is the Norse god of war. Me and my friends are into witchcraft. We're really into Odin right now."

Teter persuaded Colossus to try praying to Jesus instead. And by the end of the semester, Colossus had accepted Jesus as the sole Lord worthy of his worship. Now this new believer prays, "O great Yahweh, this is Colossus, your servant-warrior."

In a special sense, Jesus was appointed to preach good news. He acknowledged as much when he gave his inaugural sermon at a synagogue in Nazareth, which we read about in today's passage. As the Messiah, he fulfilled the prophecy of Isaiah 61:1–2.

In a more general sense, all of us are called to help others see Christ by how we live. As we allow others to see that ours is a life oriented around worshiping Jesus, we may have the joy of seeing others take our Lord as theirs. ♣

PRAYER

O great Yahweh, you are the only true Lord . . .

THE CROOKED KISS

Be merciful, just as your Father is merciful.   LUKE 6:36

In his book *Mortal Lessons: Notes on the Art of Surgery*, Dr. Richard Selzer takes readers into the hospital room where a young woman has just awakened after Selzer operated on her. In the process of removing the tumor from her cheek, Selzer unavoidably severed a nerve, causing her mouth to twist into a clownish shape. Now that she has awakened, Selzer has to inform her that the new shape of her mouth is permanent. The woman nods silently at the news. Her husband then bends to kiss her, twisting his lips to conform to the shape of hers.

We are the woman with the twisted mouth. Our lives have been distorted by the effects of sin, our own as well as others'. But because God loves us, he accommodates us anyway, and over time he even straightens out our crookedness. That's the kind of compassion God has for us. During his sermon on kingdom-living from today's passage, Jesus taught his followers then and now to be merciful. Mercy is what we need to extend to others—a compassion that meets the needs of those made repulsive by the conditions of this wicked world.

If this sort of compassion seems too hard or too costly to you, remember that God promises to crown compassion with goodness. Seek God's direction for how you can show mercy to someone today. Make a specific plan. Then do it. ✤

PRAYER

Lord, fill me with your mercy . . .

day273

THE SMELL OF WORSHIP

Therefore, I tell you, her many sins have been forgiven—as her great love has shown. But whoever has been forgiven little loves little.   LUKE 7:47

Sigmund Freud said, "The quickest way to trigger an emotional response is with scent." In fact, scents have been shown to affect the limbic portion of the brain, the center of emotion and memory. With all the personal and social implications attached to scent, it's little wonder that perfume has become a multibillion-dollar business. Perfumes were popular even in Biblical times.

In today's passage, the perfume a woman poured over Jesus' feet was contained in a small alabaster vase and was probably made from nard, an herb grown in India. Perfume was commonly offered to guests in Jesus' day, but as this honor had been withheld from Jesus by his host, the woman chose to step forward herself to sacrificially clean, kiss and anoint Jesus' feet with an expensive perfume. As the pleasing scent wafted to Christ's nostrils, he was probably reminded of the sweet odors of scented oil and incense used in Jewish worship (see Exodus 30:22–38).

We don't know the back story to this event. Presumably Jesus had recently met this sinful woman, had showed her the need to repent and had touched her heart with a pure love the likes of which she had never known before. The woman, in response, just had to do something extravagant to show her gratitude. So, she boldly barged into the dinner party Jesus was attending and performed the foot washing. Her act of worship was beautiful. Pity the religious folk at the table who were less sinful—or thought they were—and so could not know such joy in loving Jesus. ✤

PRAYER

Jesus, I want to show you love today . . .

WHO IS JESUS?

Once when Jesus was praying in private and his disciples were with him, he asked them, "Who do the crowds say I am?"   LUKE 9:18

Pope John Paul II was roundly criticized when he singled out certain entertainers for wearing a cross as jewelry while engaged in activities far removed from Christian morality. But John Paul was correctly picking up on modern culture's tendency to accept Jesus as an icon so long as we can interpret him in any manner we want. Jesus is good, but then so is the Dalai Lama, Muhammad and any number of other "spiritual" people and symbols.

In Jesus' own day, people were willing to accord him limited prestige as a prophet. It took special insight from the Father for Peter to come up with the right answer when Jesus asked him the question in today's key verse. He told Jesus, "God's Messiah" (Luke 9:20).

Some people today might be excused for giving Jesus limited praise if they really don't know any better. But how many individuals are subconsciously hoping to escape the full claims of Jesus by giving him only partial approval?

Reflect on your own response to Jesus' question, "Who do you say I am?" Worship him in the fullness of his claim as Messiah, God in human flesh. ✣

PRAYER

Jesus, you are more than a good man. You are . . .

ONLY ONE THING NEEDFUL

"Martha, Martha," the Lord answered, "you are worried and upset about many things, but few things are needed—or indeed only one. Mary has chosen what is better, and it will not be taken away from her." LUKE 10:41–42

Want to watch a movie on your Blu-ray or DVD player? Great. But first you must decide whether to watch it in standard or wide-screen format, with or without subtitles and with or without the director's commentary. And then there's a whole menu of other "special features" to explore.

Want to save money by doing your own taxes? Good for you. Just remember that the instructions for Form 1040 alone now run to more than 60 pages of small print.

Need to buy a new computer? Sounds fun. But do you want a desktop, a notebook or a tablet computer like an iPad? Which type of processor? How many gigs of memory? Hurry up and decide; we haven't even started talking about software.

Life has become mighty complex, hasn't it? It's easy to get caught up in the practical details of living, just as Martha did when preparing dinner. But while the complexity of modern life makes our preoccupation with details understandable, it does not constitute an excuse for neglecting what's most important. We are still called to be like Mary, making it a priority to sit at the feet of Jesus to take in everything he teaches and give him our adoration in return.

What is the "one" necessary thing? It's engaging with Jesus. Even now, as you are spending time with God, what details are crowding your mind? Write them down on a piece of paper and then throw it away to symbolize your desire to preoccupy yourself with God. ❖

> PRAYER

Lord, help me be like Mary, sitting at your feet ...

day276

HOW NOT TO BE A FOOL

And I'll say to myself, "You have plenty of grain laid up for many years. Take life easy; eat, drink and be merry."　　　　　　　　　　　　　　　　　　　　Luke 12:19

Just hours before dying in 2003 of a pulmonary embolism during the Iraqi war, NBC anchor David Bloom wrote the following in an e-mail message to his wife:

> *You can't begin to fathom—cannot begin to even glimpse the enormity—of the changes I have and am continuing to undergo. God takes you to the depths of your being—until you're at rock bottom—and then, if you turn to Him with utter and blind faith, and resolve in your heart and mind to walk only with Him and toward Him, [He] picks you up with your bootstraps and leads you home.*

Bloom did not know that he was about to die, but clearly he was ready for it. In that sense he presents an example opposite to the one found in Luke 12:16–21.

The farmer in Jesus' story had been blessed with a bountiful harvest and he had stored it all away. So far, so good. But his idea of what to do next reveals the problem: He did not take into account that he, like everyone else, lived day by day according to the grace of God. While he envisioned a vast vista of hedonism stretching out before him, God had other plans. The following day was marked down on God's calendar as the farmer's exit day. The lesson? "This is how it will be with whoever stores up things for themselves but is not rich toward God" (Luke 12:21).

Is your life focused on accumulating worldly wealth, like the farmer? Or is it focused on developing a rich relationship with God, like David Bloom?

Let every sign of worldly wealth you see throughout the day—banks, ATM machines, stores and so on—remind you of where true wealth is found. ✤

PRAYER

Lord, you are my treasure . . .

GATHER ME IN

Jerusalem, Jerusalem, you who kill the prophets and stone those sent to you, how often I have longed to gather your children together, as a hen gathers her chicks under her wings, and you were not willing. LUKE 13:34

The city bustled with life. Merchants bought and sold and haggled over prices. Old men sat by the gates and debated the finer points of the law. Women gathered at the wells and shared the latest news. Children laughed and shouted and chased one another down the street. And over all this, the temple loomed, dominating the city with its splendor. Jerusalem, the city of David—soon to be destroyed.

But Jesus mourned, saying, in essence, "O Jerusalem, how I long to gather you in, but you will not be gathered. Jerusalem, you who have rejected the prophets have now rejected the Son of God. You long for the Messiah, but do not recognize the anointed one standing in your midst. Come to me, come to me now, O Jerusalem, or face certain destruction."

It's easy to dismiss this dilemma as relevant only to the people of that day. Unfortunately, we face the same dilemma: Will we allow Jesus to gather us in or not? The Son of God has been revealed. He has died, he has risen and he is now glorified. Accept him now, believe in him now, worship him now. Or reject him at your peril, just as Jerusalem did.

Consider your relationship with Jesus at this moment. He longs to gather you in, but will you be gathered? His welcoming arms await you. Run to Jesus, your Savior. Draw close to him, for he is your protector. Worship him, for he is the Son of God. Bow down and give homage, for he is your King. ✤

PRAYER

Gather me in, Lord Jesus. I am willing ...

WHAT WILL YOU ENDURE?

I tell you that in the same way there will be more rejoicing in heaven over one sinner who repents than over ninety-nine righteous persons who do not need to repent.   LUKE 15:7

A shepherd searching in the wilderness for the one lost sheep that has strayed from the flock. A woman turning her household upside down to find a lost coin. A father eagerly welcoming a wayward son who, after squandering his inheritance, returns home. In each instance, Jesus tells us the end result—a celebration when the lost has been found.

In this passage, Jesus reveals the heart of a Father who tenderly searches for sinners and then joyously forgives them. It is a love that sent God's Son to not only search for the lost but to also endure the cross for their sake. It is the same extraordinary love God has for us today. He is still in the business of seeking and saving—and he calls us to do the same.

Every person we meet is precious to our Father. Every person is someone God desires to return to him. And when that person does return, oh the rejoicing! All of heaven, we are told, is involved in an angelic celebration. So what are we willing to endure, how far are we willing to search, how much will we allow our "households" to be turned upside down to seek the lost for God?

As an act of worship to the One who came and saved you, consider your neighbors today. Take time to pray for their salvation. See them today with the eyes of your Father in heaven. ✤

PRAYER

Jesus, give me a heart to seek out the lost . . .

CLING TO THE CROSS

The apostles said to the Lord, "Increase our faith!"   Luke 17:5

In the beginning it was easy for the apostles to believe. They watched Jesus heal the sick and give sight to the blind. They saw him raise the widow's son from the dead and call Lazarus from the grave. They witnessed his power when he rebuked the wind and calmed the sea. But then Jesus began to confront the religious leaders with their sin and the trouble started. Soon the leaders plotted to have him arrested, and Jesus predicted his own death. The apostles were confused, so they pleaded with Jesus, "Increase our faith!"

It's easy to trust God when times are good—but life is often difficult. Accidents, illness, job loss, broken relationships—all can leave us wondering if God's promises are true. Yet it is in these very situations that we can learn to trust God and humbly depend on him.

When we stumble in our faith, when we falter because of difficult circumstances, that's when we need to cling to the cross. Like the disciples, we need to turn to Jesus and ask him for more faith.

As you spend time with God today, tell him about the doubts and trials that threaten to erode your faith. Ask him to point you to his promises and ask him how to receive more faith. ❖

PRAYER

Lord Jesus, I cling to the cross . . .

EVEN THE ROCKS WILL CHEER

"I tell you," he replied, *"if they keep quiet, the stones will cry out."*   LUKE 19:40

See the King in his triumphal entry. Mighty is he, yet humble. Does he not ride the colt of a donkey? He comes in peace, our King. And powerful, our King is powerful. Did he not heal the blind, cure the leper, cause the lame to walk again? Did he not calm the sea? Throw down your garments in homage. Wave palm branches before him. Shout and sing as you follow him to Jerusalem. Praise God for all the miracles he performed. Bless him, for he comes in the name of the Lord.

Now the King is glorified. He reigns in majesty at the right hand of his Father. He offers eternal life to those who call on his name. Throw down your time and your talents and your possessions in service to your King. Lift your arms in worship. Praise him for all the wondrous things he has done. Sing and shout as you follow him all your life.

The Pharisees insisted that people should not give Jesus the glory due to God. Even today, some refuse to believe that Jesus is the Son of the living God. But Jesus does not need our praise. Were we to remain silent, "the stones [would] cry out." Not only stones, but all creation declares his glory. It is our privilege to glorify our King and to serve him.

Go outside today and glorify God in his creation and with his creation. Remember, even the rocks will one day celebrate his glory! ✣

PRAYER

Jesus, I lift up my arms and glorify you . . .

day281

WHAT BELONGS TO GOD

He saw through their duplicity and said to them, "Show me a denarius. Whose image and inscription are on it?"

"Caesar's," they replied.

He said to them, "Then give back to Caesar what is Caesar's, and to God what is God's."
LUKE 20:23–25

The dining room is awash in paper. Stacks of canceled checks line one side of the table. A mound of reports fills the center, and piles of receipts spill over the edge. Pay stubs mingle with bank statements, and a layer of tax forms covers the floor. Hours drag on as you calculate and re-calculate, but at last you are finished. You sign the forms and attach checks. Sighing with relief, you drop them in the mailbox. Your taxes are paid for another year.

Taxes. No more popular in Jesus' day than in our own. The leaders tried to trick Jesus into saying it was wrong to pay taxes to Rome, but Jesus said, "Give back to Caesar what is Caesar's." It is our duty to submit to the authorities God has placed over us. But as difficult as it is to pay taxes, the second half of the verse presents a greater challenge—giving everything else back to God.

"The earth is the LORD's, and everything in it, the world, and all who live in it" (Psalm 24:1). You are a child of the Lord. Do you submit to his authority or do you try to go your own way? Are you generous with the gifts God has given you or do you hold them tightly for your own pleasure?

The taxes we pay fund roads and schools and hospitals, but a life fully yielded to the Lord reaps benefits beyond measure. As an act of worship today, mentally surrender your time, your appointments, your errands, your encounters to God's authority and will. ✤

PRAYER

Lord Almighty, I submit every thought and every action to your perfect will . . .

THE TEARS OF OUR SAVIOR

And being in anguish, he prayed more earnestly, and his sweat was like drops of blood falling to the ground.   LUKE 22:44

"The dungeon became to me as if it were a palace." So says Perpetua, a 22-year-old Christian from Carthage, North Africa, martyred around AD 200. Ripped away from the baby she was still nursing, a woman of wealth and education, tortured and killed in an amphitheater. Onlookers claimed she went joyfully to her death, anticipating heaven.

We remember Perpetua for her bravery and unswerving devotion. Yet another martyr—the most famous in all of Christendom—cried out in anguish against his impending doom. As Jesus agonized, his sorrow expressed itself in what many believe were real drops of blood. Our Savior, the King of kings, overwhelmed, everything in him wanting to call off the pain that was about to sear his body and soul. And though sobs wracked the body that would soon be broken, the temptation finally subsided: "Yet not my will, but yours be done" (Luke 22:42).

Perhaps you find tears of your own as you recount the precious story. And you may wonder, "Did he really need to be the victim of torture, harassment and malicious lies? Was it really necessary that he felt separated from his Father, accompanied by friends who slept through his deepest pain?"

In a word, yes—no crucifixion, no way to the Father. If there were no heart-wrenching agony, you would never know Jesus stands with you through the suffering and temptation you face (see Hebrews 2:18). This truth transforms every sorrow into an opportunity for true intimacy.

As you worship him today, remember that he feels your hurts and provides everything you need for victory over temptation and death. ❖

PRAYER

Teach me, Lord, how to use my pain as an opportunity to draw closer to you . . .

FORGOTTEN FORGIVENESS

Jesus said, "Father, forgive them, for they do not know what they are doing."

LUKE 23:34

"I'm forgiven because you were forsaken" asserts a popular worship song by Chris Tomlin. When we first come to Christ, the words seem rich with meaning. After realizing our brokenness and separation from a holy God, our hearts overflow with thanksgiving for his forgiveness.

The funny thing about forgiveness, however, is that we often fail to remember how much we need it. Feeling that our eternal destiny is secure, we can become a bit less thankful for the mercy of God. In our honest moments, we may even admit that it doesn't move us like it used to. And it shows.

Traces of our ungratefulness poke through as we avoid Christian brothers and sisters who have offended us or spurn the co-worker who betrayed our confidence. Our forgiveness has limits. In our hearts, we cry out like Peter did. "Lord, how many times shall I forgive my brother or sister who sins against me? Up to seven times?" (Matthew 18:21). It is all too easy for us to keep a record of wrongs.

In contrast, Jesus said, "Father, forgive them, for they do not know what they are doing"—a cry of mercy for the people who had mocked, tortured and condemned him to a cruel death.

Today, allow your thinking to shift from those who have wronged you to the One who pardons all the wrongs you commit. Come to him in gratitude now for your forgiveness—then pass it on to others. ♣

PRAYER

Father God, help me to forgive ...

AN APPROPRIATE RESPONSE

While he was blessing them, he left them and was taken up into heaven. Then they worshiped him and returned to Jerusalem with great joy.   LUKE 24:51–52

On October 3, 1863, Abraham Lincoln issued a proclamation. It called all Americans to acknowledge their gratitude for God's many blessings. Even though America was still in the midst of the Civil War, the sixteenth president had recently experienced his faith in Christ in a new way. In spite of continued conflict in the country, he felt compelled to invite recipients of God's faithfulness to appropriately respond. The proclamation led to the establishment of our national Thanksgiving holiday.

Lincoln was not the first to call for a national expression of gratitude to God for his goodness. Governor William Bradford formally called the pilgrims to esteem the Almighty with worshipful hearts in what we now acknowledge to be the very first Thanksgiving in 1623. George Washington took his cue from Bradford and in 1789 proclaimed a national day of gratitude.

It's no wonder there have been multiple Thanksgiving proclamations. The principle is a timeless one. Recognition of God's gracious activity in our lives demands an appropriate response. Blessings require bowing before the One from whom they originate. But unlike our forefathers, the disciples had no need for someone to issue a proclamation. Their gratitude was automatic. Having watched the risen Jesus' ascension, they were filled with unstoppable thanks and joy.

If it has been a while since you've felt that joy, spend some time today contemplating how you have been showered with God's blessings. ✤

PRAYER

O Lord Jesus, I truly am blessed . . .

THE TRANSCENDENT, PERSONAL GOD

In the beginning was the Word, and the Word was with God, and the Word was God. He was with God in the beginning. Through him all things were made; without him nothing was made that has been made.   JOHN 1:1–3

"In the beginning was the Word, and the Word was with God, and the Word was God." What an odd way to begin an account of the life of the most important man who ever lived! What was in John's mind when he wrote those enigmatic words?

We may not know for sure all he was thinking, but a couple of predominant thoughts seem clear. John was a Jew, and when a Jew heard the words "In the beginning," he would of course think of the first words (actually, in Hebrew, the first word) of Genesis: "In the beginning God created the heavens and the earth" (1:1). Creation and existence itself—the great mystery of how the universe came into being.

John was a Jew, but he wrote in Greek, and his thinking was heavily indebted to Greek thought and philosophy. When a Greek heard the phrase "In the beginning was the Word," he heard the word *logos*—from which we get our words *logic*, *logical*, *logistics* and so on. He thought of what gave order and intelligence to the cosmos.

Creation and existence, order and intelligence—they all came together, wrapped in flesh, and entered the world through a stable in Bethlehem. What a mind-boggling idea! So incredible, so outrageous—*so scandalous*—that it set off shock waves throughout the ancient world. The ripples from those shock waves continue to this day, changing the lives of men, women, young people, entire cultures and nations and the course of history itself.

When you worship, remember that you praise the God who draws so near he became one of us. ✤

> **PRAYER**

Lord, I praise you for drawing near . . .

ONLY ONE WAY TO HEAVEN

Jesus answered, "Very truly I tell you, no one can enter the kingdom of God unless they are born of water and the Spirit. Flesh gives birth to flesh, but the Spirit gives birth to spirit. You should not be surprised at my saying, 'You must be born again.'"   JOHN 3:5-7

How does a person get to heaven? A 2011 survey of American adults by the Barna Research Group showed that

- 43% agreed and 54% disagreed with the statement, "It doesn't matter what religious faith you follow because they all teach the same lessons"
- 40% agreed and 50% disagreed with the statement, "All people are eventually saved or accepted by God, no matter what they do, because he loves all people he has created"
- And about half of adults concurred that "if a person is generally good or does enough good things for others, they will earn a place in heaven" (48% agreed, while 44% disagreed)*

But what does Jesus say? "No one can enter the kingdom of God unless they are born of water and the Spirit." Can you imagine how Nicodemus must have felt when he heard Jesus say that? Talk about a paradigm shift! All his credentials could not earn him a ticket to heaven.

The gospel of grace runs counter to our natural impulses; human beings are naturally inclined to think we will get to heaven by being good. When people understand clearly the doctrine of grace—that we are powerless to save ourselves, that God must do it all for us—it is shocking, perhaps insulting. But when we are honest about who and what we are, sinners in the presence of a holy God, it is simply overwhelming. We must, by God's grace, be born again.

Thank God today that he has made a way to do what would be impossible without him. ♣

PRAYER

Father, only you are truly good. I accept the grace you offer . . .

---

*"What Americans Believe About Universalism and Pluralism." April 18, 2011. www.barna.org.

IN SPIRIT AND TRUTH

Yet a time is coming and has now come when the true worshipers will worship the Father in the Spirit and in truth, for they are the kind of worshipers the Father seeks. God is spirit, and his worshipers must worship in the Spirit and in truth.   John 4:23–24

What is worship, really? What do we mean when we talk about it?

Worship comes from the old English word *worthship*. Worship is ascribing worth to God—giving God his due. That's the heart of worship. Notice: The focus of attention in worship is not the preacher, a choir, a group of musicians, the kids … and it's not *us*, either. We're all important, but we are not the most important part of worship. God is the audience, and we are the participants. So what does it mean for us to worship him "in the Spirit and in truth"?

In the Spirit. The Holy Spirit is not indicated here since the Greek text has no definite article, but rather human spirit. Worship certainly engages the mind, but it engages the whole person as well. Intellect, emotions, will, attitudes, bodies—our whole being is involved.

In truth. We must worship God truthfully. For Bible-believing Christians, that means we approach him in accordance with what the Bible tells us about him. It also means we must approach God on the basis of what Jesus has done for us in his life, death, resurrection and ascension. He is the truth. "I am the way and the truth and the life. No one comes to the Father except through me" (John 14:6). Just as the Bible is the written Word, Jesus is the *living* Word.

Worship is not a spectator sport. It is full-contact spirituality. Engage yourself fully today in your time of worship—read, sing, meditate, dance, kneel, bow—do whatever it takes to worship God fully. ✤

PRAYER

Father, I am fully yours today …

A TALE OF TWO VOICES

A strong wind was blowing and the waters grew rough. When they had rowed about three or four miles, they saw Jesus approaching the boat, walking on the water; and they were frightened. But he said to them, "It is I; don't be afraid." JOHN 6:18–20

Everyone has to deal with some fear in life. It comes in many different forms: fear of dying, of going to the dentist, of heights, of speaking in public.

But fear also comes in other, more personally addressed packages.

- When it's 2 a.m. and your daughter was supposed to be home at midnight
- When the doctor tells you your test results are in, and you need to come in for a face-to-face consultation
- When the bills are piled up on the desk, and there's not another paycheck in sight
- When your spouse says, "I don't love you anymore ... I want out of the marriage"

Fear may come in different packages, but we've all received at least something—one or two ... or 20 ...

Isn't it interesting that whenever God makes an appearance to a human being in the Bible—directly or in the form of the angel of the Lord—usually the first thing the angel says to the man or woman is, "Fear not"? Something about the presence of God causes fear on our part; but something in his nature also will not allow fear to stay.

First John 4:18 says, "There is no fear in love. But perfect love drives out fear." We can face our fears with confidence, knowing that God is with us, even in the storms. Take your fears to the One who alone can deal with and overcome them. ✤

PRAYER

Father, I offer you my fear(s) ...

NO MORE HUNGER AND THIRST

"Sir," they said, "always give us this bread." Then Jesus declared, "I am the bread of life. Whoever comes to me will never go hungry, and whoever believes in me will never be thirsty."   JOHN 6:34–35

Going to parties, spending time with friends and family, heading to the mall, overeating, watching or playing sports, climbing the corporate ladder, listening to music, using illegal drugs—what do all these activities, both the good and the bad, have to do with each other?

Just this: Everyone is hungry and thirsty for life. All of these pursuits, most of which are perfectly legitimate, are often the means we use to satisfy that hunger and thirst. With a couple of obvious exceptions, nothing is wrong with any of those options in and of themselves, but they can never satisfy our hunger and thirst for true life. For that, we need something much more substantial.

Jesus told the people who were inquiring of him that he himself was the bread of life they were hungry for, the living water they were thirsty for. They could search anywhere and everywhere for something else to meet those needs, but their search would ultimately be doomed to failure. Only God can satiate that hunger and quench that thirst.

The great French physicist and philosopher Blaise Paschal wrote that each person has a vacuum inside that only God can fill. Try as we may with all these other activities, objects and even people, none of them can satisfy for long. Only the bread of life and the living water can do that. Eat regularly and drink deeply from him, both individually and corporately. ❖

> **PRAYER**

Lord, I hunger and thirst for ...

SEEING IN GOD'S LIGHT

When Jesus spoke again to the people, he said, "I am the light of the world. Whoever follows me will never walk in darkness, but will have the light of life."　　JOHN 8:12

Think of all the times in the Bible when God reveals himself in light of some form, or when light accompanies God's revelation of himself.

- Exodus 3: The burning bush
- Matthew 17: The transfiguration, when Jesus became radiant to the point that his face shone like the sun and his garments became white as light itself
- Luke 2: The birth of Jesus and the radiance of God's glory in the sky
- Revelation 21: The eternal Holy City with no need for lamps or the sun or the moon, because God himself is her light

What does the light show us?

The light shows us as we really are—and it's not always a pretty picture. The Bible says, "There is no one righteous, not even one; there is no one who understands; there is no one who seeks God" (Romans 3:10–11). Yet the light also shows us that we are God's image-bearers. From the beginning, God created us in his own image (see Genesis 1:26–27).

In the light, we see ourselves as we really are—radically and pervasively sinful, yet made in the very image of God. We also see where forgiveness really comes from: the grace of God manifested fully in the cross of Christ, where the holiness of God and the sinfulness of man come together and our salvation is accomplished.

Look in the mirror and thank God that you can see yourself clearly in his light—as a sinner, yet made in his image. ✤

PRAYER

Lord God Almighty, help me see myself and others in the light of your truth . . .

THE POWER OF A CHANGED LIFE

Then the man said, "Lord, I believe," and he worshiped him.   JOHN 9:38

How did you become a Christian? Did someone answer all your questions, give you a crash course in apologetics or show you the overwhelming evidence for the veracity of the Bible? Some people do come to faith in Christ that way, but most don't. We most often come to profess Jesus as Lord because someone we trust shares with us that Jesus can meet our deepest needs: forgiveness, purpose, meaning, direction, truth, companionship and peace.

This man Jesus encountered in John 9 had an obvious need—he was born blind. He wanted to see, and Jesus gave him his sight. Is it any wonder he called him "Lord" and proclaimed his belief in him? Further, his belief in Jesus was unshakeable even in the face of intense, entrenched opposition. You might let someone who is knowledgeable or powerful talk you out of or intimidate you into renouncing your allegiance to a merely intellectual proposition. But you wouldn't renounce someone who changed your life by restoring your eyesight.

How has knowing Jesus changed your life? Different values, different principles, different lifestyle, different recreations, different ways of handling your money, time and relationships—knowing Jesus will, or should, change your life in every way. Knowing theology and apologetics is great, and you should "be transformed by the renewing of your mind" (Romans 12:2). But there is no more persuasive argument for the validity of our faith than a changed life.

Take time to reflect on the past year, the past five years or even the past ten years. Thank God for the changes he has brought to your life during that time. ✤

PRAYER

Father, may my changed life be a clear testimony to your power, grace and love . . .

PALM SUNDAYS AND PROBLEM MONDAYS

The next day the great crowd that had come for the festival heard that Jesus was on his way to Jerusalem. They took palm branches and went out to meet him, shouting, "Hosanna! Blessed is he who comes in the name of the Lord! Blessed is the king of Israel!"

JOHN 12:12–13

The events surrounding Jesus' triumphal entry into Jerusalem are familiar to anyone who has ever attended a worship service on Palm Sunday. We sing hymns and praise choruses as our own hosannas as we rejoice over the royal reception our Lord received as he entered the city. We resonate with the roar of the approving crowd, the waving palm branches and shouted praise. *At last*, we think, *the King of Israel is receiving the honor due him. It's about time!*

Behavior that publicly demonstrates our love for Christ is an important part of worship. It provides an outlet for expressing the love we carry for the One who died for us on the cross. "Hosanna!" we cry with the crowd on Sundays. "Blessed is he who comes in the name of the Lord!"

We live in a world, however, where iPads are more prevalent than palm branches—where the realities of Monday's problems quickly eclipse the passion of Sunday's praise. The challenge for the contemporary Christian is to continue to honor Jesus after the hosannas have faded and the crowd has dispersed. Worship must be more than outward passion; it must also be inward devotion.

What comes most easily for you—public worship or private devotion? Take a few moments to quietly praise God for the blessings you are currently experiencing. ✤

PRAYER

Lord, when Monday's problems arrive, I choose to exclaim . . .

THE SERVANT-SAVIOR

Now that I, your Lord and Teacher, have washed your feet, you also should wash one another's feet. I have set you an example that you should do as I have done for you.

JOHN 13:14–15

The senior pastor was only months into his tenure at his new church in the Midwest when church members made an astonishing discovery about him. Following a special dramatic presentation in the sanctuary, participants began the laborious process of putting the large room back in order for the next service. Although the church employed several full-time custodians, the new pastor rolled up his sleeves and began to move furniture and vacuum the carpet. Church members exchanged stunned glances.

Why are we so surprised when our leaders take on the role of a servant? We live in a culture where being a member of a certain group, as the credit card commercial boasted, "has its privileges." We have become accustomed to leaders who would rather ascend to a position of status than stoop to serve others.

Today's key passage reflects just the opposite principle. Washing the feet of houseguests was a job assigned to the lowliest servant, so the disciples were astounded when Jesus himself took on that humble task. Scripture tells us that Peter protested vigorously. Jesus had a point to make, however, and he taught his followers what it meant to be a servant-leader, not by preaching but by practice.

"No servant is greater than his master" (John 13:16). When we seek to model ourselves after the One we worship, we need to start from the ground up, and that means serving others in the most humble of ways. Throughout the day, look for practical, unexpected ways you can serve others with the caring and compassion of Christ. ✤

PRAYER

Lord, open my eyes to the serving opportunities before me . . .

BELONGING TO EACH OTHER

My prayer is not for them alone. I pray also for those who will believe in me through their message, that all of them may be one, Father, just as you are in me and I am in you. May they also be in us so that the world may believe that you have sent me. JOHN 17:20–21

In a *Peanuts* comic strip that appeared some years ago, Linus Van Pelt said, "I love humanity; it's just people I can't stand!"

If we're honest with ourselves, we can admit that we sometimes feel the same way. As followers of Christ we know that we are to love one another as he first loved us, but that doesn't mean we will always like each other very much. The necessity of the body of Christ remaining united is a theme that runs throughout the Bible, yet it is perhaps one of the most difficult goals for us to achieve.

Are you ever tempted to think that you can go it alone without the fellowship of other Christians? Jesus' prayer for his disciples was also a prayer for us—those who would place their faith in him in the centuries to come. He stressed again and again his passionate desire that we "be one" even as he and his Father are one. When we gather together, he has promised to be in our midst. God's union with us allows us unity with each other.

As you worship God now, imagine the countless other believers who also are bowing before him. Pray for the unity of believers both in your community and around the world. ✤

PRAYER

Lord, give me grace to accept others . . .

THE CROSS AND THE CROWN

The soldiers twisted together a crown of thorns and put it on his head. They clothed him in a purple robe and went up to him again and again, saying, "Hail, king of the Jews!" And they slapped him in the face.   JOHN 19:2−3

Ironic, isn't it? Just a few days prior, Jesus was being hailed by the people as the King of Israel. Now he was once again being hailed as a king, but this time by men intent on mocking, humiliating and physically abusing him.

It hurts to read about the torture Christ received. The One we worship was subjected to a sarcastic veneration. The soldiers were ordered only to flog Jesus, but their cruelty went beyond carrying out his court-ordered punishment. They chose instead to "worship" him by placing a painful crown on his bloody head and a purple robe on his battered body, all the while taunting and mocking his identity.

Satan counterfeits every good gift God has given us. We have the capacity to worship Christ in gratitude and reverence, yet we also live in a world that continues to mock his name and those who bear it.

The bloody crown of briers Jesus wore for our sake was not a symbol of defeat, however. It was a symbol of God's glory and total victory over sin.

How can we possibly repay the One who has the very universe at his disposal? We can give him nothing that he does not already possess—nothing, that is, except for our hearts. Reflect today on the sacrifice of the One who bore both the cross and the crown for us. ✤

PRAYER

Forgive me, Lord, when I fail to honor you . . .

day296

THE GOD OF THE SECOND CHANCE

The third time he said to him, "Simon son of John, do you love me?" Peter was hurt because Jesus asked him the third time, "Do you love me?" He said, "Lord, you know all things; you know that I love you." Jesus said, "Feed my sheep."   JOHN 21:17

The story of Peter's failure is well known. Despite Peter's confident statement that he was willing to die for Jesus (see John 13:37), he instead denied three times that he even knew the Lord, whom he professed to love.

The account of Peter's restoration in today's passage is highly significant. Three times Peter denied Christ and three times he was given the opportunity to reaffirm his love. Jesus was not only Peter's master, but he also was a master teacher. A good teacher usually knows whether his students will pass a test. The purpose of the test is so that the student will know whether or not he or she has mastered the subject.

In Peter's case, his teacher was not only fully human but also divine; Jesus had predicted how Peter would perform in the crisis that led to the cross. Now he offered Peter the chance to retake the exam. A second chance.

If we as flawed human beings take care to mend and repair what has been torn, why would God not want to see his broken ones restored?

We serve the God of the second chance. Each of us, like Peter, is offered the opportunity to pour our brokenness at the feet of the One who was himself broken for our sake. Repentance is one of the truest forms of worship, for it has the power to remove any barrier of sin that separates us from the Savior. Take a moment to thank him for that privilege today. ✣

PRAYER

Thank you for offering me a second chance, Lord ...

THE STILL SOURCE OF MOVEMENT

They all joined together constantly in prayer, along with the women and Mary the mother of Jesus, and with his brothers.
Acts 1:14

Jeremiah Lanphier, a businessman who felt called to missionary work in New York City, wondered how best to begin his new task. After praying about it, he decided to put up copies of a handbill advertising a prayer meeting to be held every Wednesday at noon. The line at the top of the handbill asked, "How often shall I pray?"

On the first day of the prayer meeting, September 23, 1857, Lanphier was ready and waiting at noon. Five minutes passed, and nobody showed up. Another fifteen minutes passed, and still nobody came. Finally at 12:30, Lanphier heard footsteps on the stairs as the first of five people entered the room to pray.

The next week, 40 intercessors showed up. Then more came. Soon Lanphier decided to make the prayer meeting daily instead of weekly. Within six months, ten thousand businesspeople were meeting daily for prayer in New York City alone. The practice quickly spread to other cities.

This prayer movement set off one of the greatest revivals in American history. According to research by Edwin Orr, one million Americans were converted in 1858 and 1859 out of a national population of 30 million.

Great acts of God arise out of the prayers of his people the way great symphonies arise out of the ready silence of musicians.

After the ascension of Jesus, the early Christians spent their time praying together, the Spirit descended upon them and they were sent out. That group of 120 believers—not much larger than the size of the average local church in America—lit the world on fire.

How often will you pray? ♣

PRAYER

Lord, today, I bring before you . . .

ON LIFE ROW

Repent, then, and turn to God, so that your sins may be wiped out, that times of refreshing may come from the Lord. ACTS 3:19

On June 13, 1983, Karla Faye Tucker and her boyfriend, Danny Garrett, both high on drugs, snuck into an apartment, intent on stealing a motorcycle. But something went terribly wrong, and the pair ended up murdering two occupants in the apartment.

Seven years later, Karla was on death row inside Mountain View Prison in Gatesville, Texas. The preaching of prison ministers had started to get through to her, so one night she snuck a Bible back to her cell and started reading. Soon she found herself on the floor, crying and asking God to forgive her.

It takes the grace of God to let us see our sins for the slop pail they are. We may not be murderers like Tucker, but we've done plenty to bring shame upon our lives. How wonderful for us when the grace of God has also helped us make the U-turn of repentance and God has cleansed us of our sins! Peter exhorted the crowd to "Repent, then, and turn to God, so that your sins may be wiped out" and find refreshment.

Let us be earnest seekers after holiness as well as ones who authentically and persistently urge others to join us on what Karla Faye Tucker called "life row."

Thank God right now that he has caused you to repent. ✤

PRAYER

God, help me run away from evil—straight into your arms . . .

day299

A WINDOW TO HEAVEN

But Stephen, full of the Holy Spirit, looked up to heaven and saw the glory of God, and Jesus standing at the right hand of God. ACTS 7:55

A number of times in Scripture we read how certain people were privileged to see angels of God. One familiar example is that of the Bethlehem shepherds in Luke 2 who witnessed a heavenly host praising God for the birth of the Savior. In such a case, the angels appeared suddenly—or perhaps they were always there but God granted the ability to see them to a few chosen humans.

Stephen, the first Christian martyr, was even more blessed. Before dying, he saw a vision of the glory of God and of Jesus by the throne. And as if Stephen were reflecting some of the light of heaven streaming down, "his face was like the face of an angel" (Acts 6:15). Perhaps Stephen's countenance was like that of Moses, who wore a veil to hide the glow of his face after meeting with God (see Exodus 34:29–35).

What would it be like to live with our spirits wide open to supernatural realities? Would it make us bold in testifying for Jesus, as Stephen was before the Sanhedrin? Would our faces betray the experience with a heaven-lit glow? Would we tune our voices to the singing of the angels?

Today, picture Jesus not as the dusty itinerant rabbi he once was, but as the Son of Man in heaven he now is, with face shining, eyes blazing, voice thundering (see Revelation 1:13–16). Worship this glorious Lord. ✤

PRAYER

Lord Jesus, bathe me in the glow of your presence . . .

GOING SOUTH

Now an angel of the Lord said to Philip, "Go south to the road—the desert road—that goes down from Jerusalem to Gaza."   ACTS 8:26

An expert in psychology and religion, Henri Nouwen spent many years teaching at Yale and Harvard. But then in 1985 he wrote the following in his journal:

> *I want to cry out loudly to my colleagues and students: "Do not serve Harvard, but God and his beloved, Jesus Christ, and speak words of hope to those who suffer from loneliness, depression, and spiritual poverty." Yet I myself have come to the painful discovery that when I am chained by ambition it is hard for me to see those who are chained by poverty. Therefore this is not a time to play the prophet, but a time to listen more carefully to the voice of God calling within me.*

In response to the voice of God, Nouwen left Harvard for Toronto to care for mentally challenged people in a household connected with the Communities of L'Arche. Later, in a moving speech at Harvard, Nouwen reported that the apparent demotion of working with a severely handicapped young man had changed his understanding of God's love.

Perhaps the apostle Philip thought it a demotion when the Lord told him to head for Gaza. After all, Philip had been leading a wildly successful ministry in Samaria. Now God wanted him to talk to a single foreigner in the desert? But he obeyed the Lord and wound up sending an enthusiastic new believer back to Ethiopia, further extending the infant church.

As with Philip and Henri Nouwen, God's call on us may not meet our expectations. Yet prestigious or obscure, publicly successful or personally humbling, our ministry is the right one if God has called us to it. We are his to direct. Faithfulness is what matters most in a minister. ♣

PRAYER

Lord, send me where you will …

GOD IN MOTION

When he arrived and saw what the grace of God had done, he was glad and encouraged them all to remain true to the Lord with all their hearts.   ACTS 11:23

We all encounter ideas that are difficult to understand. For the earliest Christians—all of them Jews—one such idea was that God might accept Gentiles on an equal footing with Jews through faith in Christ. That's why leaders of the mother church in Jerusalem sent Barnabas to verify reports of Gentiles becoming followers of Jesus. Barnabas was a good choice. When this good man saw that God had indeed been moving among Gentiles in Antioch, he rejoiced in the work and did his little bit to push it along, encouraging the believers "to remain true to the Lord with all their hearts."

We have our own ideas of what the church should be, and sometimes the movement of God in the world surprises us. How do we feel when a celebrity who has political views opposed to our own is born again and doesn't change her politics? How do we feel when we hear of growth in a church movement that includes some secondary doctrinal beliefs that make us uncomfortable? The point is not that others are right and we are wrong. The point is that God may be moving among others even though they are different from us and no more perfect than we are.

God ranges about the earth freely, acting in ways we cannot always predict. Let us not be worried by this but instead open our eyes and our minds to what God might be doing. Rejoice today in the work the Lord is doing in your community. ✤

PRAYER

Holy Spirit, move through my community . . .

DANCING YOUR WAY TO HEAVEN

And the disciples were filled with joy and with the Holy Spirit.　　　Acts 13:52

When burdened by the constant pressure of his studies while a seminary student, W. A. Criswell would sometimes pause to pray, read a passage from the Bible or sing a cheerful gospel song. On one occasion right before midterm exams, Criswell began singing the old gospel tune "It Pays to Serve Jesus"—not out of discouragement but from pure joy

When he was preaching years later at the First Baptist Church in Richmond, Virginia, a fellow pastor spoke to him after the service with tears in his eyes. This pastor explained how he was about to leave seminary out of discouragement, when he suddenly heard a voice singing "It Pays to Serve Jesus." The young man was forever changed as he heard Criswell's unrestrained joy.

The new converts in Antioch of Pisidia—today's central Turkey—had that kind of joy. The apostles who had brought them the gospel, Paul and Barnabas, were chased out of town. But the local Christians were not discouraged; they were "filled with joy and with the Holy Spirit."

What does it take to possess a joy that bubbles up despite trouble? A fixation on God and the salvation he grants through his Son. We can be like David dancing before the ark of God (see 2 Samuel 6:14–15) if we have experienced the forgiveness Christ offers and have the Holy Spirit living within us.

How long has it been since you felt joy? If it has been a while, might there be a problem in your relationship with God? If you do have joy, find a way to express it today. ✤

PRAYER

Lord, let me share in the joyful mood of heaven . . .

AN AUDIENCE OF ONE

About midnight Paul and Silas were praying and singing hymns to God, and the other prisoners were listening to them.   ACTS 16:25

Jerome Hines (1921–2003) thrilled audiences in opera houses around the world when he sang the bass lead in such operas as *Boris Godunov* and *Faust*. He also became a Christian in young adulthood. In his autobiography, *This Is My Story, This Is My Song*, Hines recalled the first time he sang for a Christian gathering, at a Salvation Army meeting in London.

> *It was announced that we would have a solo. I started to get up from my chair, but the officer in charge introduced a lady-officer from another corps who arose and began to sing.*
>
> *"Why," I thought, "do they let her sing? What a terrible sound. It's strange that they'd let her sing, knowing there's a Metropolitan Opera singer on the program."*
>
> *Then my attention was caught by the radiant, beautiful look on her face and the impact of the words she was singing struck me. She sang with such dedication and sincerity that I began to forget the unpleasant scratch of her voice.*
>
> *"Lord," I whispered, "it may sound bad to me, but I'll bet that is beautiful music to your ears."*

We do not make our joyful noise to the Lord because the sound of our voice is a treat for God. We do not necessarily sing praises because we're feeling happy, for like Paul and Silas in prison, things may not be going well for us. And if others are listening who might be blessed by our singing, that's great; if not, we sing anyway. We sing because our audience is the One who has filled our hearts with a joy that must come out. ✤

PRAYER

I will sing unto you, Lord ...

LIFTING UP THE DOWN-AND-OUT

In everything I did, I showed you that by this kind of hard work we must help the weak, remembering the words the Lord Jesus himself said: "It is more blessed to give than to receive."
ACTS 20:35

Where do we direct our eyes? Do we look upward in envy at those who have more than we have? Or do we look downward in compassion at those who are less fortunate and so stoop to give them a hand?

The apostle Paul chose to look downward. He knew a trade—tent making. And he put it to good use by earning enough money not only to support himself—thereby relieving fledgling congregations of that responsibility—but also to give to the poor. He makes a good model for us, embodying as he did the spirit of generosity that permeates the teachings of Jesus.

While many today are fascinated by the lifestyles of the rich and famous, others are following the example of the apostle Paul by caring for the poor. Mary Jo Copeland is one such individual.

Copeland grew up in a desperately poor home, then married and raised 12 children of her own amid difficult circumstances. But she could not ignore those still needier than she was. In 1985, she started a ministry to the homeless in the Twin Cities called Sharing and Caring Hands. Tireless in her efforts, Copeland has built a complex of services that gives shelter, hot meals, bus tokens, showers, clothing, medical and dental care, legal aid, counseling and referrals to more than one thousand people a day. The "Mother Teresa of Minneapolis" is known for personally washing the filthy, blistered feet of the street people who come her way.

Mary Jo Copeland saw the poor and didn't look away. Let us, likewise, give to and get involved in the lives of the poor. A blessing awaits us when we do. ✤

> **PRAYER**

Show me, Lord, where to offer your love . . .

day305

TRUTH BE TOLD

Brothers and fathers, listen now to my defense.   ACTS 22:1

As a young woman, Rebecca Manley Pippert was talking with a new acquaintance on the campus of the University of California, Berkeley. The conversation turned to God, and Becky began going on and on about her Christian faith. Meanwhile, the other woman fell silent.

Finally Becky interrupted herself and said, "Look, I feel really bad. I am very excited about who God is and what he's done in my life. But I hate it when people push 'religion' on me. So if I'm coming on too strong, will you just tell me?"

The other woman said, "I never knew Christians were aware that we hate being recipients of a running monologue."

"Listen," Becky responded, "most Christians I know are very hesitant to share their faith precisely because they're afraid they'll offend."

"But as long as you let people know that you're aware of where they're coming from, you can say anything you want!" the other woman responded.

And thus an unbeliever gave Becky—and now us—a lesson in evangelism. We need to be respectful to unbelievers, certainly, but there's an interchange of ideas going on out there all the time; we don't have to be ashamed to put in our comments about Christ. Who knows? God may use our words to revolutionize the life of another.

The apostle Paul found himself in an opportune situation when he was accused of violating temple protocol. Caught in the spotlight, he used the occasion to boldly yet respectfully tell his own story of encountering Christ.

You can do the same whenever you receive spoken or unspoken permission from another to share what's closest to your heart. ✤

PRAYER

Use me, Lord, to boldly witness for you ...

CRAZY FOR JESUS

At this point Festus interrupted Paul's defense. "You are out of your mind, Paul!" he shouted. "Your great learning is driving you insane."   Acts 26:24

Reports filtering out of North Korea suggest that incarcerated Christians in this officially atheistic society have been treated more harshly than other prisoners. U.S. State Department reports frequently accuse North Korea of torturing and executing Christians because of their faith. One former North Korean prison guard also testified that "those believing in God were regarded as insane." In this, North Korea has stolen a page from the former Soviet Union, which for decades committed Christians to insane asylums where they were subjected to cruel and unnecessary "treatments."

We are fortunate to live in a society in which Christian faith is not equated with lunacy. Or at least not seriously. Some may still shout, "You've got to be nuts!" when we testify for the Lord. That's the sort of reaction Paul got while giving his defense before a pair of local rulers, Festus and Agrippa. When Paul got to the part of the story where Jesus rises from the dead, Festus blurted out his views on Paul's mental health, and the proceedings came to a crashing halt. Perhaps it was experiences like this that led Paul to write about how God's wisdom seems foolish to the world (see 1 Corinthians 1:18–25).

It all has to do with the inclination of one's thinking. Academics tell us that we all have mental "paradigms," or sets of assumptions about reality. It takes a powerful exposure to new truth to cause a "paradigm shift." In fact, it takes the Holy Spirit to shift a person from worldly mindedness to heavenly mindedness. When others think we're crazy for believing as we do, our response should be to pray that God will enable them to believe in Jesus too (see Acts 26:29). ✤

PRAYER

Lord, help me lay down whatever is preventing me from being a "fool" for you . . .

CHANGE OF ITINERARY

For this reason I have asked to see you and talk with you. It is because of the hope of Israel that I am bound with this chain.   ACTS 28:20

Dayna Curry and Heather Mercer were young Americans who wanted to tell people about Jesus. But they went to Afghanistan as missionaries at a time when the extremist Muslim Taliban ruled much of the nation. So on August 3, 2001, after showing a film about Jesus in a Kabul home, the two young women were picked up by Taliban operatives and thrown into prison.

Instead of putting an end to the women's Christian influence, their imprisonment multiplied it. As they state in the book *Prisoners of Hope*, while in prison Curry and Mercer were able to live closer to Afghan women than they ever had before. And following their rescue by American troops, their media popularity enabled them to tell about the love of God to many in the U.S. who would otherwise never have heard of them.

In a similar situation, the apostle Paul may have been disappointed to see his plans to minister in Rome seemingly derailed when he was arrested in Jerusalem and then spent years incarcerated in Caesarea. But he later wound up in Rome anyway, arriving on a different timetable, with a different set of people to witness to and with a more poignant testimony to give. As he told the Jewish leaders of Rome, he was in chains for the sake of the Messiah.

One way to respond to an unexpected turn of events is to become angry and fearful. Another is to assume that God has something better—though not necessarily easier—in mind for us and to look for the opportunities he is putting in our way. If our desire is to live for him, he will make it happen in the way that best suits his purposes. ✤

PRAYER

Father, tell me where, and I will go . . .

A SILENCE THAT SPEAKS VOLUMES

For since the creation of the world God's invisible qualities—his eternal power and divine nature—have been clearly seen, being understood from what has been made, so that people are without excuse. ROMANS 1:20

The sun rises in the east and sets in the west. Summer follows spring, which follows winter, which follows autumn, which follows summer. Orion, Pleiades and Ursa Major move in their bejeweled glory across the night sky in the same pattern, night after night, millennium after millennium. The tide ebbs and flows, ebbs and flows.

All of creation bears witness to its Creator. If you had never read a Bible, attended a church service or heard the term *general revelation*, you would still know that this world was planned and placed here by an intelligent designer. As Psalm 19:1–2 puts it, "The heavens declare the glory of God; the skies proclaim the work of his hands. Day after day they pour forth speech; night after night they reveal knowledge."

Today's verse makes this point even more emphatically. Paul states that all people everywhere can look at this marvelous planet and the skies above it and know that it must have been created by Someone. Furthermore, we can discern some character traits about that Someone, namely, that he is powerful, orderly, beautiful and creative. These qualities are mirrored, if rather imperfectly, in his creation. No, nature alone cannot impart the whole gospel to us, but it can and does point unmistakably to its origin.

As you consider the majesty and beauty of the cosmos, pause to praise and adore its artist. Spend a few moments today in God's creation—at a nearby park, at a conservatory or simply in your backyard. Worship the Creator of all that you see. ❖

PRAYER

Lord of creation, thank you for . . .

FROM ENEMIES TO FRIENDS

For if, while we were God's enemies, we were reconciled to him through the death of his Son, how much more, having been reconciled, shall we be saved through his life!

ROMANS 5:10

In C. S. Lewis's *The Lion, the Witch and the Wardrobe*, a boy named Edmund commits a terrible act of treachery and is condemned to die by the laws of Narnia. According to this law—the Deep Magic from the Dawn of Time—all traitors are the rightful property of the evil White Witch. But Aslan the lion, the Christ-figure in the series, frees Edmund by dying in his place. The Witch exults, believing she now has Narnia in her unchallenged grip. The next morning, however, Aslan comes back to life. He explains to Edmund's sister Susan what the Witch didn't know: When an innocent, willing victim is killed in place of a traitor, death itself begins to work backward. The Deeper Magic from Before the Dawn of Time is a law of sacrifice, atonement and redemption.

What Lewis illustrates in his masterful tale is what in Romans 5:6–10 Paul says happened in reality in the life, atoning death and resurrection of Jesus. Sinful humanity stood justly condemned before a holy God. Lawbreakers all, we deserved judgment and condemnation, but an innocent substitute took our place and gave us the opportunity to be redeemed from the penalty of the law.

From enemies to friends, from estranged to reconciled, from orphans to beloved children—the grace of God manifested in the cross of Christ has accomplished this amazing transformation in us and for us. Can we respond with anything less than total gratitude to God for all he has done? ✤

PRAYER

Jesus, thank you for your sacrifice . . .

day310

LOOKING FROM THE OUTSIDE IN

What a wretched man I am! Who will rescue me from this body that is subject to death? Thanks be to God, who delivers me through Jesus Christ our Lord! So then, I myself in my mind am a slave to God's law, but in my sinful nature a slave to the law of sin.

ROMANS 7:24–25

Have you ever seen a snakeskin without a snake in it? Snakes cast off their skin every so often by a process known as molting. Sometimes you can find a complete skin whose owner has slithered off in its brand-new covering. Wouldn't that be wonderful—to be able to shed your external shell like that and start over in a brand-new one? Just one problem: The snake that molts and leaves behind its old skin *is still a snake.*

When we try to reinvent ourselves—through exercise, meditation, 12-step programs or any other form of self-help—we can end up just like our reptilian friends. We may look better, dress better, talk better and even think and feel better, but we still end up just slightly modified versions of the same old people we were before. We need help from something—or Someone—outside of ourselves.

That's Paul's dilemma in Romans 7:24–25. He had given his best effort at remaking himself and had ended in despair. He was like a snake that shed its skin only to realize it was still a snake. That despair then drove him straight to the grace of God as manifested in Jesus Christ.

Has that powerful grace changed you in ways you could never change on your own? In what significant ways has God changed you since you became a Christian? Have you thanked him for what he's done—and is doing—in you, with you, for you and through you? Take a few moments to thank God for helping you make real changes in your life rather than just "shedding your skin." ✣

PRAYER

Father, thank you for changing me from the inside out . . .

314

THE OTHER SIDE OF THE DARKNESS

For I am convinced that neither death nor life, neither angels nor demons, neither the present nor the future, nor any powers, neither height nor depth, nor anything else in all creation, will be able to separate us from the love of God that is in Christ Jesus our Lord.

ROMANS 8:38–39

Do you sometimes find yourself in circumstances that cause you to question whether or not God really loves you? A divorce, a death in the family, financial difficulties, a rebellious child, illness or injury—all these can make us wonder if God has lost our address.

Yet Paul assures us that regardless of the crisis or calamity, we can never be lost to God's love. Nothing can separate us from his love. Nothing.

Why then does God allow us to undergo such difficulties and such pain? Often, the best answer is, we just don't know. His ways are not always our ways, and his thoughts are not always our thoughts (see Isaiah 55:8–9). Perhaps an even tougher question is, Why does he love us so tenaciously in the first place? Again, it's hard to fathom that a holy God could love sinful men and women.

It's natural to question his love when times are tough. It is supernatural to see through the tough times and discern the face of a loving Father.

An old Puritan prayer says, "My Father, I trust thee, even when I do not understand thee." Make that your prayer in the dark places. ✤

PRAYER

Father, help me to see your love through my pain ...

ALL I KNOW

Therefore, I urge you, brothers and sisters, in view of God's mercy, to offer your bodies as a living sacrifice, holy and pleasing to God—this is your true and proper worship. Do not conform to the pattern of this world, but be transformed by the renewing of your mind. Then you will be able to test and approve what God's will is—his good, pleasing and perfect will.　　　　　　　　　　　　　　　　　　　　　　　　ROMANS 12:1–2

Can you picture an Old Testament worship service?

- The splendor of the temple
- Priests dressed in glorious garb
- A gold-plated altar
- Fire, smoke and sacrificial animals being led, uncomprehending, to their deaths

Now think about a worship service under the New Covenant:

- Buildings become irrelevant (see John 4:19–24)
- The whole idea of a separate priesthood is superseded by the reality of the priesthood of all believers (see 1 Peter 2:4–10)
- The system of animal sacrifice is done away with because of the sufficiency and finality of Jesus' sacrifice on the cross (see Hebrews 9)

If there is no "temple" and there are no "priests" offering animal sacrifices for the people, what exactly are we to offer to the Lord in worship? Paul puts it very straightforwardly in the passage above: Ourselves. Our forebears used to offer animal sacrifices for their sin; now we offer ourselves for *holiness*. The animals went unknowingly; we offer ourselves knowing what we're doing.

Worship is not for wimps. It is an all-encompassing, all-engaging, all-consuming offering of ourselves before our triune God. Consider your hands, your feet, your mouth—use them today as an act of sacrifice to the Lord. ✤

PRAYER

Father, bring me, by your grace, to that point where I can truly offer myself as a living and holy sacrifice . . .

WITH ONE VOICE

May the God who gives endurance and encouragement give you the same attitude of mind toward each other that Christ Jesus had, so that with one mind and one voice you may glorify the God and Father of our Lord Jesus Christ.   ROMANS 15:5–6

You've heard it before. A duet, a trio, a quartet or even a whole choir that just can't quite find the right notes, can't quite blend their voices into the harmony they were aiming for. Or maybe they weren't even close. Either way, it is a very unpleasant, uncomfortable experience for the listeners. The song can't end fast enough.

God must feel something like that when we squabble in our churches over issues that, more often than not, are not really all that important. Instead of being of "the same attitude of mind toward each other" and "with one mind and one voice [glorifying] the God and Father of our Lord Jesus Christ," we warble off in our own key, our own pitch, our own melody, our own tempo. Individually, it might sound fine. But when it's time to blend together with other believers, it's dissonant and discordant. Worse, it's unworthy of our magnificent Lord.

Coming together as Christians means not only accepting Jesus' view on the authority of Scripture, the nature of heaven and the reality of the resurrection; it also means adopting the attitude of love toward other Christians that Jesus has for us. Only then can we truly join together in praising him with "one voice."

Are there people for whom you have a hard time showing consideration? Do you tend to focus on the things that divide and distract from God and his glory? Pray today that he will give you the attitude Paul described above so that you will be better able, both individually and corporately, to praise him with one voice. ✤

PRAYER

Lord, I long for unity in this relationship ...

THE FOOLISH PLAN OF GOD

We preach Christ crucified: a stumbling block to Jews and foolishness to Gentiles, but to those whom God has called, both Jews and Greeks, Christ the power of God and the wisdom of God. For the foolishness of God is wiser than human wisdom, and the weakness of God is stronger than human strength.   1 CORINTHIANS 1:23–25

Perhaps you've heard the haunting Christmas song by 4 Him, "A Strange Way to Save the World," that imagines Joseph surveying the Bethlehem stable on that first Christmas night and wondering why. Why him, a simple man of trade? Why a stable? Why a baby? Why an ordinary girl? The chorus ends, "Now I'm not one to second guess what angels have to say, but this is such a strange way to save the world."

Strange indeed. Jesus, the baby "Savior," grows up in obscurity, not even making a public splash until he's 30. And even then, his ministry is a mixed bag. He gathers far more enemies than followers, until his surprising words and unpredictable actions at last earn him a date with the executioner. When rich friends put his battered body in a grave, what's he got to show for his three-plus years of effort? A ragtag group of frightened men and a few weeping women.

The whole thing is odd, bizarre beyond words. But it gets even stranger. The grave can't hold Christ. He emerges from the tomb, gives his followers new hope—eternal hope—and then departs. Before he goes he commissions them, a motley crew of messed-up misfits, to take the message of his life and death and resurrection to the whole world. He calls them to live sacrificially and to overcome evil with good.

Today, rejoice that you are part of this amazing and strange story. Think of the odd events God used to save you. Imagine how he might want to use you to pull someone else into his forever family. ♣

PRAYER

Lord, thank you for letting me be part of your "foolish" plan . . .

POWER IN THE BLOOD

Get rid of the old yeast, so that you may be a new unleavened batch—as you really are. For Christ, our Passover lamb, has been sacrificed. 1 CORINTHIANS 5:7

The old Isaac Watts hymn "Not All the Blood of Beasts" is a great worship song about Christ, our Passover Lamb. The first two stanzas go like this:

> *Not all the blood of beasts*
> *On Jewish altars slain*
> *Could give the guilty conscience peace*
> *Or wash away the stain.*
>
> *But Christ, the heav'nly Lamb*
> *Takes all our sins away;*
> *A sacrifice of nobler name*
> *And richer blood than they.*

Passover's origins are found at the end of the Jews' 400-year period of Egyptian bondage (see Exodus 12). Under the leadership of Moses, the Jews watched God bring a series of ever-worsening plagues on their oppressors. Finally, each Hebrew family was instructed to take an unblemished male lamb, slaughter it and sprinkle its blood above the doorframe of their home. They were then to eat a meal of roasted lamb and unleavened bread and prepare to depart. As judgment fell upon Egypt, those "under the blood" were spared. Death "passed over" their houses. But in every home not covered by the blood of a Passover lamb, the firstborn son (and firstborn of all their animals) died.

This is nothing less than a preview of the gospel—a sneak peak at the One who would come almost 15 centuries later, and about whom John the Baptist would proclaim, "Look, the Lamb of God, who takes away the sin of the world!" (John 1:29).

Here then is one more reason to worship: Christ died on our behalf. Are you willing to live for him? ♣

PRAYER

Lord Jesus, I am willing ...

day316

KEEP YOUR EYES ON THE PRIZE

Do you not know that in a race all the runners run, but only one gets the prize? Run in such a way as to get the prize. Everyone who competes in the games goes into strict training. They do it to get a crown that will not last, but we do it to get a crown that will last forever.　　　　　　　　　　　　　　　　　　　1 CORINTHIANS 9:24–25

Those who watched the 1976 Summer Olympics may remember the exploits of a Japanese gymnast named Shun Fujimoto. In his quest for the men's all-around gold medal, the 26-year-old shattered his right knee during the floor exercise. Yet, amazingly, he continued to compete, even in what many regard as the most grueling event of all—the rings. Onlookers were stunned by his flawless routine and flabbergasted when he nailed a perfect triple somersault twist dismount, landing squarely on his feet, further injuring his knee.

Interviewed later about his feat, Fujimoto said, "Yes, the pain shot through me like a knife. It brought tears to my eyes. But now I have a gold medal and the pain is gone."

It is this mindset that Christians need to embrace and live out—a dogged determination to suffer and persevere for the faith. An absolute refusal to cut corners or "cheat" in any way. A never-say-die commitment to go the distance for Christ, no matter what that requires.

No athlete becomes a champion through ordinary effort. He or she takes home the top prize by putting forth extraordinary effort. And if they're willing to go to such lengths for a medal or trophy, for short-lived athletic glory, how much more committed should we be to receive eternal spiritual glory?

As you go through your day, imagine the errands, tasks and work you do while "running the race" for Christ. Commit your best efforts to him as your act of worship. ✤

PRAYER

Lord, grant me the perseverance to run this race . . .

LOVE CONQUERS ALL

No temptation has overtaken you except what is common to mankind. And God is faithful; he will not let you be tempted beyond what you can bear. But when you are tempted, he will also provide a way out so that you can endure it.   1 Corinthians 10:13

The premise of the 1983 hit movie *Mr. Mom* is what happens in a family when the husband gets laid off and becomes a stay-at-home dad and the mother of the family's young children reenters the workplace. It's a funny film that also includes a powerful lesson about temptation.

The temptation scene comes at the end of the movie. Due to a whole series of misunderstandings, the stressed-out husband and wife are barely speaking. To make matters worse, both are being seduced—she by her annoying boss, he by a sultry neighbor. Jack, the husband, is clearly torn. Given the sad state of his marriage, the forbidden fruit is very tantalizing. The grass on the other side of the marital fence definitely looks greener. But after wrestling with his options, he reminds himself of his love for his wife, which keeps him from giving in to temptation.

Notice that the Bible assures us that temptations will come. They are a fact of life in a fallen world. Notice also that we're not unique in the kinds of temptations we experience. Others wrestle with the same kinds of messes. The key verses today remind us that God is faithful. He will never allow a temptation so strong that we are unable to resist. In every inducement to evil, God will show us a way out, a way of escape.

The best escape, as we've already noted, is love. When we love Christ above all else, when he is the great desire of our lives and the One we want most to please, it becomes much easier to say no to sin. ❖

PRAYER

Father, increase my love for you as I face the temptations in my life . . .

ALL YOU NEED IS LOVE

It always protects, always trusts, always hopes, always perseveres. Love never fails. But where there are prophecies, they will cease; where there are tongues, they will be stilled; where there is knowledge, it will pass away.   1 Corinthians 13:7–8

The final verse of the hymn "The Love of God" reads:

> *Could we with ink the ocean fill,*
> *And were the skies of parchment made,*
> *Were every stalk on earth a quill,*
> *And every man a scribe by trade;*
> *To write the love of God above*
> *Would drain the ocean dry;*
> *Nor could the scroll contain the whole,*
> *Though stretched from sky to sky.*

God's love is wondrous. As today's passage teaches, God's love "always trusts, always hopes, always perseveres." No wonder the apostle Paul prayed for his Ephesian brothers and sisters in the faith. "I pray that you, being rooted and established in love, may have power, together with all the Lord's holy people, to grasp how wide and long and high and deep is the love of Christ, and to know this love that surpasses knowledge — that you may be filled to the measure of all the fullness of God" (Ephesians 3:17–19).

God's stunning love alone has the power to change us. No strings. No conditions. No getting our acts together first. He doesn't love us only if we measure up to certain standards. He just sets his perfect affection on us — or, we could say, he sets us permanently in the warmth of his absolute care and favor.

This immense and endless love, which liberates us from our prisons of fear and self-protection, results in our finding a new capacity to love others. Spend some time meditating on God's great love for you. Then, in the overflow of that love, share it with someone else today. ✤

> **PRAYER**

Lord Jesus, thank you for your amazing love …

THE GOD OF ALL COMFORT

Praise be to the God and Father of our Lord Jesus Christ, the Father of compassion and the God of all comfort, who comforts us in all our troubles, so that we can comfort those in any trouble with the comfort we ourselves receive from God.   2 Corinthians 1:3–4

People like comfort. Consider these comments given to the staff of the Bridger Wilderness Area in Wyoming:

- Too many bugs and leeches and spiders and spider webs. Please spray the wilderness to rid the areas of these pests.
- Chair lifts need to be in some places so that we can get to wonderful views without having to hike to them.
- Escalators would help on steep uphill sections.

When Scripture speaks of comfort, it is not referring to plush surroundings. Today's passage teaches us, instead, about the true nature of comfort—the sort of solace and consolation that can only come from God himself.

Like the loving parent he is, God models comfort for us so that we in turn can reach out to others with the comfort of Christ. He never promises to remove all difficulties from our lives, but rather to give us consolation and encouragement to endure them.

Human comfort often comes in the form of a hug or a hand to hold. When we "hold" others in their times of sorrow through words of solace or acts of kindness, we are redeeming our own troubles by allowing them to be used for God's purposes.

Worship flows freely from the heart that has received divine comfort. How has God embraced you in comfort? Extend that kind of embrace to a family or friend who is in need of encouragement today. ❖

PRAYER

Lord, teach me to comfort others . . .

NEVER GIVE UP OR GIVE IN

Therefore, since through God's mercy we have this ministry, we do not lose heart.

2 CORINTHIANS 4:1

Winston Churchill once delivered what became a famous speech at Harrow, his former prep school. He is often quoted as having stated, "Never give up. Never give up. Never give up!" What Churchill actually said was, "Never give in, never give in, never, never, never, never—in nothing, great or small, large or petty—never give in except to convictions of honour and good sense."

Giving up or giving in—is there a difference? Let's face it—sometimes it feels like the same thing. We try to serve others only to have our motives misunderstood or our methods questioned. Ministry is tough, and at times we honestly wonder whether it is worth it.

That's when the words of the apostle Paul serve to strengthen our spirit just as Churchill stiffened the spines of the young men at Harrow. "We do not lose heart," writes Paul.

Do you notice the descriptor used here? "Through God's mercy we have this ministry." It is a magnificent extension of God's mercy that he allows us to minister to others in the name of his own Son.

Are you tempted to give up in discouragement or give in to doubt? Take heart from the Scriptures and set aside any thought of quitting. Remember that "we have this treasure in jars of clay to show that this all-surpassing power is from God and not from us" (2 Corinthians 4:7).

Allow God's light and power to shine through you today in the attitude and way you serve others. Rejoice in the wonderful ministry to which he has called you. ❖

PRAYER

Lord, help me to see that wherever you have placed me, I am to persevere for your honor and glory . . .

A HARVEST OF GENEROSITY

Now he who supplies seed to the sower and bread for food will also supply and increase your store of seed and will enlarge the harvest of your righteousness. You will be enriched in every way so that you can be generous on every occasion, and through us your generosity will result in thanksgiving to God.   2 CORINTHIANS 9:10–11

John Wesley practiced what he preached when it came to giving. He limited his expenditures by not buying the kinds of things generally considered essential for a man in his station of life. In 1776, the English tax commissioners inspected his return and wrote back, "[We] cannot doubt but you have plate for which you have hitherto neglected to make an entry."

They assumed that a man of his prominence certainly had silver dinnerware in his house, and they wanted him to pay the proper tax on it. Wesley wrote back, "I have two silver tea-spoons at London, and two at Bristol. This is all the plate I have at present and I shall not buy any more while so many around me want bread."

Today's passage teaches that God himself is the source and supply of every blessing we have, including the material ones. We are not to keep what we are given for ourselves alone, but rather we're to use our resources wisely so that a "harvest of generosity" will be produced from which we can bless others.

When we donate to charity or write a check to support our local church, we are not simply fulfilling a religious obligation. God does not desire our sacrifices but rather our hearts. According to Paul's second letter to the Corinthian church, giving is not only an act of worship itself but results in worship. Those who benefit from our giving "will break out in thanksgiving to God."

Offer your blessings back to God as a love gift today. ♣

PRAYER

Lord, help me glorify you through giving generously . . .

THANKFUL FOR THE THORNS

Therefore, in order to keep me from becoming conceited, I was given a thorn in my flesh, a messenger of Satan, to torment me.   2 CORINTHIANS 12:7

Many have speculated about the nature of Paul's thorn. It could have been a chronic physical condition, such as failing eyesight, or even a person or group of people who were opposed to his ministry (see the end of chapter 11). Whether Paul was dealing with a physical disability or a person who became a psychological liability, it seems clear that his focus was not on his thorn, but rather on why God had allowed it.

How can it be possible to not only accept our human frailties but also to literally praise God because of them? Rather than bemoan his plight, Paul was able to "delight" in his weaknesses (see 2 Corinthians 12:10) because he recognized that his condition provided a showcase for God's divine power to be displayed through his life.

Do you have a thorn or two in your garden of relationships, or perhaps a physical weakness that never seems to improve? Take your cue from Paul and respond by thanking God for your thorn. In the book of Ephesians, Paul puts it very plainly: "always giving thanks to God the Father for everything" (5:20).

Author Beth Moore has said that whether or not God chooses to remove a thorn depends on the point. He will either choose to demonstrate his supremacy—that he can do it—or his sufficiency—that he can get you through it. Regardless of how God answers our plea for help, our response should be to praise him for the grace that allows his power to work through us. ✤

PRAYER

Lord, in regard to the thorn in my life, I . . .

day323

THE GOD WHO CHANGES LIVES

They only heard the report: "The man who formerly persecuted us is now preaching the faith he once tried to destroy." And they praised God because of me. GALATIANS 1:23–24

Author Lee Strobel, who was at one time a staunch atheist, now serves as a pastor. When asked to describe the difference God made in his life, he shared the following story.

> *My daughter Allison was 5 years old when I became a follower of Jesus, and all she had known in those five years was a dad who was profane and angry. I remember I came home one night and kicked a hole in the living room wall just out of anger with life. I am ashamed to think of the times Allison hid in her room to get away from me. Five months after I gave my life to Jesus Christ, that little girl went to my wife and said, "Mommy, I want God to do for me what he's done for Daddy." . . . God changed my family. He changed my world. He changed my eternity.*

We worship a God who has the power to change human lives. The same resurrection power that raised Jesus from the dead can also transform those who are spiritually dead into fully awakened followers of Christ. As today's passage illustrates, God did it with Paul, a persecutor-turned-preacher. He did it with Lee, who once profaned the very gospel he now proclaims. No one is beyond the reach of God's grace.

If you struggle with feelings of self-defeat or failure, thinking you lack the ability to make a new start, take heart from the fact that this same life-changing power is available to you as well. The most powerful testimony on earth is that of a transformed life. ✤

PRAYER

Lord, help me to become like the One I worship . . .

AIMING AT HEAVEN

But now that you know God—or rather are known by God—how is it that you are turning back to those weak and miserable forces? Do you wish to be enslaved by them all over again?   GALATIANS 4:9

In today's passage, the apostle Paul is writing to those who have become followers of Christ and should be enjoying the rights and privileges of their faith. Instead, they are returning to legalism—placing themselves once again in bondage to works and religious rituals.

This temptation to place our trust in our own achievements still marks our world. Worship should be a celebration of the glorious status we have in Christ, whose sacrificial death for us on the cross paid the penalty for our sins once and for all. Our old nature, however, resists this freedom and at times beckons us to return to the way of life we left behind.

Cyprian, a bishop of Carthage in the third century, explained it this way: "Don't look to things behind us that the devil calls us back to. Instead, look to things ahead of us that Christ calls us to. Let us lift our eyes up to heaven, lest the earth deceive us with its delights and enticements."

Worship allows us to fix our focus not on the things we can see around us, but on the unseen realities of the spiritual world. Meditate on the glorious inheritance that is waiting for you in eternity. Take aim at heaven; your faith has already shown you the way. ❖

PRAYER

Lord, help me live within eternity's value system and not that of this world ...

BE A BURDEN BEARER

Carry each other's burdens, and in this way you will fulfill the law of Christ.

GALATIANS 6:2

No one enjoys suffering, and it's quite natural to ask God to remove our burdens from us. Do we recognize the presence of divine intervention, however, when others come along to share our pain?

In today's key verse, the apostle Paul instructed the Galatians to lift each other's burdens, for in this way they would be fulfilling the law of Christ. Bearing one another's burdens is not an option for believers; it is a command. Shared joy is doubled joy; shared sorrow is halved sorrow.

How can we learn to be more sensitive when it comes to sharing the needs of others? It begins with learning to listen to quiet instructions from the Father, who cares for his children. We hear his voice when we worship—when we deliberately set aside time to communicate with him on the most intimate of levels. Scripture is clear that God intends for us to care for one another.

Lactantius, one of the early church fathers, explains this principle. "He has given us the affection of compassion so that we can protect lives by helping one another. If we are created by one God, descended from one man, and, therefore, are thus connected by the law of kinship, we should love everyone. Our frailty is prone to many accidents and inconveniences. Expect that what you see happening to someone else may also happen to you. You will be excited to help someone if you shall assume the mind of those who, being placed in danger, beg for your help."

We need to pray for stronger backs—backs fit to bear the burdens of a world that needs to know the strength we find in Christ. ✤

PRAYER

Lord, give me insight into the burdens of others and the wisdom to know how to help them . . .

ADOPTED BY GOD

He predestined us for adoption to sonship through Jesus Christ, in accordance with his pleasure and will—to the praise of his glorious grace, which he has freely given us in the One he loves.   EPHESIANS 1:5–6

In her autobiographical book *Amazed by Grace*, author Lucinda Secrest McDowell relates the story of the adoption of her three oldest children, whose biological mother had died of cancer some years before. To her surprise, each of the children was given a newly revised birth certificate with her name on the line for "mother" as well as her place of residence at the time of their births. Even though Lucinda was living elsewhere in the U.S. during the years when the children were born in Seattle, that did not alter the fact that she was now their mother—legally and in every other way. God had brought them together and made them a family.

Today's passage brings the wonderful news that those who belong to Christ have been adopted by God into his family. Where we were born and into what circumstances no longer matters; for God has chosen us to be his own. Our advocate, Jesus Christ, provided the way and the means for our adoption to take place.

Our status as children of God gives us both the right and the privilege to lay claim to "every spiritual blessing in Christ" (Ephesians 1:3). Notice the passionate praise in the beginning of this same verse: "Praise be to the God and Father of our Lord Jesus Christ."

Just as an adoptive father or mother becomes a parent by choice, God draws us into his spiritual family. Let that reality take root in your life. You are God's beloved child, and as his heir you stand to receive an eternal inheritance one day.

Celebrate your birthright as God's adopted child today. ❖

PRAYER

Lord, I can never thank you enough for adopting me into your heavenly family . . .

BIND US TOGETHER

There is one body and one Spirit, just as you were called to one hope when you were called.

EPHESIANS 4:4

There is one word—one beautiful word—that sums up the principle described above: *unity*. This verse in Ephesians specifies three reasons we should exhibit unity as believers in Christ: We are one body with one Spirit destined for one common future.

So what could possibly divide us? We are born with a sin nature, and even those who sincerely profess a common faith in Christ can still find themselves at odds over differences in doctrine or practice. One of the greatest privileges we have as believers is that of worship itself, yet disagreements over worship styles or music preferences have at times caused serious division within the body.

Little wonder, then, that Paul urged the Ephesians to "Make every effort to keep the unity of the Spirit through the bond of peace" (Ephesians 4:3).

Saint Chrysostom explained it this way: "What is this *unity of Spirit*? In the human body there is a spirit which holds the several parts together, and forms in some sort into one which exists in different members. So is it also here; for to this end was the Spirit given; that He might unite those who are separated by race and by different manners."

A simple chorus pleads, "Bind us together, Lord, bind us together, / With cords that cannot be broken." Let's not debate the use of this song in a worship setting, but rather live by its truth.

Spend time praying for "cords that cannot be broken" in your own church, your ministry and among believers in your community. ✣

PRAYER

Father, thank you for the Holy Spirit, who binds us together with peace . . .

day328

EYES WIDE OPEN

And pray in the Spirit on all occasions with all kinds of prayers and requests. With this in mind, be alert and always keep on praying for all the Lord's people. EPHESIANS 6:18

The late songwriter and Christian recording artist Keith Green was known for his passion for missions and ministry. A song entitled "Make My Life a Prayer to You" expressed his plea for his life to contain no empty words, no white lies, no token prayers and no compromise.

In today's key verse, Paul is instructing believers to pray continually, at all times and on every occasion. Live constantly in a spirit of worship, he urges us. Stay fully alert; pray with unrelenting faith. It's almost as if he's saying, "Pray with the eyes of your heart wide open!"

As we learn to be continually watchful in prayer, offering up each anxious thought and every situation to his sovereignty, we will find that Keith Green's plea has been realized in our own lives. Even when asleep, our hearts are awake to God's will. Our very lives have become a prayer to him.

Find different times of the day to pray than are your usual habit. Spend time in prayer before you enter your place of work or right before your children get home from school. Let this break in routine refresh your prayer life and keep you alert. ✤

PRAYER

Lord, open the eyes of my heart . . .

day**329**

A GROWING APPRECIATION!

And this is my prayer: that your love may abound more and more in knowledge and depth of insight.   PHILIPPIANS 1:9

Remember thinking ...

- Your college roommate was a real loser ... and she became your best friend!
- The salesman had nothing to offer ... but you bought his product and it was amazing!
- The restaurant looked like a hole in the wall ... but served reasonably priced gourmet meals.
- Your neighbor was pretentious ... but he turned out to be a down-to-earth guy.
- The women's Bible study was filled with cliques ... and they warmly embraced and accepted you.

First impressions can indeed be misleading. When you take the time to know someone deeply, that relationship changes your attitudes about the other person or product or place. It also changes you. That's why the apostle Paul let the Christians in Philippi know that he was praying that their knowledge of God would increase. He knew that as we grow in our awareness of our heavenly Father we come to a deeper appreciation of his glory and greatness. The more we appreciate him the more we want to please him. As a result, our lives, relationships and choices are impacted in a positive way.

Celebrate as many attributes of Christ as you can think of in the next five minutes. Focus on these attributes throughout the day to worship him. ❖

> **PRAYER**

Lord, I celebrate the fact that you ...

TOWERING ABOVE THE TRASH

What is more, I consider everything a loss because of the surpassing worth of knowing Christ Jesus my Lord, for whose sake I have lost all things. I consider them garbage, that I may gain Christ and be found in him. PHILIPPIANS 3:8–9

Thousands who travel by cruise ships through the Inside Passage of Alaska annually visit the old gold rush town of Nome. But few visitors would label it an attractive tourist spot. Garbage lines the streets. Due to harsh winters, permafrost and limited landfill area, litter is left in front of many houses.

Amid the debris and litter that has come to define Nome's landscape is the community's Christian radio station that broadcasts Biblical teaching and praise and worship songs, as well as Russian programs that are heard 150 miles to the west in Siberia. KICY's transmitter tower stands 250 feet in the air, pointing toward the One above in whose name they broadcast daily. The contrast between the garbage on the ground and the tower in the air is striking.

According to what Paul is saying in this passage, our firsthand knowledge of Jesus elevates us to a level of living that towers over everything else in this world. We have a choice each day to preoccupy ourselves with the "litter" of this world— career advancement, material possessions and wealth, family life—or we can reach upward to what truly counts—a relationship with Christ.

All our other pursuits—including job, education, family life, hobbies and future plans—are like the litter in Nome. They may represent valid experiences and meaningful accomplishments, but they are an eyesore in contrast to the beautiful relationship the Lord has invited us to experience with him.

Take out the litter today—remove everything that is preventing you from living for Jesus. ✤

> PRAYER

Lord, I will fix my focus on you . . .

ENEMIES NO LONGER

But now he has reconciled you by Christ's physical body through death to present you holy in his sight, without blemish and free from accusation. Colossians 1:22

When Wayne Messmer was shot in the throat by a teenage thug in April 1994, he thought his career was over. In addition to singing the national anthem at various sporting events, the Chicago businessman made his living as a motivational speaker. Doctors doubted if Wayne would speak again—let alone sing—if he even survived.

Miraculously, Mr. Star Spangled Banner was at the mike six months later, honoring America at the start of the Chicago Blackhawks' game. What was an even greater miracle was Wayne's decision to seek out his assailant to offer forgiveness. After driving to the Galesburg Correctional Center, this Christian celebrity extended his hand to James Hampton and said, "I bid you peace."

Amazing? Yet that is exactly the action God has taken in response to our malicious thoughts and behavior. The offended holy One, with every reason to consider us his enemies, has welcomed us as his friends. It's more than a truce. The lines of separation have been erased. Relationship exists where once there was alienation and condemnation. That's how Paul describes God's disposition toward us in this verse. In his infinite mercy, God has drawn us to himself as friends.

It's totally unexpected and undeserved. Apart from that love, there is no way our sin could be removed or forgiven—or that we could offer that same love and forgiveness to another.

You are God's friend. Celebrate that truth today by renewing that friendship. ♣

PRAYER

Heavenly Father, to know that I am blameless before you means . . .

day332

A STADIUM CHOIR

Let the message of Christ dwell among you richly as you teach and admonish one another with all wisdom through psalms, hymns, and songs from the Spirit, singing to God with gratitude in your hearts.　　　　　　　　　　　　　　　　Colossians 3:16

In the last decade of the twentieth century, an amazing phenomenon began to occur in sports stadiums across the country. Hundreds of thousands of men gathered in stadium venues to do something other than cheer on their favorite teams. They were cheering their Creator with Christian music. The Promise Keepers movement saw arenas and stadiums packed to capacity with men acknowledging their need for God. The two-day events were filled with testimonies, Biblical teaching and extended times of singing.

What occurred during those events is exactly what Paul describes in this letter to the Colossian Christians—the rich words of Christ so embedded in the soul that they find expression in "psalms, hymns, and songs from the Spirit." With tears rolling down their upturned faces, big burly men sang "O for a Thousand Tongues to Sing" and "Amazing Grace." But they also sang lyrics they had learned for the first time—songs like "Open the Eyes of My Heart" and "Give Thanks." It was an awesome sound.

But even if you never attended a Promise Keepers event, you can experience the power of praise music in your personal worship time. Go ahead and crank up your iPod with your favorite Christian music. Close your eyes and close out the demands of your calendar or "to do" list. Sing along. Open your Bible and let the words of God take root in your heart. ✤

PRAYER

Jesus, accept my vocal offering—even if it's somewhat out of tune—as my gift of love...

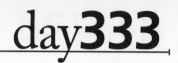

MORE THAN MERE WORDS

For we know, brothers and sisters loved by God, that he has chosen you, because our gospel came to you not simply with words but also with power, with the Holy Spirit and deep conviction. You know how we lived among you for your sake. I THESSALONIANS 1:4–5

In 1992, a community choir from Magadan, Siberia, traveled to California on a tour. It was one of the first cultural exchanges following the fall of Communism. In addition to performing Russian folk songs, the chorus also sang Eastern European hymns they had only recently learned. Because of the oppressive regime under which they had lived, the choir had never heard the rich songs of their nation's previous Christian heritage. These anthems had been locked in vaults for over seven decades.

As they stood before their American audiences, it was obvious the musicians had learned the music well. Their performance was technically correct. But their faces did not reflect the joy of faith the hymns' lyrics suggested. For the atheistic choir, the words wed to the melodies were only words. It was obvious that they didn't believe the truth they were singing about.

This isn't only true of Siberian singers; we see that all around us. It's easy to say the right words or mouth worshipful lyrics without meaning what we say. Talk is cheap, right? As Paul writes these words to the Thessalonians, he is aware that words of faith don't always translate into lives of faith. His desire for them—and God's desire for us—is that Bible reading or Scripture memory not be an end in itself. What matters is the impact those words have on our lives by putting them into practice.

Store up God's powerful truths in your heart today. Read aloud this passage or another that addresses your situation and circumstances. Speak powerfully and with expression. ✤

PRAYER

Lord, I long to live out the words I read . . .

THANKFUL NO MATTER WHAT

Rejoice always, pray continually, give thanks in all circumstances; for this is God's will for you in Christ Jesus.   1 THESSALONIANS 5:16–18

Shortly after Fanny Jane Crosby was born in 1820, the family doctor made a tragic mistake. Instead of irrigating her infant eyes with prescribed drops, he inadvertently used a toxic substance. The result? Fanny was blind for life. Amazingly, she lived without resentment or bitterness. This gifted poet, who penned several thousand poems that were set to music, was known for her cheerful outlook and this customary greeting: "God bless your dear soul." Her remarkable hymns are a chronicle of gratitude for the blessings from God that she experienced in her 95 years.

Although Christians still sing several of her well-known hymns a century after her death, one song in particular has universal appeal. The first stanza begins with these words: "To God be the glory, great things he has done." Isn't that something? How could Fanny attest to God's goodness when she was the victim of such a horrendous injustice? Obviously, she had reached the spiritual destination Paul held out as a worthy goal for all believers. In spite of unpredictable circumstances, the apostle calls us to express our gratitude. He says it's God's will.

The tragic events we are exposed to in an imperfect world are not necessarily the will of the Lord. But he does will that our response to those events be sprinkled with thanksgiving, knowing that he is still in control. That's not an easy assignment. But that's why we need to make time for God sometime during each day. Bringing the difficult circumstances of our lives into the Lord's presence somehow defuses them. Laying our concerns at the Lord's feet reminds us that Someone greater than we are concerned about what we are going through. ✤

PRAYER

Lord, may I respond today in a God-honoring way ...

A DAILY DRESS REHEARSAL

They will be punished with everlasting destruction and shut out from the presence of the Lord and from the glory of his might on the day he comes to be glorified in his holy people and to be marveled at among all those who have believed. This includes you, because you believed our testimony to you.   2 THESSALONIANS 1:9–10

Jerome Hines was a bass soloist with the Metropolitan Opera for many years. His renditions of classic arias brought audiences to their feet. It was obvious to all who heard him that he had a musical gift. But being endowed with an exceptional ability did not relieve Jerome Hines from the necessity of rehearsing.

When the well-known Presbyterian pastor Dr. John A. Huffman Jr. invited Jerome to sing at a special occasion at his church, the opera star stayed in the Huffman home. Early Sunday morning Jerome could be heard throughout the house as he warmed up his voice with melodic scales and then rehearsed the song he was to perform later that day. Although he was a gifted singer, rehearsing was a prerequisite to performance.

In much the same way, salvation is a gift God gave us when we believed what we heard about Jesus. But, as with Jerome Hines and his gift for singing, being gifted doesn't mean we don't have to exercise our gift. That's why we spend time with the Lord each day. Practicing our spiritual "scales" helps to fine-tune our understanding of what the Lord has done for us.

Our personal worship time is a dress rehearsal for the day Paul talks about in this verse. So, when you crank up the stereo and sing along to "Worthy Is the Lamb" or "Awesome God," you aren't just making noise. You are getting in tune for the performance you will offer to an audience of one. Rehearse today the many blessings you received when you exercised your gift of salvation. ♣

PRAYER

Lord Jesus, I long for the day when I see you face to face . . .

HATCHET MAN OR HALO-WEARER?

Here is a trustworthy saying that deserves full acceptance: Christ Jesus came into the world to save sinners—of whom I am the worst.   1 TIMOTHY 1:15

Chuck Colson has become an authoritative moral voice among Christians in America. Thousands of Christians read his articles and columns in Christian magazines and listen to his daily radio commentaries. His leadership of a ministry to those behind bars means his growing constituency includes converted prisoners and their families. But Chuck Colson has not always been a Christian leader or viewed as a moral voice.

When Richard Nixon occupied the White House, Colson was his chief counsel. He was also the president's willing pawn. Known as the "hatchet man," Colson was called on to do what the chief executive didn't relish doing himself even if he could. Chuck had a reputation for dirty tricks and deception. But that changed when Colson accepted Jesus as his Lord and Savior when he was in prison. When news of Colson's conversion to Christianity leaked to the press in 1973, *The Boston Globe* reported, "If Mr. Colson can repent of his sins, there just has to be hope for everybody."

That's the picture we have of the apostle Paul in this passage. Aware of his sinful past, he calls attention to it. Lest we think of him as some larger-than-life saint, he reminds us of his true identity—the worst sinner of them all. But Jesus came into the world to do God's bidding for him. He came to reach out to the Pauls and Chucks of a fallen planet. Except for his grace, we all would still be lost in our sin and trapped in reputations we well deserve.

Take time to compose a mental picture of yourself "before" and "after" meeting Christ. Then worship the One who "came into the world to save sinners." ♣

PRAYER

Lord Jesus, thank you for coming into the world to save me . . .

A STANDING OVATION FIT FOR A KING

I charge you to keep this command without spot or blame until the appearing of our Lord Jesus Christ, which God will bring about in his own time—God, the blessed and only Ruler, the King of kings and Lord of lords, who alone is immortal and who lives in un-approachable light, whom no one has seen or can see. To him be honor and might forever. Amen.　　　　　　　　　　　　　　　　　　　　　　1 TIMOTHY 6:13–16

George Frederic Handel wrote his masterpiece oratorio *Messiah* in a mere three weeks. He wrote nonstop night and day as if driven by a power greater than himself. He neglected food, sleep and friends to accomplish what he viewed as a God-given goal. Picture the composer seated at his piano with sheets of music strewn around him. No doubt tears were streaming down his face. Handel, having encountered the majesty of a holy God while composing music for the scriptural lyrics, said, "I do believe I have seen all of Heaven before me, and the great God Himself."

When the composer introduced his oratorio to a London audience, King George was in attendance. Unable to restrain himself when the orchestra and choir sang the "Hallelujah Chorus," the king stood to his feet in adoration of God because he knew his position paled in contrast to the King of kings. Since then, audiences follow the monarch's example and continue to stand whenever that familiar chorus is sung. And based on what the apostle writes in today's passage, kings, princes and citizens of all nations will have an opportunity to pay homage to the Messiah in person when he returns to earth someday.

In this passage Paul reminds us that God's holiness is "unapproachable." The only means we have to come before God is through his Son. Only he is able to stand before God totally blameless. Only through his work on the cross and out of his love for us are we able to draw near to God. ✤

PRAYER

Lord Jesus, I can stand before God because of you . . .

RUNNING WITH A PURE HEART

Flee the evil desires of youth and pursue righteousness, faith, love and peace, along with those who call on the Lord out of a pure heart. 2 TIMOTHY 2:22

Eric Liddell's God-honoring life is the basis for the movie that won the Academy Award for best picture in 1982. In *Chariots of Fire* we meet a sprinter from Scotland who loves to run almost as much as he loves his Lord. Eric qualifies to be part of Great Britain's team in the 1924 Paris Olympics. When he discovers that his qualifying event at the Games is scheduled for a Sunday, he is faced with an issue of conscience.

Given his personal interpretation of the fourth commandment, he does not feel the personal liberty to compete on the Lord's Day. In the film version, Eric's decision to give up his spot on the Olympic team rather than dishonor the Lord is unexpectedly rewarded. A teammate who has already won a medal offers to let Eric take his place in another event that will be held midweek. Gratefully, Eric accepts the offer and wins the race.

In Eric Liddell we find a godly athlete who not only runs around a track, but runs toward God, determined to keep his heart pure and his relationship with his Lord unblemished. That is what Paul has in mind when he refers to pursuing faith and love and peace. Paul uses words such as "flee" and "pursue." Our faith is one of action, not passivity. It means running on a daily basis with our eyes focused on pleasing God.

Run toward God. Confess whatever is causing you to stumble and falter. Use the times when you wash your hands today as an opportunity to purify yourself through personal confession. ✤

PRAYER

Lord, give me the desire to remain pure in heart ...

THE JOY OF WAITING

Now there is in store for me the crown of righteousness, which the Lord, the righteous Judge, will award to me on that day—and not only to me, but also to all who have longed for his appearing. 2 TIMOTHY 4:8

Dietrich Bonhoeffer was a Lutheran pastor in Germany during the days of the Third Reich. He was arrested for his part in a Christian resistance movement. A month before the Allied forces freed Germany, the 39-year-old pastor was executed. Some months before his death, Bonhoeffer's fiancée surprised him with a visit. He pleaded with her not to come unannounced again. For him, the ability to anticipate a longed-for reunion was a gift too precious to be denied.

Isn't that something? When you stop and think about it, you can understand his logic. You can almost put yourself in that Nazi cell and feel the prisoner's longing for the day when he could look his loved one in the face. In the same way, as Paul neared the end of his life, he began to think of being in the presence of Jesus. This passage reveals his longing for the day of his reunion with the Lord while calling us to anticipate when we too will stand before the lover of our souls.

In all honesty, how eagerly are you looking forward to Jesus' glorious return? No doubt your life is dotted with deadlines and "to do" lists. But how much do you think about the second coming? That's a worthy aim in our daily personal worship times. The more we anticipate what is to come, the greater our satisfaction and fulfillment when we see Christ. You can count on that! ✣

PRAYER

Jesus, I can't wait to see you . . .

LIVING OUR WORSHIP

Remind the people to be subject to rulers and authorities, to be obedient, to be ready to do whatever is good, to slander no one, to be peaceable and considerate, and always to be gentle toward everyone. Titus 3:1–2

It's said that the following sign was on the wall of Gandhi's home: When you are in the right, you can afford to keep your temper; and when you are in the wrong, you cannot afford to lose it.

Today's passage in Titus reminds us that the reverence we hold for God should extend into the way we treat other people. If we worship the Lord faithfully on Sunday but behave contentiously on Monday, we are not allowing our faith to filter our conduct. A follower of Christ is not usually recognized by his or her worship style, but rather by his or her behavior toward others. It's pleasant to praise God when those around us behave agreeably; the real test of character, however, comes when we rub shoulders with those who are difficult.

Even those who serve the Lord vocationally are not immune from occasional feelings of annoyance toward others in the Christian community. Titus instructs us not to let these feelings get the best of us. Instead, our lives are to be characterized by a submissive, obedient spirit toward those in authority and gentle humility toward everyone else. Jesus, quite certainly, would like us to do that.

Today, as an act of worship, pray specifically for your employer or others in authority over you. Treat them with added respect, as if they were the people you love best in the world. ♣

PRAYER

Lord, grant me the grace to demonstrate a gentle spirit . . .

GENEROUS FAITH

I pray that your partnership with us in the faith may be effective in deepening your understanding of every good thing we share for the sake of Christ. PHILEMON 6

In 1908, explorer Ernest Shackleton led an expedition to Antarctica to reach the South Pole. They came close, but they had to turn back 97 miles short of the pole. On the return trip, food supplies had dwindled to one last ration of hardtack for each man. In his diary, Shackleton recorded that some men consumed their ration immediately; others, however, stowed it away, saving it for a last moment of hungry desperation.

Shackleton was almost asleep when he noticed one of his most trusted men sitting up in his sleeping bag, looking around to see if anyone was watching. Shackleton's heart sank as he watched the man reach over to the food sack of the man next to him—until he realized that the man was actually putting his own hardtack into the other's food sack!

Such acts of generosity stir our emotions. It is what Paul wrote about to his friend Philemon. Every good deed becomes an act of worship, for in serving others, we serve Christ.

Paul encouraged Philemon to extend kindness to his runaway slave. Paul was confident that Philemon would do all he asked and even more, because now Onesimus was part of the family of God.

Our generous giving not only is an outward demonstration of our faith; it also brings glory to the One we worship. Look for opportunities to give generously today—whether it's monetary or material, your talents or your time. Give out of your faith and love for God. ✤

PRAYER

Lord, show me ways to be outrageously generous . . .

THE ESSENCE OF EMPATHY

Because he himself suffered when he was tempted, he is able to help those who are being tempted. HEBREWS 2:18

How often have you heard someone say, "Oh, how awful. I know exactly how you feel"? But it's not true. You know this person does not know even *approximately* how you feel, much less exactly. The presumption only adds to the pain. No one could possibly know.

Then there is Jesus. He is the Son of God, the high and lofty One, seated at the right hand of the Father Almighty, who became a human being. The impossible is true. There *is* One who knows exactly how you feel.

The letter to the Hebrews is the epistle of empathy, good news of the most personal nature. "For this reason he had to be made like them, fully human in every way, in order that he might become a merciful and faithful high priest in service to God, and that he might make atonement for the sins of the people" (2:17).

Jesus understands our weakness. Consider the 40 days in the wilderness, the three years of struggle, the prayers in the Garden of Gethsemane. Physical suffering, mental anguish, emotional upheaval, loss, abandonment. Temptation to grab the glory, to rush ahead of the Father's plan, to give up entirely.

"Fully human in every way." His identification with you is complete. He does not understand *approximately* how you feel, but *exactly*.

What will you do with this truth? Hebrews offers this invitation: "Let us then approach God's throne of grace with confidence, so that we may receive mercy and find grace to help us in our time of need" (4:16). Tell him what you have not revealed to anyone else. He knows. Exactly. ✤

PRAYER

Lord Jesus, you alone know my struggles ...

CUTTING DEEP, CUTTING TRUE

For the word of God is alive and active. Sharper than any double-edged sword, it penetrates even to dividing soul and spirit, joints and marrow; it judges the thoughts and attitudes of the heart. Nothing in all creation is hidden from God's sight. Everything is uncovered and laid bare before the eyes of him to whom we must give account.

HEBREWS 4:12–13

Then the lion said—but I don't know if it spoke—"You will have to let me undress you." I was afraid of his claws, I can tell you, but I was pretty nearly desperate now. So I just lay flat down on my back to let him do it.

The speaker is Eustace, a boy whose greed turned him into a dragon in *The Voyage of the Dawn Treader*. The lion, Aslan, is the Christ-figure in C. S. Lewis's Chronicles of Narnia series. Eustace goes on to describe the agonizing process of removing all the dragon skin.

The Word was made flesh. The Word cuts through flesh, through the façade, through the falsehood. Nothing is safe from the sharp knife of Christ, but nothing is truly safe without it; the frightening claws of Aslan are both the ultimate weapon against the dragon hide and the only tool to give Eustace new skin, new life.

The Scriptures can cut to the quick and cut to the heart. But the wounds are not malicious. Rather, the knife of God's Word slices through and slices away our own malice, our own layers of sin and excuses. The knife is the sharpest, used by the only surgeon able to do the job.

Do you shrink from the knife of the Word? Only Aslan's claws could cut through to a new life for Eustace. Only God's Word cuts deep but true.

Take a few moments to reflect on what areas of your life most need the sharp edge of God's Word. Prayerfully give him your consent and your thanks. ❖

PRAYER

God, wield the knife of your Word in my life . . .

PERFECTLY CLEAR, CLEARLY PERFECT

How much more, then, will the blood of Christ, who through the eternal Spirit offered himself unblemished to God, cleanse our consciences from acts that lead to death, so that we may serve the living God!   HEBREWS 9:14

The perfect gift. A perfect 4.0 GPA. The perfect match. A perfect score from the Olympic judges. A perfect fit.

Christy, the oldest daughter of alcoholics, coped with perfectionism's illusion of control. "If I could just be the best little girl there ever was" changed to "If I could just get all A's," then became "If I could just be the perfect wife" and "If I could just work harder and be the Employee of the Year instead of just the Month." And on and on, through all the roles in her life.

She started going to Al-Anon and found it helpful. One slogan caught her ear—"Progress, not perfection"—but she had many years of habitual thinking to conquer. And at church, pleas for perfection also caught her ear. Didn't Jesus exhort, "Be perfect" (Matthew 5:48)? "Okay, so I'll be the perfect Christian," she promised herself.

Then during a communion service one day, Christy heard some words she had heard before but never absorbed: "He stretched out his arms upon the cross, and offered himself, in obedience to your will, a perfect sacrifice for the whole world."

It had already been done. Perfection had been reached. Tears of relief joined tears of gratitude down her cheeks. Jesus was the perfect sacrifice for the whole world, the perfect sacrifice for her.

Jesus is also the perfect sacrifice for you. Allow that truth to release you from the tyranny of perfection today. Lift up a praise of thanksgiving for his holiness. ✤

PRAYER

Lord Jesus, you alone are the perfect One...

ALL, ALL IS WELL

So do not throw away your confidence; it will be richly rewarded. You need to persevere so that when you have done the will of God, you will receive what he has promised.

HEBREWS 10:35 – 36

Confident trust, patient endurance. Chapters 10 and 11 of the letter to the Hebrews form "A Guide to the Care and Feeding of Faith." Faith is defined indirectly in today's verses and directly in Hebrews 11:1: "Faith is confidence in what we hope for and assurance about what we do not see."

Then there is the Hall of Fame of Faith (Hebrews 11), examples of Old Testament individuals through the centuries who placed their faith in God. Their lives are an inspiration.

Little is known about Mary Bowley Peters. The wife of an Anglican rector in Gloucestershire, England, in the early 1800s, she may have been constrained by the expectations of society. Still, she wrote *The World's History from the Creation to the Accession of Queen Victoria* (in seven volumes) and more than twenty hymns.

Only 43 when she died, her living out of her faith encourages us to do the same. Consider the third and final verse of her best-known hymn, "Through the Love of God Our Savior": "We expect a bright tomorrow, All will be well; / Faith can sing through days of sorrow, All, all is well; / On our Father's love relying, Jesus every need supplying, / Or in living, or in dying, All must be well."

Run to him. Worship the One who rewards faith, no matter what.

Reflect on your favorite inductee into the Hall of Fame of Faith. What about that person's faith walk encourages you? Use that person as a model for your own journey. ❖

PRAYER

Holy Lord, help me live out my faith in you . . .

ONE AND THE SAME

Jesus Christ is the same yesterday and today and forever.   Hebrews 13:8

Is this ever different, Jeff thinks. *It's nothing like our old church. Just like Chicago is nothing like the last city.*

Jeff and his family have moved around the country. A lot. He is sick of it.

"Could this place get any older?" he whispers to his mother. She shrugs; she is sick of change too. They find some seats and look around. Finally, their eyes focus on the large lettering way above the altar: *Jesus Christ is the same yesterday and today and forever.* They gulp. They blink. They close their eyes and thank the changeless One.

The current Moody Memorial Church building was completed in 1925, itself a product of great change. Started as a Sunday school by the evangelist Dwight L. Moody, it was organized as a church in 1864 but burned in the Great Chicago Fire of 1871. The words of Hebrews 13:8 echo in the hearts and minds of all worshipers there.

Only there? Limitations of time and geography vanish in the verse. The verb tense is past, present and future.

The truth reaches back to the second century, to Saint Irenaeus as recorded in "Irenaeus Against Heresies" in *The Apostolic Fathers, Justin Martyr, Irenaeus*: "For, although the languages of the world are dissimilar, yet the import of the tradition is one and the same. For the Churches which have been planted in Germany do not believe or hand down anything different, nor do those in Spain, nor those in Gaul ... For the faith being ever one and the same."

What changes are you facing today? Rest in the One who remains wonderfully the same. Praise his changeless name. ✣

PRAYER

Christ Jesus, I rejoice that you are the same ...

ASKED AND ANSWERED

But when you ask, you must believe and not doubt, because the one who doubts is like a wave of the sea, blown and tossed by the wind. That person should not expect to receive anything from the Lord.   JAMES 1:6–7

In the 1880s, George and Sarah Clarke opened the Pacific Garden Mission of Chicago—a ministry to homeless and downtrodden men—with little more than their personal funds and faith that God would provide. As the ministry expanded, expenses grew and the couple's resources dwindled. Eventually, the day came when they could not pay the rent. With only 24 hours to pay the rent or lose the lease, the couple began to pray.

Throughout the night, the Clarkes prayed for God's guidance and provision. They reminded him of the souls being saved. They asked why their work—God's work—was in such straits. But they were determined to trust God and stayed before the throne of grace in simple faith until dawn. When they emerged from their house, the couple discovered their lawn was covered in white—mushrooms of the very best quality! The Clarkes gathered the mushrooms and carted them to the chefs of the Palmer House, a famed hotel in Chicago. The receipts for the mushrooms were enough to pay the rent, with enough left over to meet other ministry expenses.

The Clarkes' faith-filled prayers exemplify what today's passage exhorts believers to do: Pray believing that God will answer. People of prayer are people who pray *before* things get desperate; before the well runs dry, the doorways are blocked or every other possible remedy is tried twice. People of prayer come before the throne of grace, like the Clarkes, trusting, believing, anticipating.

So go to God's throne in prayer. Be confident that he will hear you. ✤

PRAYER

O God, I come before you asking for . . .

TAKE COURAGE FROM HIM

Be patient, then, brothers and sisters, until the Lord's coming. See how the farmer waits for the land to yield its valuable crop, patiently waiting for the autumn and spring rains. You too, be patient and stand firm, because the Lord's coming is near. JAMES 5:7–8

Surely there are better ways to celebrate a saint's life than getting drunk, hanging shamrocks and turning rivers green. Saint Patrick was not even Irish. Pirates kidnapped and took this 16-year-old British boy to Ireland. Sold into slavery, he was sustained by his faith in Christ. Six years later he escaped to England, but God called him back to Ireland to spread the gospel around AD 400.

"Take courage," God told him, for his life was under constant threat as he traveled the entire island. But the former slave convinced nearly the entire population to become slaves of Christ.

Scholars are uncertain whether or not he wrote "Saint Patrick's Breastplate." But the prayer was composed around the time that he lived and certainly is in keeping with his trust in the Trinity and in Christ's protection. One translation begins, "I arise today through a mighty strength, the invocation of the Trinity." It continues, "Christ be with me, Christ within me, Christ behind me, Christ before me, Christ beside me, Christ to win me, Christ to comfort and restore me. Christ beneath me, Christ above me, Christ in quiet, Christ in danger, Christ in hearts of all that love me, Christ in mouth of friend and stranger."

Lean into the Lord Christ. Know that he is all around you. Praise his name for the courage and protection he offers. ♣

PRAYER

Lord Christ, please give me your courage as I serve you wherever you lead me . . .

O GRACIOUS LIGHT

But you are a chosen people, a royal priesthood, a holy nation, God's special possession, that you may declare the praises of him who called you out of darkness into his wonderful light.

1 PETER 2:9

The flames leaped higher, yet still he sang. In the third century, the emperor Diocletian's reign claimed yet another martyr. The bishop and theologian Athenogenes was burned alive along with ten of his students. But the beautiful song he sang as he entered the flames lives in our liturgy today. Called the *Phos Hilaron* in its original Greek, it praises God's "wonderful light" about which Peter wrote in today's passage.

Ever since Athenogenes's death, the hymn attributed to him has been used in the Orthodox tradition as part of its evening vespers liturgy. It was not translated into English until the 1600s, but soon became part of Anglican and later Roman Catholic vespers services. Sung or read aloud, the beauty and brilliance of God's wonderful light shines through.

> *O Gracious Light,*
> *Pure brightness of the everliving Father in heaven,*
> *O Jesus Christ, holy and blessed!*
>
> *Now as we come to the setting of the sun,*
> *And our eyes behold the vesper light,*
> *We sing your praises, O God: Father, Son, and Holy Spirit.*
>
> *You are worthy at all times to be praised by happy voices,*
> *O Son of God, O Giver of life,*
> *And to be glorified through all the worlds.*

God has called us out of darkness into his wonderful light. Consider the brightness of his ways. Close your eyes and imagine the purity of the flame of his love for the world, his love for you. ❖

PRAYER

Jesus, I'm grateful that you have called me out of darkness into your wonderful light . . .

day350

SEE HIM IN THE CLOUDS

Humble yourselves, therefore, under God's mighty hand, that he may lift you up in due time. Cast all your anxiety on him because he cares for you. And the God of all grace, who called you to his eternal glory in Christ, after you have suffered a little while, will himself restore you and make you strong, firm and steadfast.　　　　1 PETER 5:6–7,10

In some places the sun always shines, or nearly so. In other places, the weather seems to change significantly by the hour. Some places seem to have only one season. Others seem to have only two seasons: the rainy season and the rainier season.

But there is no place on earth where the clouds of bad times signal God's absence. The very clouds we think push out the sunshine of his care are, in his forecast for our lives, his means of arrival. Just as meteorologists can sometimes be surprised by the significance or timing of the weather, we are sometimes way off in our interpretations and predictions of what—and Who—the clouds bring.

Steven Curtis Chapman wrote the song "Sometimes He Comes in the Clouds." At times "his face cannot be found," go the lyrics. And when the sky is all manner of dastardly colors, it is only then that our faith can grow. Sometimes he does come in the clouds, in the rain, "and we question the pain."

Yet he *is* there. *In* the rain and the pain, not despite it. In the words of Peter's letter, "he may lift you up in due time." Ready to restore, support, strengthen. Time will show us, in the words of Chapman's song, "He was right there with us."

The clouds come. But rejoice and thank God, who not only allows them but also accompanies them. ✤

PRAYER

Heavenly Father, help me to trust your care and your timing . . .

MAKE EVERY EFFORT TO REMEMBER

For this very reason, make every effort to add to your faith goodness; and to goodness, knowledge. But whoever does not have them is nearsighted and blind, forgetting that they have been cleansed from their past sins.   2 PETER 1:5,9

She walks into the kitchen to get something. Problem is, nearly ten seconds have elapsed and she has no idea what she wanted.

Alzheimer's patient? Possibly. But more likely a middle-aged woman with middle-aged memory challenges and 30 things on her mind. And she never was good at multitasking.

Our walk with God often encounters memory challenges. We forget that his promises to care for us are not conditional. That prayer really does work. That, as Peter expresses it, God has cleansed us from our old life of sin.

The apostle James also exhorts us to remember better when he says this: "Anyone who listens to the word but does not do what it says is like someone who looks at his face in a mirror and, after looking at himself, goes away and immediately forgets what he looks like. But whoever looks intently into the perfect law that gives freedom, and continues in it—not forgetting what they have heard, but doing it—they will be blessed in what they do" (James 1:23–25).

Charles Wesley, the cofounder of the Methodist movement with his brother John, could relate. Sure, he wrote an unbelievable number of upbeat hymns that we still enjoy today, but he was also a poet. One poem that was never set to music is "Times Without Number Have I Pray'd," with its theme of relapsing—a forgetting, intentionally or not, of what life in Christ means.

Return to God. Remember. And worship him today by your repentance and gratitude for your new life. ✤

PRAYER

Lord God, forgive me when I fail to remember ...

THE PICTURE OF PATIENCE

The Lord is not slow in keeping his promise, as some understand slowness. Instead he is patient with you, not wanting anyone to perish, but everyone to come to repentance.

2 PETER 3:9

"What's wrong with that idiot?! Where are the police when you need them?!" we yell in traffic, wishing for instant justice for a reckless driver. Waiting isn't easy, especially when we witness or experience injustice. Politicians, police and other authorities all seem to move slowly, if at all, especially to deal with our problems.

When we learn of tragic national and world events, injustice on an international scale, our impatience moves to a higher level. "Where is God?" we ask. "What's he waiting for? Why doesn't he step in and end all of this?" God's response time does not seem to be one of his better attributes.

Yet where would we be if God were not patient with all sinners, including ourselves? Clearly, the Bible teaches us that the world as we know it will come to an end. But our patient God is not willing to see anyone perish in the destruction to come.

The fact that we worship a patient, longsuffering God should give us cause for rejoicing every day of our lives. It is still not too late to embrace the Savior who came "to seek and to save the lost" (Luke 19:10).

Second Peter cautions us that the day of the Lord is coming when the heavens and the earth will be consumed by fire and the ungodly will perish. But it is not here yet because of God's compassion for those he created and his wonderful patience.

As you read today's headlines or listen to the news, thank God for his merciful patience and his perfect timing. ✣

PRAYER

Lord, I celebrate your patience ...

SHOWERS OF BLESSING

If we confess our sins, he is faithful and just and will forgive us our sins and purify us from all unrighteousness. If we claim we have not sinned, we make him out to be a liar and his word is not in us. 1 JOHN 1:9–10

Military personnel stationed overseas often comment that one of the things they most looked forward to after weeks of enduring the dust and dirt of the battlefield is a shower. Imagine the layers of grit washing away under the steady stream of refreshing and restoring water.

In the same way, God has provided a way for us to be spiritually cleansed. Today's passage teaches one of the most important principles in all of Scripture, that of confessing our sins. Confession has been described as agreeing with God about the things we have done that violate his commandments and his will for us. No human intermediary is necessary. God knows every secret of the human heart, and he stands ready to forgive us. There is only one condition: We must confess our sin.

Sin separates us from the One who longs to enjoy unbroken fellowship with us. When Adam and Eve first sinned in the Garden of Eden, their disobedience caused them to hide from the Lord. It's often been noted that the first recorded question in the history of the universe was not "God, where are you?" but one that God asked Adam: "Where are you?"

No one can hide from God. God observes us through eyes of love, much like a father who carefully watches to see if his child will own up to wrongdoing. Have your times of personal worship felt lifeless and dry? If your actions or attitudes have erected a barrier between you and your Lord, confession will knock it down. A heavenly shower of blessing awaits you. ✤

PRAYER

God, I confess . . .

LOVE IS NOT OPTIONAL

Whoever claims to love God yet hates a brother or sister is a liar. For whoever does not love their brother and sister, whom they have seen, cannot love God, whom they have not seen. And he has given us this command: Anyone who loves God must also love their brother and sister.
1 JOHN 4:20–21

Pastor Mike, a New England pastor, was preaching a series of sermons one winter on what it means to truly love God. When he polled his congregation, most responded that they demonstrated their love for God through faithful church attendance, tithing and service on various committees. An elderly woman, however, rose to her feet a bit unsteadily. "I am here this morning," she said quietly, "because my friend was willing to drive me. We were able to get out of my driveway because a neighbor came over to shovel the snow. My home has heat because the church paid my bill. I don't need to ask what it means for people to love God, because I have already seen it."

Today's passage stresses again and again the importance of loving one another. If loving others were a simple matter, though, perhaps so much of this letter from John wouldn't be devoted to the subject.

Let's face it. Not everyone is easy to get along with, including ourselves! Scripture provides a powerful reason for loving others, however. If we say we love God, then he commands us to love the other members of our family in Christ. It is not optional.

Identify the person who is the most difficult for you to love right now. As an act of worship to the One who is love, show your love to that person today in a concrete way. ❧

> **PRAYER**

Lord, grant me the humility to love . . .

WATCHING AND WORKING

Watch out that you do not lose what we have worked for, but that you may be rewarded fully.
                                                                    2 JOHN 8

The infamous criminal Willie Sutton was once asked why he robbed banks. His reply? "Because that's where the money is."

A parallel reasoning motivates our enemy. Why does Satan work so hard at deceiving believers in Jesus? Why, in every generation, does he continually unleash legions of false teachers on the church? Answer: Because that's where the worship is. The devil hates to see God honored. He will do anything to stop this. In fact, he would really like to steal this affection for himself.

Like so many of the New Testament letters, 2 John warns believers to "watch out." We need to pay attention and be on our guard. Without vigilance and diligence, we can easily get off track and shift our focus and affection to unworthy things. Suddenly we find ourselves valuing that which is not God.

A fully devoted life of worship encompasses more than just attending praise services. Worship is more than singing exuberantly and praying fervently. Worship involves watching. We must be alert to the schemes of the enemy. Like a cosmic terrorist, he is always looking for an opening. Therefore, we cannot afford to be careless. Worship involves watching, and watching requires work. Guard the treasure of worship that God has given you. ✤

PRAYER

Lord God, make me watchful and give me a diligent heart ...

NEIGHBORHOOD WATCH

It gave me great joy when some believers came and testified about your faithfulness to the truth, telling how you continue to walk in it.   3 JOHN 3

A disturbing number of modern Christians do not understand—or simply do not embrace—the concept of Biblical community. They prefer to view their faith as a private, personal matter. Interacting with others, being a vital member of a church, sharing life as a body of believers (see 1 Corinthians 12)—being a part of the community of believers is seen as optional, unnecessary or undesirable.

This was never God's intent. The Bible both describes and prescribes a spiritual existence in which people of faith live and serve together (see Acts 2:42–47). Third John is another example of Christian community. It's essentially a postcard—a window into true spiritual friendship. It depicts believers not just coexisting, but co-laboring for a great cause. And why? Because we need each other. God purposely designed us to be interdependent. Left alone we are vulnerable and incomplete. Even worse, we will forget what's true, stop doing what's important and stop ordering our lives and activities around the One who is worthy of all that we are and have.

Check your habits of interaction with other believers. Are you deeply involved in your church? Do you attend? Participate? Serve? Give? Do you have Christian friends who continually motivate you to love Christ better and better?

Practice Christian community today. Call one or two friends and spend time in prayer, Bible reading or encouraging one another. ❖

PRAYER

Lord, forgive me for thinking I can live independently from the rest of your body, the church . . .

BE A LIFEGUARD

Be merciful to those who doubt; save others by snatching them from the fire; to others show mercy, mixed with fear—hating even the clothing stained by corrupted flesh.

JUDE 22–23

The beach is a beautiful place, and also a dangerous one. Every summer we hear grim stories of shark attacks or tragic tales of swimmers being pulled out to sea by strong undertows. Perhaps you've even experienced dozing off on a raft, only to wake up and find that you've drifted. The wind and waves have gently pushed and pulled you far from where you began floating.

The beauty and danger of the beach provides a good metaphor for life. The world is beautiful—and dangerous! At times our enemy can be more vicious and deadly than the giant shark in the movie *Jaws*. And if he doesn't attack us in overt ways, then he uses more subtle means to get us to drift away from God and from what is true. It happens so gradually that we don't even notice—until we "wake up," far from where we need to be.

The short New Testament book of Jude warns readers about the enemy and his diabolical tactics. Not only are we urged to pay attention to our own safety, we are also called to look out for others—to be *lifeguards*, in the most critical sense of the term.

A big part of what it means to worship God is to care for his people. By protecting those who are called to worship him, we enhance his glory and the honor due his name. Today, make it your goal to throw a lifeline to someone in trouble. Be a prayer warrior. Speak words of encouragement. Pull someone toward the safety of Christ, our rock. ✤

> **PRAYER**

Lord Jesus, help me be a lifeguard today . . .

IT'S WORTH IT!

Do not be afraid of what you are about to suffer. I tell you, the devil will put some of you in prison to test you, and you will suffer persecution for ten days. Be faithful, even to the point of death, and I will give you life as your victor's crown. REVELATION 2:10

The young mother-to-be watches as her schoolgirl figure changes before her eyes. Morning sickness, weight gain, stretch marks, the pain of labor. Is motherhood worth all this trouble? Ask her as she lies there smiling through the tears at the miracle of her newborn child.

The football player endures grueling twice-a-day practices in the 90-degree heat of late summer. He then plays all season long through countless aches and pains. What's the point? Ask him as he hoists the championship trophy above his head in front of hundreds of screaming fans.

Painful preparation is not limited to the birthing center or the football field. We are in a contest of eternal proportions. Everything is on the line. We can find comfort and new strength by remembering that God is watching. He keeps records and has pledged to reward faithfulness. This is what he promised the Christians in the ancient church at Smyrna (in what is now modern-day Turkey). It is also what he guarantees us (see Ephesians 6:8). We *will* one day enjoy glory, but first we must pass the test. And that test involves suffering.

When you endure suffering, when you continue to enthrone God in your heart and life no matter what, then you will one day be crowned with glory by the glorious One who owns all glory. In short, it pays to walk with God.

This Christmas Eve make it your goal to cling fiercely and stubbornly to God. Instead of letting suffering and trials drive a wedge between you and the Lord, let your troubles be an opportunity to turn to him in praise. ♣

PRAYER

Father, I need the courage to push on and not quit . . .

HE'S AT THE DOOR

Here I am! I stand at the door and knock. If anyone hears my voice and opens the door, I will come in and eat with that person, and they with me.   REVELATION 3:20

Before he died in a tragic plane crash on July 28, 1982, Keith Green was the biggest name in contemporary Christian music. He had the heart of a David and the prophetic message of a John the Baptist. His song "You Love the World," written as a message from Christ, is typical of Keith's radical style. Consider some of the lyrics: "You prefer the light of your TV. / You love the world, and you're avoiding me." The songwriter goes on to ask from Jesus' point of view if it is right to ignore him after he "gave my blood, to save your life."

These are hard-hitting words, but certainly not a new message. These uncomfortable lyrics communicate the same message we find in Revelation 3:20. Speaking to and through the apostle John, Jesus describes himself as being at a "door," knocking and desiring to come in.

Christians typically use this verse in evangelism, urging unbelievers to "open their hearts to Jesus." While it is certainly true that Christ wants non-Christians to receive him in faith (see John 1:12), this particular verse is actually addressed to Christians! A group of believers in Laodicea (modern-day Turkey) had become spiritually indifferent. They were going through the motions of Christianity, but in their attitudes and by their actions, they had actually shut Christ out of their lives! Is this true today as well?

Christmas is the perfect day to examine your heart. Have you shoved Christ over into the margins of your life? Has he become a bit player in the drama of your life? He wants to be central in your thoughts and plans. He wants to fellowship with you and be your closest friend. Are you letting him? ♣

> **PRAYER**

Lord Jesus, please come and fellowship with me ...

THE SWEET SMELL OF PRAYER

Another angel, who had a golden censer, came and stood at the altar. He was given much incense to offer, with the prayers of all God's people, on the golden altar in front of the throne. The smoke of the incense, together with the prayers of God's people, went up before God from the angel's hand. REVELATION 8:3–4

Surveys show that an overwhelming majority of Americans pray. Believe it or not, even many self-described atheists admit to sending an occasional spiritual smoke signal toward heaven. Yet to a large number of people, prayer feels like nothing more than religious self-talk, mixing up a lot of words and aiming them toward God, all in an elaborate attempt to trick ourselves into feeling better about our lives.

Does God hear our prayers? Does prayer make a real difference? Not according to some. "I felt like my prayers were falling on deaf ears or bouncing off the ceiling," is a common complaint. Perhaps you've felt this or said this yourself. So what can we conclude? Is prayer nothing more than superstition? Is it merely a fancy kind of religious mumbo jumbo, a silly exercise in wishful thinking?

Look again at the passage above. Notice the prayers of the saints mixed with incense and ascending into the very presence of God. Not sweet-smelling incense alone, not mere religious ritual, but sacrifice permeated with prayer. Desperate cries. Longings for God. Fervent expressions of love and trust. No wonder the Scripture says, "The LORD detests the sacrifice of the wicked, but the prayer of the upright pleases him" (Proverbs 15:8).

Today, if your heart is right, your prayers will be too. By communing with God and leaning on him as you work and play and rest, you are worshiping. ✣

PRAYER

Lord, may this prayer be a pleasing offering to you . . .

day361

NO DISPUTE

And the twenty-four elders, who were seated on their thrones before God, fell on their faces and worshiped God, saying: "We give thanks to you, Lord God Almighty, the One who is and who was, because you have taken your great power and have begun to reign."
REVELATION 11:16–17

So much about the book of Revelation is disputed. What is the purpose of this odd series of visions? How literally should we interpret all the imagery in the book? When will the events prophesied in these 22 chapters take place?

But so much about Revelation is not disputed. There is no disputing its claims of who is in charge. Time and time again, the curtains of heaven are pulled back, so to speak, to reveal Almighty God on his throne, reigning over the heavens and ruling over human affairs.

The creatures and inhabitants of heaven have no confusion about worship. Interestingly, everyone (and everything) is described in terms of where they are in relation to the triune God. The elders are described as being "before him who sits on the throne" (Revelation 4:10). Millions of angels "encircled the throne" (Revelation 5:11). Countless other creatures are revealed to be "standing before the throne and before the Lamb" (Revelation 7:9). God is the worthy One, the celebrated One. The Lord is central. He is adored and honored.

Will you do that today? Wonder at all these breathtaking peeks into eternity? Wonder at a God who holds time in his hands and who has the whole cosmos on a perfect schedule? Wonder at the opportunity to know the Creator who desires to make his home in you and to reign over your heart with perfect love and mercy?

Wonder. ✣

PRAYER

Lord, you are worthy . . .

THE LANGUAGE OF HEAVEN

And they sang a new song before the throne and before the four living creatures and the elders. No one could learn the song except the 144,000 who had been redeemed from the earth. REVELATION 14:3

Imagine a world filled with noise but no music. Not a single choir. No violin concertos or chirping birds. No pianos or three-part harmony. It's hard to fathom, isn't it?

Thankfully, we do enjoy God's gift of music. And in the scene described above, we are reminded that heaven is filled with gorgeous, otherworldly praise music. Anthems, hymns and songs forever new and that take away your breath. Angelic choruses that fill heaven with joy and gladness.

God is good enough to give us little previews of this on earth. You've had the experience. You hear a new song that sets your toe a-tapping. It puts a bounce in your step and a smile on your face that lasts all day. Or you hear an instrumental arrangement or a beautiful solo, and for some inexplicable reason tears fill your eyes. What can this mean?

Today, why not surround yourself with praise music? Turn off the news or sports radio and let music fill your day. Be transported into the presence of God and then just try to keep from singing. ✤

PRAYER

Father in heaven, let my whole life be a song of praise to you . . .

CAUGHT OFF GUARD?

Look, I come like a thief! Blessed is the one who stays awake and remains clothed, so as not to go naked and be shamefully exposed. REVELATION 16:15

A TV commercial showed workers throwing an all-out party to celebrate the company president's going away on business, only to then find out that he had canceled his trip and would be arriving at the office any minute.

An old cartoon featured an obviously angry boss standing over the desk of a clearly surprised employee. The employer is saying, "Why aren't you working!?" And the underling's reply? "Because I didn't know you were here!"

Anyone who's ever held a job smiles at these glimpses of office humor. Funny how a person's efficiency increases when the boss is in the building.

Revelation 16:15 echoes a theme found throughout the New Testament. It is imperative that Christians live for God each and every moment because Jesus Christ could return at any time. We cannot afford to slack off or get sloppy in our faith. In fact, we are warned to faithfully watch and wait—even as we work hard and serve well. We are to "remain clothed"—which we might interpret as keeping our souls full of love and worship and anticipation for the Lord's coming. In one of his letters, the apostle John puts it this way: "And now, dear children, continue in him, so that when he appears we may be confident and unashamed before him at his coming" (1 John 2:28).

What's the status of your heart today? Take a few minutes to reflect on your readiness to receive Jesus. ❖

PRAYER

Lord, make me ready for your return . . .

day364

THE ROAR OF THE CROWD

Then I heard what sounded like a great multitude, like the roar of rushing waters and like loud peals of thunder, shouting: "Hallelujah! For our Lord God Almighty reigns."

REVELATION 19:6

Kevin is a 43-year-old believer in Jesus. He leads a men's group, works as an accountant and is a husband and the father of two teenagers. One Saturday he went to watch his alma mater play a big conference basketball game. Talk about exciting! Down by 18 at halftime, his team came roaring back to win in double overtime. Kevin was ecstatic. He behaved like a wild man, jumping up and down, even high-fiving total strangers!

Today at church, as the worship team sings songs about the greatness of God and the wonder of his love, Kevin barely sings. During one especially upbeat chorus, a group of college students begins to clap enthusiastically. Kevin contemplates joining in, but then feels sheepish. So he shoves his hands in his pockets.

Why do so many Christians get excited about their secular activities yet remain unexcited when celebrating their faith? Furthermore, why shouldn't our weekly church services be as thrilling as a great sporting event?

What the apostle John experienced when he saw his visions of heaven was anything but tame. Loud worship. A wild celebration. Unbridled joy.

What are your expectations for worship—personal and corporate—this week? Remember—wherever you worship, you will be in the presence of our great God Almighty. What will you do differently to lose yourself in reverence and praise?

Stand up and shout. Clap your hands. Raise your arms in praise. Do something to express your excitement about being in God's presence. ❖

PRAYER

Lord, may my whole life roar with praise for you . . .

OPEN AT LAST

He who testifies to these things says, "Yes, I am coming soon." Amen. Come, Lord Jesus.
REVELATION 22:20

The gates to paradise are opened. The curse of Eden is broken. "'He will wipe every tear from their eyes. There will be no more death or mourning or crying or pain, for the old order of things has passed away" (Revelation 21:4). All things are restored. John's finite, stunned mind scrambles feverishly to come up with adequate words to describe all that he sees unfolded before him. But not even an unabridged thesaurus can do eternity justice.

Beauty, purity, newness. Heaven is a marvel—filled with exquisite wonders and infinite mysteries. But chief among them all is the promise that we "will see his face" (Revelation 22:4). No wonder John cries out at the end of his book, "Amen. Come, Lord Jesus." This is the cry of every worshiper. This is the deepest desire of our hearts—to be swept up into perfect intimacy with God. This is the great hope of the believer. Only this promise can sustain us in a fallen world.

Today, let the reality of heaven give you a newer, truer perspective on this world. ✤

PRAYER

Come, Lord Jesus . . .

SCRIPTURE INDEX

TOPICAL INDEX

Also available in the
Once-A-Day Devotional Collection

Once-A-Day Devotional for Women

Once-A-Day Devotional for Men

Once-A-Day Walk with Jesus Devotional

Once-A-Day Men and Women of the Bible Devotional

Go deeper with NIV Once-A-Day Bibles

NIV Once-A-Day Bible

NIV Once-A-Day Bible: Chronological Edition

NIV Once-A-Day Bible for Women